The Economics of QWERTY

The Political Economy of the Austrian School Series
General Editor: Mario Rizzo, New York University

Although long associated with a deep appreciation of the free market, the Austrian School has not been fully recognized as a unique approach in analyzing the role of government in the economy. A major contribution of the Austrian School was to demonstrate, as early as 1920, the impossibility of economic calculation under socialism. Recent events in the former Soviet Union and Eastern Europe have dramatically illustrated the cogency of this argument. In more recent times, and in contrast to conventional static analyses, Austrian research has been concerned with the impact of government control on entrepreneurial discovery. To what extent does the impact of such control go beyond the firm's static pricing decision and reach into the very discovery of new opportunities and hence the transmission of knowledge in society? Austrians are also concerned with the dynamics of state intervention – the degree to which one intervention induces further interventions and, conversely, the degree to which one decontrol "necessitates" further steps in the process of deregulation. Finally, the Austrian School is firmly committed to the value-freedom of economics: that is, the separation of the analysis of policy consequences from the moral and political values inherent in the *advocacy* of particular economic policies.

The Economics of QWERTY

History, Theory, and Policy

Essays by

Stan J. Liebowitz and Stephen E. Margolis

Edited and with an introduction by

Peter Lewin

NEW YORK UNIVERSITY PRESS
Washington Square, New York

First published in the U.S.A. in 2002 by
NEW YORK UNIVERSITY PRESS
Washington Square
New York, N.Y. 10003
www.nyupress.nyu.edu

This book is printed on paper suitable for recycling and
made from fully managed and sustained forest sources.

Library of Congress Cataloging-in-Publication Data
The economics of QWERTY : history, theory, and policy / essays by
Stan J. Liebowitz and Stephen E. Margolis ; edited and with an introduction by
Peter Lewin.
p. cm. — (The political economy of the Austrian school series)
Includes bibliographical references and index.
ISBN 0–8147–5178–4 (alk. paper)
1. Technological innovations—Economic aspects. 2. Economics—Research.
I. Liebowitz, S. J., 1950– II. Margolis, Stephen, 1950– III. Lewin, Peter, 1948–
IV. Political economy of the Austrian school.
HC79.T4 E263 2001
338'.064—dc21 2001030705

Printed in Great Britain

Contents

THE INDEPENDENT INSTITUTE is a non-profit, non-partisan, scholarly research and educational organization that sponsors comprehensive studies of the political economy of critical social and economic issues.

The politicization of decision-making in society has too often confined public debate to the narrow reconsideration of existing policies. Given the prevailing influence of partisan interests, little social innovation has occurred. In order to understand both the nature of and possible solutions to major public issues, The Independent Institute's program adheres to the highest standards of independent inquiry and is pursued regardless of prevailing political or social biases and conventions. The resulting studies are widely distributed as books and other publications, and are publicly debated through numerous conference and media programs.

Through this uncommon independence, depth, and clarity, The Independent Institute pushes at the frontiers of our knowledge, redefines the debate over public issues, and fosters new and effective directions for government reform.

List of Figures

List of Tables

Preface

If one is to believe the popular press, recent technological developments pose an unprecedented threat to the functioning of the market economy and the well-being of free citizens. New technologies have been seen as a mixed blessing, conferring benefits to those who produce and use them, but also posing threats to those who would compete with and those who might be held captive by them. All change is painful to some degree as it challenges old ways of doing things and requires costly adaptations. The presence of alarmists in our midst is not a new phenomenon. Apprehension and paranoia have, however, been fueled by recent developments in the academic economics literature. The imagination of economists has been spurred to discover (and invent?) evidence of new types of "market failure" associated with the special nature of new technologies. This general area of research has been coined the "economics of QWERTY" – after a suggestion that the layout of the standard typewriter keyboard according to the QWERTY pattern on the top left-hand side is an inefficient layout, an unfortunate accident of history, to which we are now irretrievably and unfortunately committed ("locked-in").

In a series of articles and other publications between 1990 and 2000, especially including their seminal book, *Winners, Losers & Microsoft: Competition and Antitrust in High Technology* (The Independent Institute), Stan Liebowitz and Stephen Margolis have critically examined the various aspects of the "economics of QWERTY" and its implications. These contributions are remarkable for their eloquence and relevance. They call into question the historical accuracy of the standard account of the QWERTY case and of similar "myths" of lock-in. In fact they contend that no plausible case of sub-optimal lock-in has ever been satisfactorily documented. Yet the conventional wisdom remains that it is widespread and much recent antitrust activity and legislative policy discussion is based on that assumption. Liebowitz and Margolis question the historical evidence for the theoretical basis of, and the policy implications drawn from, the economics of QWERTY.

Eight of Liebowitz and Margolis' articles are reprinted in this book. Together with their important companion book, *Winners, Losers & Microsoft*, this combined work constitutes a complete account of the critique of the economics of QWERTY. For those interested in this area of research it will hopefully be extremely convenient to have a cogent treatment of the issues at stake and to get a sense of how the critique has developed over the decade 1990–2000. In the introductory Chapter 1 I provide a summary and a discussion of the issues from a somewhat broader perspective.

I have reprinted the articles with minimal editing. Although each article contains relevant new material there is some repetition (for example, concerning some of the historical evidence – in a few places I have, indeed, decided to omit repetitive passages). I wish to thank the publishers of the following journals for their permission to reprint articles: *Journal of Law and Economics* (Chapter 2), *Journal of Economic Perspectives* (Chapter 3), *Research in Law and Economics* (Chapter 4), *Journal of Law, Economics and Organization* (Chapter 5), and *Harvard Journal of Law and Technology* (Chapter 6). I would like also to thank the following for permission to republish extracts and chapters: Macmillan Publishers (for extracts from the *Palgrave Dictionary of Law and Economics* – Chapters 7 and 8); The Cato Institute (for the *Policy Analysis* 324 reprinted in Chapter 9); and The Independent Institute (for the adaptation of chapters 7, 8 and 9 from *Winners, Losers & Microsoft* for Chapter 10).

Many people have helped me with this project, by reading parts of the introductory chapter or by discussing various aspects of Liebowitz and Margolis' work with me. I am particularly grateful to Mario Rizzo, who (once again) provided not only insight but also encouragement; to Peter Boettke for an invitation to present my views on this general subject area to the J. M. Kaplan Workshop in Politics, Philosophy and Economics at George Mason University and to the participants of the workshop (especially Peter Boettke, Mario Rizzo, Don Lavoie, Richard Wagner, Jerry Ellig, Rebecca Menes, Marc Brady, and Nicola Tynan) for very helpful comments; to Steven Horwitz (once again) for reading early manuscripts and providing much-needed direction; to Sam Weston for helpful suggestions; and to Stan Liebowitz and Stephen Margolis with whom I have had invaluable discussions, but whom I must also clearly distance not only from my errors but also from any presumed association with any of the views I have expressed.

I have been most fortunate to have had the expert copy-editing services of Keith Povey and Barbara Docherty. Because of their keen eyes and common-sense approach I have been able to avoid numerous errors and inconsistencies. Any that remain are most decidedly my own fault. I am very grateful to them.

In everything that I do, especially the things that are important to me, I benefit from the help and encouragement of my family, my children Dan, Andy, Shiralee and Gabbi, and my wife Beverley – a debt I gratefully and affectionately acknowledge.

Acknowledgements

The editor and publishers wish to thank the following publishers for permission to reprint articles, monographs or chapters: The University of Chicago Law School, publishers of *The Journal of Law and Economics*, for "The Fable of the Keys," 33 (1990): 1–25; The American Economic Association, publishers of *The Journal of Economic Perspectives*, for "Network Externality: An Uncommon Tragedy," 8 (1994): 133–150; Elesevier Science, publishers of *Research in Law and Economics*, for "Are Network Externalities a New Source of Market Failure?," 17 (1995): 1–22; Oxford University Press, publishers of *The Journal of Law, Economics and Organization*, for "Path Dependence, Lock-in, and History," 11 (1995): 205–226; Harvard Law School, publishers of *Harvard Journal of Law and Technology*, for "Should Technology Choice be a Concern for Antitrust?," 9 (1996): 283–318; Macmillan/St. Martin's Press, publishers of *The New Palgrave Dictionary of Economics and Law*, edited by Peter Newman (London, 1998) for "Path Dependence," 17–23; Macmillan/St. Martin's Press, publishers of *The New Palgrave Dictionary of Economics and Law*, edited by Peter Newman (London, 1998) for "Network Externalities (Effects)," 671–675; The Cato Institute, publishers of *Cato Policy Analysis*, for #324 "Dismal Science Fictions: Network Effects, Microsoft, and Antitrust Speculation," (Washington, DC, 1998); Cambridge University Press, publishers of *Dynamic Competition and Public Policy: Technology, Innovation, and Antitrust Issues*, edited by Jerry Ellig (Cambridge, 2001) for "Network Effects and the Microsoft Case"; The Independent Institute, for the reprinted figures and adapted text from chapters 7, 8 and 9 of its book, *Winners, Losers & Microsoft: Competition and Antitrust in High Technology*, by Stan J. Liebowitz and Stephen E. Margolis (The Independent Institute, 1999 and 2001): 135–233, which form chapter 10 of this book.

The jacket-design is by Jorge De La Canal.

1

Introduction: The Market Process and the Economics of QWERTY

Peter Lewin

Introduction and overview

Some recent claims that high-technology markets fail to operate efficiently have become very influential, not only among economists (theorists and economic historians) but also in the popular press and in public policy. This is a new type of "market failure" mostly associated with the goods (sometimes known as "information goods") that are related to many of the technological advances regarding the generation and use of information in one form or another. In economics, the literature is known generally by association with the technical concepts of "network-effects," "path dependence," and "lock-in." These concepts suggest that the outcomes we observe (for example, in the generation of products to record and play video images, process data, or simply type book chapters) may not be particularly efficient. In this view of the world, random events may "lock us in" to a path and, therefore, an outcome that is socially inferior to an alternative one that is, or was, available. This view of the world has come to be known generally as "the economics of QWERTY." This general field of inquiry in economics is associated with parallel developments in the fields of mathematics and statistics having to do with topics like "chaos" and "complexity."

In the essays reprinted here, Stan Liebowitz and Stephen Margolis have critically examined the various aspects of the economics of QWERTY (to be defined below) and its implications. With eloquence and relevance they call into question the historical accuracy of the standard account of the QWERTY case and of similar "myths" of lock-in. They contend that no plausible case of sub-optimal lock-in has ever been satisfactorily documented. While the conventional wisdom has been that such inefficiency is widespread and much recent antitrust activity (including the recent Microsoft case) and legislative policy discussion is based on that assumption, Liebowitz and Margolis question the historical evidence, the theoretical basis, and the policy implications drawn from the economics of QWERTY.

Taken by themselves the publications by Liebowitz and Margolis over the last decade (1990–2000) constitute a remarkably comprehensive and accessible account of this literature As such, they can be read with great profit by anyone wishing to understand what path dependence, lock-in, network effects, etc. are all about and how they relate (if at all) to the recent lawsuit involving Microsoft.

Some brief comments on context

The economics of QWERTY derives from the assertion that the inherited typewriter keyboard, with its layout of keys according to the QWERTY configuration, is an archetypical representation of unfortunate accidents of history leading to inefficient results. The QWERTY keyboard design is claimed to be inferior to more rational designs that should, in a more ideal world, have been adopted. This particular historical example has served as a widely quoted and accepted paradigm case for what is seen as a general phenomenon, namely, the lock-in to inferior standards.

This book's organization of articles reflects the historical progression of Liebowitz and Margolis' research. They began, in 1990, by examining the historical accuracy of the QWERTY story and, stimulated by what they found there, were led to examine other historical cases, like the Beta/VHS videocassette case (see Chapter 5) and the Macintosh/Windows case (see Chapter 6). In each instance they found the evidence for sub-optimal ("inefficient") outcomes wanting. They also re-examined the theoretical basis underlying the conventional wisdom and provided an accessible but rigorous understanding of the concepts involved. Liebowitz and Margolis show also that the concepts of "network externalities" "path dependence", and "lock-in" are ill-defined and inconsistently used and they provide a definitive taxonomic clarification.[1]

In the process of considering both history and theory, the relationship between the two comes into question. Liebowitz and Margolis raise important questions about the proper role of economic modeling. They show that almost all of the discussion in the literature is about alternative economic models and not about the real world. There are an infinite number of possible economic models, many of which exhibit lock-in. The important question is which models are relevant to economic reality and, even more importantly, to economic policy?

Concerning policy, the literature on network-effects underlies much of the new antitrust policy initiatives that have been manifested in the ongoing case of the Justice Department against Microsoft. Liebowitz and Margolis have analyzed the Microsoft case and the implications for antitrust more generally. They find that these new initiatives make little sense if the objective is to benefit consumers, and are fraught with dangers to the competitive process and the dynamics of innovation (Chapters 9 and 10).

A brief history of the history

Chapter 2 of this volume is a reprint of the article that started it all (Liebowitz and Margolis 1990, provocatively titled "The Fable of the Keys"). It is a critical examination of assertions made by economist Paul David and others that lock-in is historically important. I therefore begin with a brief look at these assertions.

The origin of QWERTYnomics

Paul David (1985) tells us that the QWERTY story is a story of path-dependence. Because, "history matters," sometimes in an irrational way, the historical path that a particular technological development takes can be decisive in locking in an alternative that is, in some meaningful economic sense, inferior to another that is available. This was what happened with the adoption of the QWERTY keyboard. A rival design, by August Dvorak and W. L. Dealey was superior, but lost out to QWERTY. This was because of "*technical interrelatedness, economies of scale,* and *quasi-irreversibility of investment.* They constitute the basic ingredients of what may be called QWERTY-nomics" (David 1985, 334, italics in original).

This unfortunate outcome was not the result "of custom, conspiracy or state control." Rather it reflects the behavior of individuals "held fast in the grip of events long forgotten and shaped by circumstances in which neither they nor their interests figured." They were, to quote Tolstoy, held "in bondage to the whole course of previous history" (David 1985, 332). The whole thing was the result of an attempt to place the keys in such a configuration that would avoid the tendency for them to become jammed. When, with later technology, typewriters no longer used jammable keys, so that this was no longer a relevant consideration, it was "too late" to change. The installed base of software in the form of typist-human-capital was too great a barrier in the way of introducing the more rational DSK.[2]

David explicitly links his work with the theoretical contributions of Brian Arthur (1983) and Michael Katz and Carl Shapiro (1983). This literature features situations in which "essentially random transient factors are most likely to exert great leverage" and a "particular system *could* triumph over rivals merely because the purchasers of the software (and or hardware) expected that it would do so" (Katz and Shapiro 1983, 335, italics added).

> From the viewpoint of the formal theory of stochastic processes, what we are looking at now is *equivalent* to a generalized "Polya urn scheme" ... [A]n urn containing balls of various colors is sampled with replacement, and every drawing of a ball of a specified color results in a second ball of the same being returned to the urn; the probabilities that balls of specified colors will be added are therefore increasing (linear) functions of the proportions in which the respective colors are represented within the urn ... [W]hen a generalized form of such a process (characterized by unbounded increasing returns) is extended indefinitely, the proportional share of one of the colors will, with probability one, converge to unity. (David 1985, 335, italics added)

Which of the colors (or rival typewriter keyboards) will gain dominance, however, is "likely to be governed by 'historical accidents,' which is to say, by the particular sequencing choices made close to the beginning of the process" (David 1985, 335).

The "Fable of the Keys"

Two things are of note in David's account. One concerns the historical accuracy and completeness of the QWERTY story. The other concerns the characterization of it as *equivalent* to a particular stochastic dynamic process. Both of these motivate the essays in this book. I consider the second later.

Concerning the history, Liebowitz and Margolis devote most of their 1990 article (Chapter 2 in this volume) to a careful examination of the historical record. They provide considerable detail, with extensive citations. They point out that the evidence from the many typewriter experiments is ambiguous at best and plausibly tainted by serious conflict of interest and methodological shortcomings. They document the many typewriter competitions that occurred with mixed results and the rivalrous competition among typewriter producers. In all, the assertion that QWERTY is an inferior standard cannot be sustained.

The case of the typewriter keyboard would appear to be especially suited to an assessment of "efficiency." This is because "what counts" for consumers of typewriter services can be boiled down mainly to two readily measurable dimensions – speed and accuracy in producing text. (Other dimensions, for example, the durability of the typewriter, can be standardized easily for comparison.) So, if tests in these dimensions produced results that clearly contradicted the "market's choice," this would, at the very least, give us pause. One would have to wonder why obvious cost savings had been passed up. Other cases are generally not so readily reducible to clearly measurable dimensions. And when many dimensions are involved, it is hard to know what the relative importance of each is for the consumer. (For example, in videocassettes, consumers care about picture quality, playing time, cassette size, and product durability in ways that are not immediately apparent without resort to observation of their market behavior.) In this respect, the typewriter case is, indeed, a sort of paradigm case.

An early work looking at typing speed was conducted by Dvorak and some coauthors. The detailed examination by Liebowitz and Margolis reveals that, in general, the Dvorak book lacks both sound experimental method and objectivity. A Navy study that held a prominent place in David's telling of the history also fared poorly under scrutiny. Liebowitz and Margolis reveal various deficiencies in the experimental methodology, including a serious truncation of the testing period, but most tantalizing is the objectivity and authorship of the study, which I will not give away here. Perhaps more important was the discovery by Liebowitz and Margolis of a 1956 General Services Administration study by Earle Strong that had been neglected by almost all writers on this subject even though it had considerable national prominence during its undertaking. Liebowitz and Margolis conclude: "Strong conducted what appears to be a carefully controlled experiment designed to examine the costs and benefits of switching to Dvorak. He concluded that retraining typists on Dvorak had no advantages over retraining on QWERTY" and "would never be able to amortize its costs" (see below 37; unless otherwise noted, page numbers will refer to this volume). Liebowitz and Margolis do not consider Strong's study to be without faults, but contend that it should be taken seriously instead of being ignored. Even a current proponent of the Dvorak, like Yamada (1980, 1983), "as much as admits that experimental findings reported by Dvorak and his supporters cannot be assigned much credibility" (38).

Liebowitz and Margolis also consider evidence from the ergonomics literature, which is more current and arguably more "scientific." "The consistent finding in the ergonomic studies is that the results imply no clear advantage for Dvorak" (40). In fact, these studies suggest that there is a strong possibility that "the limitations of typing speed ... [may] have something to do with a mental or, at least, neurological skill and fairly little to do with limitations on the speeds at which fingers can complete their required motions" (41).

Competitions between expert typists provide another type of (limited) evidence. "[T]yping contests and demonstrations of speed were fairly common" at one time involving "many different machines, with various manufacturers claiming to hold the speed record" (43). In the 1880s Remington's champion Frank McGurrin won a number of victories for the QWERTY keyboard. There were other types of machines besides the Dvorak but the evidence is complicated by the lack of standardization of the abilities and training of the various contenders. Touch typing was not common. Suffice it to say that there is absolutely no presumption indicated that QWERTY was an intrinsically inferior design.

The final, and perhaps the most important, type of evidence pertaining to conclusions about the QWERTY standard relates to the details of the market process by which QWERTY emerged. As Liebowitz and Margolis tell us it "was not invented from whole cloth." Quoting Yamada (1983, 177): "Examination of these materials reveals that almost all ideas incorporated into Sholes' [QWERTY] machines, if not all, were at one time or another already used by his predecessors" (41). The emergence of QWERTY was in fact the result of a fairly long and complex rivalrous process between numerous competitors. It is very important to be clear about *exactly* what it is that Liebowitz and Margolis assert in Chapter 2 (the 1990 article) and what they are not asserting. They explicitly state that they are *not* asserting "that QWERTY is proven to be the best imaginable keyboard." Neither are they claiming "that Dvorak is proven to be inferior to QWERTY." Rather their claim is simply *"that there is no scientifically acceptable evidence that Dvorak offers any real advantage over QWERTY"* (Chapter 2, n. 20, my italics).

The theory

In "The Fable of the Keys" Liebowitz and Margolis introduce the subject with a critical survey of the relevant theory of lock-in and discuss it again in the conclusion, and it forms a large part of the other essays in this book. It is the subject also of a large and growing literature in the journals and advanced texts.

The basics

The relevant theory can be broadly characterized as the theory of *network-effects*. (Liebowitz and Margolis introduced the term "network-effects" to substitute for the formerly more common term network *externalities*, to account for the possibility, indeed the likelihood, that these effects are often internalized.) Network-effects, relating to the consumption of a particular good or service, occur whenever the benefits of consuming that good or service depend positively on the number of individuals who do so. So an additional consumer adds benefits to the consumption of other participants. This phenomenon is not new and is extremely common. Indeed the social institution of "the market" itself is a network. The benefits to all participants often, as Adam Smith realized, depend on its extent. Languages are networks. The value of learning a particular language often depends on how many speakers there already are. In fact, network-effects occur whenever benefits are related positively to the interaction of individuals within the network. Others examples are telephone networks, local area computer networks, clubs, trade associations, and of course the internet.[3] Network-effects are an example of economies of scale (increasing returns to scale) on the demand side as distinct from the more traditional economies of scale in production, with which they sometimes are, but should not be, confused.

Though common, network-effects are more important for some types of goods than others. (I shall use the word "good" to refer generically to a good or service, any "economic good.") They have been given prominence recently because of the proliferation of so called "knowledge-goods," though, as Liebowitz and Margolis point out knowledge is a dimension of every good. The connection between knowledge-goods and network-effects, however, has been related to the fact that the usefulness of any knowledge possessed, often depends on how many others have similar knowledge (demand-side economies of scale), *and* (not always correctly) to the fact that knowledge consumption is non-rivalrous and that it can often be duplicated without cost (or almost without cost). One person's use does not preclude another's (implying supply-side economies).[4] I discuss this further in a moment.

There is, therefore, a strong connection between networks and *standards*. A standard is a "shared way of doing things, of interacting."

Standards serve to coordinate individual activity by reducing costs of interacting. A common language is a prime example. Common software would be another. Obviously the relative benefits of a particular common standard are related to the presence or absence of devices for cheaply converting from one standard into another – analogous to the presence of a competent language interpreter. Standards may be fixed or flexible to some greater or lesser degree. Many standards, like languages, legal systems, operating systems, etc. evolve over time. Their benefits are a complex function of the degree of stability and flexibility that they exhibit.[5]

Liebowitz and Margolis point out that networks likewise come in many shapes and sizes and vary along a few dimensions. First, networks may be literal or notional. An example of a literal network is a telephone exchange. An example of a notional network is the network of Yale Law School graduates (55). Second, networks may be owned or unowned. This may be crucial in assessing the economic properties of the network. For example, an owned network does not exhibit any "externality problem," even though some of the benefits of consumption of the good involved are "external" to the individual. Though each individual fails to take account of the benefit that he/she confers on others by being in the network, the owner of the network has an incentive to do so and will charge for "membership" accordingly. In contrast an unowned network presents properties that are more interesting and challenging from the standpoint of static allocational efficiency.

As mentioned above, network-effects are economies of scale in demand. As such their existence is an "empirical" matter. Actual networks may exhibit economies or diseconomies of scale. The same is true of supply-side (or production) economies. "The currently popular association of new technology with increasing returns may well be faulty, at least for some technologies" (Liebowitz and Margolis, 1999, 81). In particular, as suggested above, network-effects should not be confused with the decreasing costs of production that occur with time as a result of product-specific learning and general technological advance. Such cost declines have characterized many new industries in the past (like refrigeration, automobiles, etc.) and have been attributed to many of the new "information age" industries of today. Decreasing returns to scale for the latter should also not be simply presumed. For example, it is sometimes argued that software production exhibits a high degree of increasing returns in production. Once the product has been developed, and once production is in place, the marginal cost of producing an extra copy is negligible so that it is possible to "spread" the fixed setup and development costs over a larger and larger volume of production forever reducing average costs. This, however, is only part of the story. Typically, increases in software consumption eventually imply increases in costs from other sources. As Liebowitz and Margolis illustrate:

> Assume ... that there is one technical-support specialist for each 25,000 users [of] ... Windows 95. If the hiring of additional technical-support personnel tended to bid up their wages, this diseconomy alone could overwhelm the decreasing average fixed cost. Suppose, for example, that hiring an additional technical-support specialist (for 25,000 additional users) increased the wages of technical-support specialists by $22 a year, or an hourly wage increase of a penny. This small change in wages would be sufficient to make overall average costs increase, not decrease with output. (1999, 81–82, endnote omitted)

Generally, knowledge-goods, like software, are produced and consumed together with a complex of other goods (sales, marketing, public relations, management, distribution, etc.) that may not be subject to increasing returns, and increases in software production may thus be associated in increasing costs from a variety of sources. Bottom line, "without investigation, it is unreasonable to accept that the law of diminishing returns somehow takes a vacation in new-technology industries" (90). Some of what is observed as economies of scale is no doubt explained instead by phenomenal improvements in the technology of production as a result of successful innovative activity, something that is much more difficult to characterize and analyze.

It is undeniably true that the production of software and similar contemporary goods exhibits a particular structure that is worthy of note, namely, instant scalability (a term coined by Liebowitz and Margolis) – the ability to expand production with little or no time lag (213). Replication of these goods is relatively easy. This may be important in considering firm and industry structure and the nature and types of competition one is likely to observe.

The question of efficiency

All this is interesting and relevant to an understanding of the modern economic landscape with its bewildering variety of new "information age" products. But its relevance has been substantially enhanced by recent discussions about economic efficiency and related policy implications. These discussions take the form of abstract theoretical speculations about the efficiency properties of various processes usually (although not necessarily always) associated with network-effects – processes that exhibit path-dependent lock-in. Crucial to an assessment of these discussions is clarity on the concepts of efficiency, equilibrium, path-dependence, and lock-in. Some brief critical remarks follow, however this is not intended as a comprehensive treatment of these terms.

Efficiency

Economists have searched long and hard for a concept of efficiency that is "objective" or value free. Economic outcomes consist of an array of goods and services and states-of-being of different individuals that are in themselves incommensurate. In order to pronounce one outcome more or less efficient than another one has to have a way of overcoming this "apples and oranges" problem. Commonly one resorts to attempting to appeal to the valuations placed on the outcomes by the affected individuals themselves. One appeals, that is, to individual preferences in deriving efficiency criteria. This obviously involves the decision that individual preferences ought to be what counts when deciding efficiency issues. In itself, however, this is merely a *definition* of efficiency. No value judgment is involved (beyond that of supporting a definition) unless one says something like, "efficiency is good" or "a more efficient outcome is a *preferred* outcome." When we do take this step, as we often do in policy discussions, what we are saying is that we believe that individual preferences ought to count in deciding what economic outcomes are preferable. This will perhaps strike readers as eminently reasonable. If what is "efficient" is defined as what the "people prefer," how could we not be for it? Is it not the quintessence of "economic democracy"?

As is well known, however, there are numerous practical difficulties in deciding what "people prefer" and, indeed, what this means. When changes are contemplated in which all of the individuals who are involved clearly gain from the change (that is, can be confidently said to prefer that the change be made), then there is little ambiguity and we have the well known Pareto improvement. (So, for example, in the typewriter case discussed above, one may be able to argue that, other things constant, a keyboard layout that is able to unambiguously deliver a faster typing speed would definitely be preferred by *everyone* concerned.) The most common difficulty comes from situations in which some individuals gain and others lose. In such "mixed" situations, we have to resort to so-called compensation tests – that is, somehow judging whether the gains outweigh the losses. If we take this leap, we are, in effect, saying that, in deciding matters of efficiency, the distribution of gains between individuals is not relevant. Of course, a standard defense is that it might be relevant, but that it is a separate issue – we ought to make the pie as large as possible before we consider how it ought to be divided up. This involves a new additional value judgment and clearly is a much less plausible and easily defensible position than one that simply says "people prefer the change." To be sure, it is still a kind of economic democracy – it says something like "more people prefer it" or "the intensity of the preferences for outweigh the intensity of the preferences against." (Again, in the keyboard case, we would not consider it reasonable for holdouts of "inferior" keyboard layouts to be able to block the adoption of a "superior" layout. This judgment may be couched in Pareto efficiency terms by noting that the truly "superior" keyboard would be able to deliver cost savings in excess of the losses suffered by those wedded to an "inferior" one.)

This efficiency standard is widely accepted in economic discussions and has penetrated deeply into the policy and legal environments. The situation is complicated because the word "efficiency" has a very strong colloquial connotation and in economic policy discussions is often confused with what is meant by efficiency in the natural sciences where inputs and outputs are so much more easily identified and evaluated and no compensation criteria are necessary. It lends to economic policy discussions a spurious aura of being "scientific."

Economists encourage this impression in spite of the fact that they are well aware of the insurmountable obstacles to arriving at unambiguous decisions about which changes are efficient and which not. These involve the well-known impossibility of discerning individuals' preferences, having to use *hypothetical* market valuations instead, and of having to posit unknowable counterfactuals, often having to do with unknowable (even unimaginable) futures. The real drawback, however, of this traditional efficiency standard, I suggest, has not so much to do with its theoretical conception *per se*, as it does with the way in which it is traditionally used in economics, that is, in *the context of the static model of resource allocation*. It is in this context that it has encouraged the kind of attacks, in the name of efficiency, on the unfettered emergence and development of products and standards that we are witnessing in this literature.

In a static context, in which the value of all potential resource uses are known (either with certainty or "probabilistically"), in which technology is unchanging, the set of products is fixed, and there are no external effects of any kind or any elements of monopoly, it is well known that a "competitive solution" is also Pareto optimal and, therefore, efficient in the sense discussed above. This idealized situation of neoclassical "perfect competition" has unrealistically and unreasonably served as a standard of comparison for actual real-world situations. In particular, in the context of network-effects and standards, economists have thought it relevant and meaningful to argue that the presence of such effects suggests that private markets might provide an "inefficient" result. The works reprinted in this book suggest that these attacks are ill-informed and based on an unwarranted presumption of knowledge as well as an irrational concept of efficiency.

Equilibrium

Equilibrium is closely connected to the concept of efficiency. It is, however, even more widely and less self-consciously used. I have elsewhere dealt at some length with the different possible meanings of equilibrium and their implications (Lewin 1997, 1999, Chapter 2). Of particular interest to us here is the tendency for writers to make connections between theoretical processes that end in some sort of equilibrium with actually existing and observed processes and outcomes in the real world.

As with the concept of efficiency, the concept of equilibrium has migrated from the natural sciences, where it connotes some type of stasis, a stable configuration of variables. In economics one cannot understand equilibrium without reference to human behavior and, therefore, to human cognition. Following Hayek many theorists define equilibrium in terms of the plans and expectations that individuals have. A situation is said to be in equilibrium when people's plans are mutually consistent and realistic; that is to say, when people have plans that are mutually compatible and can be successfully carried out. In such a situation there are no surprises, no one has any reason to "change his/her mind." There is no change in an economically meaningful sense.

Such an equilibrium never exists as such, though aspects of individual plans must be consistent if we are to have life as we know it. In the realm of economic activity, however, and particularly in the area of the "new technology" industries there is no equilibrium to speak of. The whole process is driven by *differences* in opinion and perception between rival producers and entrepreneurs. Where people have different expectations about the same situation, at most one of them can be right. The values they place on the resources at their disposal or which they trade, are not, in any meaningful sense, equilibrium values. They reflect only a "balance" of expectations about the possible uses of the resources. One cannot use such values meaningfully in any assessment of efficiency (in the sense discussed above).

Path-dependence

The concept of path-dependence is also not new and it also has links to the natural sciences. In economics it gives expression to the common sense idea that equilibrium values might depend on the path taken to get to equilibrium. This is most obvious already in the realization that "false trading" may imply income effects that affect the final prices and quantities of a set of products in a general equilibrium system. But it is much more general and, one suspects, ubiquitous. One should surely not be surprised to find that the equilibrium values of most economic systems are likely to be affected by events that lead up to the attainment of equilibrium, that is, the equilibrium values are not insensitive to the path taken to get to equilibrium. The fact that, as explained, we may never get to equilibrium speaks to the relevance of the whole discussion. May we assume that it is relevant to an assessment of which path is chosen even if equilibrium is never attained?

Lock-in

In the current discussion path-dependence gains added relevance because it is seen to attach to systems that exhibit network-effects. In particular, the fact that the benefits of being in the network depend, in part, on how many individuals already belong, suggests that, among competing networks, whichever gets started first may foreclose the development of the others simply by virtue of being there first, and not from any economic merit. This could then be seen as a "market failure," a failure of the market to unfailingly deliver the "best" standard. To be sure, lock-in may or may not be a problem. It is a problem only if one becomes locked-in to an inferior standard.

We are now in a position to consider some of the theoretical contributions in this field and the role of Liebowitz and Margolis in all of this.

Theory and efficiency

It is fair to say that the theoretical contributions in this field of economics are almost exclusively in the form of a series of exercises designed to show how various types of sub-optimality can occur. A typical example is the set of articles collected in the *Journal of Industrial Economics* (March 1992). In the introductory overview, Richard Gilbert (the editor of the symposium articles) provides a sampling of the findings:

> The need for standardization is a constraint on product variety ... The five papers that appear in this symposium address how successfully markets make this tradeoff[6] ... Unfortunately, coincidence between the compatibility choice that is best for producers and the choice that is *best for economic performance* is not likely to hold in many real situations. (Gilbert 1992, 1, italics added)

For example (it is worth quoting at length to get the flavor of the assertions made):

> Katz and Shapiro (1992) showed that in a market with network externalities, the sponsors of technologies that differ in the size of the installed base may have different preferences for compatibility. For example, a dominant firm might prefer a technological design that is incompatible with other alternatives, thereby denying a new entrant the benefits of the installed base ... [We may require] firms to produce products that conform to set standards ... [but this] is a potentially costly requirement. Standards limit flexibility ... [and] may constrain technological progress ... [an alternative is] the development of products that allow consumers to use different technologies. Farrell and Saloner (1992) study the economics of (two way) "converters" ...
>
> *Markets fail* to give consumers the right incentive for investment in imperfect converters ...
>
> *Markets may fail* to give consumers the correct incentives to join one network instead of another. As a result, the success of a network is likely to be determined by consumers' expectations about which network will prevail and by choices made in the past ...
>
> [*C*]*onverters can exacerbate the problem* [italics in original] of incorrect market incentives. Converters encourage consumers to choose the technology that best suites their private preferences. But consumers fail to take account of the benefits that their patronage would confer on an alternative network [and this] ... does not generate as much total benefit for society as a whole. In Farrell and Saloner (1992) standardization provides greater total surplus unless

> consumers have sharply differentiated preference for different technologies. (Gilbert 1992, 1–3, italics added, except where noted)

And so on.

> [There is] a common theme. When production and consumption decisions are interrelated, either through network-effects or through complementary products, a competitive market does not necessarily send the right signals to firms and consumers for the delivery and purchase of goods and services. The *market fails* to reward consumers for the benefits they bring to a network or for the costs they impose by leaving the network. As a result, consumers who follow their own private interests may support more (incompatible) competing products than *would be desirable for total economic surplus*. The market would make the wrong tradeoff between product variety and network economies of scale, sometimes leading to too much variety and not enough technological compatibility. (Gilbert 1992, 7, italics added)

Note that either too much or too little variety my emerge from these models – they are models in which sub-optimal "lock-in" *and* "lock-out" may occur. Sub-optimal standards may be adopted too early (as with QWERTY) or the adoption of an optimal standard may be sub-optimally delayed – there may be too much or too little variety as opposed to uniformity. So uncertainty about the emergence of optimality applies on both sides of the issue and would necessarily also be attached to any remedial policy. It is noteworthy that nowhere in Gilbert's introduction, nor in the papers are we told how we could identify such "market failures" or what we could or should do about them. Almost as an afterthought Gilbert adds two caveats:

> Market forces might produce new institutions, *not addressed in these models* to deal with these inefficiencies ... In addition there are a myriad of unknowns concerning the performance of new technologies, the ability of firms to deliver desired services, and consumer behavior, *all of which could influence the efficient structure* of supply in markets with network-effects and complementary products. (Gilbert 1992, 7, italics added)

Models and methods

The above is offered as typical of the kind of work that is being done in this area. It is this type of work that Liebowitz and Margolis criticize in much of their work. In doing so, they raise crucial questions not only about this work, but also about the relationship between models, methods and reality in general.

Their attack proceeds on two broad fronts:

1. They point out that the building of models is not a substitute for empirical, historical research – the investigation of real case studies in order to decide which of the infinite types of models that can be constructed is likely to be relevant, and they provide a number of such studies.
2. They subject the prevailing theory to in-depth examination and demonstrate that a much wider range of results than those typically derived (and illustrated above) is not only possible but is likely. Applying what we know about the historical functioning of markets there are theoretical (in addition to empirical reasons) for doubting the existence of the so-called inefficiencies purported to be characteristic of these situations.

I consider these in turn, the first point more briefly.

"Economists often like to make their work appear to offer the same certainty as mathematics, presenting much of their work as 'proofs'" but "proofs in economic models are not proofs about the world. However much a model may prove, it can never prove that the assumptions it starts off with are the right ones" (Liebowitz and Margolis, 1999, 50). An examination of the historical case record suggests that "QWERTY worlds are awfully hard to find" (1999, 50). They look at a series of cases including the VHS versus Beta case for videocassettes, the WindowsDOS versus Macintosh case, and a whole series of cases in the software industry (to which we shall return). In each case they find no evidence for any kind of inefficient lock-in such as the dominance of early starters, lack of rivalrous activity, absence of technological innovation, or even the diminution of competitive activity.

Of course this raises the basic methodological issue, alluded to above, of how such investigations should proceed in the first place. This is an issue we shall have to examine at some length below.

Concerning the second point, Liebowitz and Margolis provide a series of crucial theoretical insights. Let us begin with the concept of path-dependence. Liebowitz and Margolis link this concept with its potential policy relevance. It is not hard to agree that "history matters." In this context, and in a number of their other comments, Liebowitz and Margolis concede the serious limitations of the model of perfect competition and related constructs. Outcomes in the world depend in a variety of ways on history. So much is clear from observing that the capital stock consists of durable items that are often highly specific in form and function. "Mistakes" in investment endure over time. That is a form of simple path-dependence. Persistence in human affairs can be called *first-degree path dependence* (97). It has no obvious policy implications. This does not imply it should be ignored, quite the contrary an understanding of the present (without any necessary efficiency judgment) demands an examination of the past.

A slightly "stronger" form of path-dependence follows from the observation that many outcomes are (in whole or in part) the subject of regret. That is to say, a retrospective evaluation of an outcome may evoke the opinion that it is not the most preferred of the alternatives that *were* available. This is called *second-degree path-dependence* (97). It is also likely to be quite common, although not so common as first-degree path dependence. We should note that its identification relies on the (necessarily speculative) identification of counterfactual historical alternatives. Except insofar as an assessment of the past is informative for the future, it too has no obvious policy implications. History is history, what's done is done.

A much stronger form of path-dependence refers to outcomes that are judged to be inferior *and were known to be inferior when the past decisions that led up to them were taken*. This is referred to as *third-degree path dependence* (98). Liebowitz and Margolis point out that this type of path-dependence implies the notion of *remediability*, that is, because of some remediable impediment, like the costs of coordinating decision-makers, an outcome that is less preferred by everyone concerned nevertheless emerges. It is only third-degree path dependence that has any possible policy relevance. As they argue: "for an inefficiency to be economically relevant, there must be some better alternative that is *feasible* in light of the *information* the we have at the time that we are making a decision" (1999, 54, italics added).

This simple taxonomy has at least two very important implications:

1. It focuses attention on the key ingredient of any discussion of policy and inefficiency, namely, *the importance of knowledge and who has it*. Asserting that one path is economically inferior to another must presume some knowledge on behalf of the economic-theorist-cum-policy-maker. And if that knowledge is available to the policy-maker, it is presumably also available to the economic agents concerned. This suggests the second implication.

2. If a path-dependent inefficiency is known *ex ante* to exist, then, by definition of efficiency as discussed above, this implies the potential that a Pareto improvement can profitably be made. That is, there is scope for someone to profitably remedy the inefficiency, since the gains available outweigh the losses that would be produced by such a remedy.

What this discussion clearly does is to place these issues firmly within the realm of familiar Coasian transaction costs economics (Coase 1960). The Coase theorem suggests that, absent transaction costs and transaction-impeding wealth effects, apparent externalities and other inefficiencies would spontaneously be removed by the market process. The identification of any such inefficiencies thus must be seen to rely on these broadly construed "transaction costs." This is relevant to third-degree path-dependent inefficiencies. If such inefficiencies exist, that is, if everyone would prefer, for example, the adoption of a particular standard, but because they expect everyone else to adopt an inferior standard, themselves all choose the inferior standard, so that we become locked-in to a standard that is Pareto dominated then such an inefficiency may be said to exist because of the high costs of coordinating the activities of the numerous agents around the adoption of the "correct" standard, that is, because of high transaction costs. More generally, if such a lock-in exists because the agents are ignorant of the advantages of the alternative standard, this too may be characterized as a transaction cost problem, since, if it were possible to cost-effectively inform such agents of their errors and to facilitate a coordinated alternative, it would be done. In fact, from one perspective, all transactions costs are *information costs* (Dahlman 1979). In sum, "it must be possible for someone to have credible information that a better allocation [of resources] is available" (Liebowitz and Margolis, 1999, 56) for path-dependence to be policy relevant.

Liebowitz and Margolis are clearly skeptical of claims regarding the existence of policy remediable inefficiencies, or "market failures." This skepticism reflects their conviction that "mechanisms exist to obviate such failures" (1999, 68). Where networks can be owned, benefits will tend to be internalized. Where this is not possible, other mechanisms exist to internalize (in whole or in part) the benefits available, for example, through the provision of complementary goods. In addition, the literature on network-effects is misleading to the extent that it tends to emphasize the possibilities for the emergence of inefficiencies. Liebowitz and Margolis provide an extensive examination of the relevant theory, one that reveals a much wider range of possibilities, even while staying within the static allocative framework.

Concerning the benefits of particular standards, Liebowitz and Margolis point out that often these benefits are tied less closely to the total number of other users of the standard and more closely to the number of users who actually interact. What concerns them are ways to achieve greater coordination and synchronization with this smaller subset. These "synchronization effects" (network-effects) may coexist with increasing, decreasing or constant returns to scale. Increasing the number of interactors in a network may add to the value of being in the network, though these additions may diminish. To obtain the total value to the consumer of any good, subject to network-effects, one must add this total "synchronization value" to the value that the consumer would place on the good as a sole user, the "autarky value." If the good has a positive supply price then its net value will be the difference between its total value to the consumer and its supply price. "[I]t is only when the net-value function slopes upward that choices between standards are fundamentally different in character from choices of other goods" (133–134). And if the supply curve slopes upward it is possible that the net-value function will slope downward.

Liebowitz and Margolis use this analysis to show that network-effects do not necessarily, or even probably, imply increasing returns to one standard that can be expected to dominate. Multiple formats are not uncommon and theoretical considerations are quite compatible with this. Niche formats are examples (Macintosh, linex, Betamax, all exist in smaller specialized markets). This result is reinforced if we assume that consumers have different tastes. Thus, "the mere existence of synchronization (network) effects is insufficient to establish the winner-take-all choice with respect to standards" (Liebowitz and Margolis, 1999, 99) and in fact the case for single dominance is quite weak.

This suggests that one may expect to see competitive strategies in which entrant firms try to specialize in their products that appeal strongly to particular groups of consumers, while incumbents, on the other hand, might try to create products that appeal to the widest possible audience attempting to foreclose opportunities for competitors (Liebowitz and Margolis, 1999, 106).

They show further that even when there are increasing returns and/or network-effects more than one standard may emerge.

Economic models are like recipes. You tend to get what you put into to them, but the way they taste depends crucially on how you mix the ingredients. Even models that stay within the static allocative equilibrium framework can vary a great deal in their implications. Liebowitz and Margolis show that winner-take-all dominance is in no way a necessary property of models that incorporate network-effects. The bias observed in the literature in that direction is a result of the presumptions of the modelers. There is no way to assess their relevance for economic policy without some way of deciding how closely they correspond to reality.

Policy

The static welfare framework is difficult to apply in the modern market environment. Market processes are truly dynamic in the sense that they take place in "real time," they are evolutionary processes that are driven by the diversity of perceptions and expectations that individuals have of the value of resources and of the process itself. They are processes that are "open ended" and are never in equilibrium. They are processes that are characterized by "radical uncertainty" and *novelty*, their outcomes are inherently unpredictable. For such processes the traditional types of efficiency assessments based on static models of resource allocation are completely meaningless. There is no way, for example, of applying the traditional utility calculus to choices among technologies that are not yet available, but that might emerge as a result of becoming "locked-in" to a particular dominant standard. Such a standard may appear to be inferior to others that are available, but it also may lead in the future to the discovery and application of complementary technologies that are vastly superior in a number of dimensions. How are we to assess the likelihood that policy action *itself* may be an "accident" that locks us into an inferior path? Insofar as new technologies are based on future knowledge and insofar as future knowledge cannot be available in the present, we cannot consider future technologies as part of today's choice-set. Neither can we include the new products, new methods of production, and new modes or organization that they bring with them. Technological change emerges from the complex interaction of individual visions (including those of the policy-makers) that are partial and incomplete and that are subject to the trial-and-error processes of the market.

Can one then say anything about efficiency? If one can it will have to be at another level and it will have to be analytically less precise than (though not entirely unrelated to) static Pareto criteria. It is at the level of the institutional framework that efficiency judgments will have to be made. If we can learn anything from history perhaps it is that certain kinds of social, legal, moral, and economic institutions are generally more conducive to the generation of innovation and prosperity that are others. Policy regimes rather than policies should perhaps be the context for this discussion.

An example is the issue of monopoly policy in high-technology industries (for an in-depth survey see Teece and Coleman 1998). Teece and Coleman argue that the nature of these industries has made the current antitrust environment obsolete. "[A]ntitrust policy cannot realistically aspire to produce 'optimal' outcomes, where 'optimality' is measured against some theoretically defined efficiency or consumer welfare criteria" (Teece and Coleman 1998, 815). What is required is a new way of thinking attuned to the truly dynamic processes of rapid and unpredictable innovation and change, in which competition and monopoly do not necessarily mean the same things as they used to.

If Liebowitz and Margolis are correct in arguing that network-effects are seldom if ever an effective mechanism for isolating firms from competition, then the kind of criteria by which we should judge the presence or absence of monopoly are not the usual market share criteria. As they point out "in this world, the firm competes not to take its share of today's market; it competes to take the market for its share of days. Legislators and courts may choose to make some ways of competing legal and some not, but the old structuralist approaches to antitrust will only be misleading" (1999, 13). The old notion of competition as a state of affairs needs to be replaced by competition as a process over time in which some firms displace others, sometimes as the dominant or only firm in the industry. Competition may indeed show up as "serial monopoly." "Competition here takes a very different form from that found in text book models of perfect competition ... There really is no 'competing' by firms in models of perfect competition, except to keep costs down" (1999, 63–64).[7] We should not base policy "on a worldview that is taken a bit too literally from an intermediate macroeconomics textbook. In the real world, information is not perfect; the future is not known with certainty; products are not perfectly homogeneous; and sometimes what we like is influenced by what others like ... From the perspective offered by ... the textbook model of the ideal economy, we might well be confused by strategic alliances, by technology-sharing agreements, by long-term guarantees, or by the continuous addition of functionality to a product." And they reject the claims "that winners might more appropriately be chosen by policymakers than by people making choices in a free market" (1999, 233).

Implicit in Liebowitz and Margolis' work is the role of knowledge – how it changes over time and how it is related to information. Much more can be said about this. In particular, innovative environments are ones where people are free to make mistakes, that is, where expectations at any time are wrong. Put another way, when we realize that at any point of time different entrepreneurs have different and inconsistent expectations about the same business environment, we must realize that at most only one of them can turn out to be right. Knowledge, unlike information, cannot be shared, and what one perceives as knowledge another will see as (an unjustified) expectation. This is fundamentally a disequilibrium situation (meaning that different people have different expectations). *In such an environment why should one assume that policy-makers are ever in possession of privileged knowledge?* Why are they likely to be right more often than any particular entrepreneur about which technology will turn out to be the best standard for consumers? More to the point, is it not likely that they are in a worse position than private businesses in this regard? In this way their work is in sympathy with some much more fundamental and far-reaching critiques of mainstream economics.

"Testing" the market process

How then does one evaluate the market process? Liebowitz and Margolis have provided a variety of in-depth historical examinations. They uncover the "problematic" nature of such "evidence" for traditional antitrust economics.[8] For example, if we "define standard A to be superior if, for all consumers and any given market share the net value of A is higher than the net value of B when B has the same market share" then it is likely that standards that create greater "social wealth" would tend to dominate and market share winning behavior may appear to be "predatory." Furthermore, "if a clearly superior technology were offered [to the market] first, we would be unlikely to see a sustained attempt to dislodge the leader by owners of inferior technologies, unless they expect that they can achieve their ends through political means, inasmuch as their expenditures in the market are likely to be futile" (Liebowitz and Margolis, 1999, 109–110). In fact, there is no presumption that policy attempts to remove a particular firm's dominance may not *itself* be responsible for us getting locked-in to an inferior standard.

This is relevant to the case of Microsoft. In order to investigate whether claims that Microsoft has achieved an inefficient monopoly are credible, Liebowitz and Margolis investigated a variety of different software products by looking at market shares in relation to reviews in consumer reports (Chapter 10). Computer magazines frequently and extensively evaluate rival products for quality and functionality. They are obviously not "objective" measures of quality, but they probably come as close as one can to ascertaining whether the products consumers use most fulfill their requirements better or worse than the alternatives. It is possible to argue that consumer reports actually provide a self-fulfilling confirmation of the tests, because consumers buy those products that the reports recommend, but this would be an extreme stretch. It is probably true that most computer users don't read the reports but become aware of the characteristics of the products by use or word of mouth over time.

Liebowitz and Margolis looked at spreadsheets, word processors, (both stand-alone and in suites), financial packages, desktop publishers, online services, and browsers. They found that (see Chapter 10 below):

- "[T]he products that have prevailed have always been the products that were regarded as best by software consumers and by the reviewers in specialist magazines" (1999, 237).
- "[A] large market share, even an extraordinarily large market share, is not a good predictor of a price increase" (1999, 238).
- Changes in market share are smooth and continuous. There is no evidence of "tipping" (the reaching of a threshold beyond which lock-in sets in).
- In many products Microsoft achieved dominance in the Macintosh market considerably earlier than in the PC market.
- Microsoft tended to charge lower prices in the market where it was dominant than in the market where it was competing.
- Rivalrous competition continues to be vigorous.

All in all, the evidence that Liebowitz and Margolis present strikes this writer as sufficient to cast substantial doubt on the case that the US government has brought against Microsoft. In some products Microsoft does not dominate, in others it has won its dominance by producing (often with extreme effort) better products. Where it does dominate, "one does not need to appeal to other factors such as those the government has focused on in its case against Microsoft ... to explain Microsoft's increasing share of the market" (Liebowitz and Margolis 1999, 202–203).

Concluding remarks

In the final analysis, Liebowitz and Margolis' work is noteworthy for its solidity (its groundedness). They do not plumb the depths of methodology. Yet at the same time, their work transcends their idiom and is pregnant with profound and far-reaching implications. Common-sense and basic historical research leads quickly to highly significant theoretical results and empirical generalizations, not to mention political implications. The hidden (and no doubt unconscious) message is much more revolutionary than it appears.

Liebowitz and Margolis provide a formidable array of objections to some standard arguments. Anyone interested in the issues surrounding the emergence of new technologies and standards and the related policy questions cannot afford to be ignorant of their work. One may hope that this book will at the very least stimulate discussion and further research.[9]

Notes

1. They also argued that, far from this literature constituting a "new economics" that moves beyond the old obsolete macroeconomics, the latter is fully capable of explaining everything that these situations presented. The economics of natural monopoly, of externalities and public goods, of transactions costs and other related well-established themes serve to establish that these new "information age" industries present nothing that is really new in principle, though some interesting new perspectives do emerge. (For example, in reexamining the alleged market failure due to consumption scale economies – the fact that the value of the product depends in part on how many people use it – they point out that this can be interestingly interpreted as the traditional "tragedy of the commons" in reverse.) This general line of reasoning is capable of being misunderstood. To claim that traditional microeconomics can be made to incorporate almost every imaginable case is probably true, but this does not contradict the criticism of the use of perfect competition as a standard in policy discussions.
2. "The occurrence of this 'lock-in' as early as early as the mid-1890's *does* appear to have owed something also to the high cost of software 'conversion' and the resulting *quasi-irreversibility of investments* in specific touch-typing skills. Thus, as far as keyboard conversion costs were concerned, an important asymmetry had appeared between the software and the hardware components of the evolving system: the costs of typewriter software conversion were going up, whereas the costs of typewriter hardware conversion were coming down" (David 1985, 335–6, first italics added).
3. In a sense, network-effects are complementarities in consumption and production and were anticipated by Marshall in his work on industrial districts, trade alliances, etc.
4. Actually, this discussion conflates "knowledge" with "information" in an illegitimate way. Information is public in a way that knowledge is not (Lewin 1997, 1999 Chapters 3 and 12). This will become more important below when I discuss the role of knowledge in policy and research.
5. Of course a vast literature on this exists. The work of Hayek (1988) on the evolution of social institutions is relevant as is that of North (1990). See also Lewin (1997) for a discussion of the connection between stability and flexibility in evolved institutions.

6. This is a typical misstatement. The papers do not address anything about real-world markets. There is no real "history" in them. Instead they address how it is possible to produce sub-optimality in theoretically conceived simulations of real world markets.
7. Cf. Hayek (1978).
8. "[A]nything that a firm does to compete can be, at some point, viewed as an attempt to monopolize. And anything that a firms does to improve its products, extend its standards, or reach additional markets will look like an attempt to monopolize" (Liebowitz and Margolis, 1999, 11).
9. For more information on the debate between Liebowitz and Margolis and Paul David see Lewin (2000) and Chapter 11 below.

References

Arthur W. B. 1983. "On Competing Technologies and Historical Small Events: The Dynamics of Choice Under Increasing Returns." Technological Innovation Program *Workshop Paper*, Department of Economics, Standford University, (November).

——— 1989. "Competing Technologies, Increasing Returns, and Lock-in by Historical Events," *Economic Journal*, 99: 116–131.

Coase, R. H. 1960. "The Problem of Social Cost," *Journal of Law and Economics*, 3: 1–44.

Dahlman, C. 1979. "The Problem of Externality," *Journal of Law and Economics*, 22: 141–163.

David, P. A. 1985. "Clio and the Economics of QWERTY," *American Economic Review*, 75: 332–337.

Farrell, J. and Saloner, G. 1992. "Converters, Compatibility, and Control of Interfaces," *The Journal of Industrial Economics*, 40: 9–36.

Gilbert R. J. 1992. "Symposium on Compatibility: Incentives and Market Structure," *The Journal of Industrial Economics*, 40: 1–8.

Hayek, F. A. 1978. "Competition as a Discovery Procedure," in Hayek, F. A., *New Studies in Philosophy, Politics and Economics and the History of Ideas*, London: Routledge.

——— 1988. *The Fatal Conceit: The Errors of Socialism*, Chicago: University of Chicago Press.

Katz, M. L. and Shapiro, C. 1983. "Network Externalities, Competition and Compatibility," *Woodrow Wilson School Discussion Paper in Economics*, 54, Princeton University September.

——— 1992. "Product Introduction with Network Externalities," *The Journal of Industrial Economics*, 40: 55–84.

Lewin P. 1997. "Hayekian Equilibrium and Change," *Journal of Economic Methodology*, 4: 245–266.

——— 1999. *Capital in Disequilibrium: The Role of Capital in a Changing World*, New York and London: Routledge.

——— 2000. "The Market Process and the Economics of QWERTY: Two Views," *Review of Austrian Economics*, forthcoming.

Liebowitz, S. J. and Margolis S. E. 1990. "The Fable of the Keys," *Journal of Law and Economics*, 33: 1–25.

——— 1999, 2001 rev. ed. *Winners, Losers and Microsoft: Competition and Antitrust in High Technology*, Oakland: The Independent Institute.

North, D. C. 1990. *Institutions, Institutional Change and Economic Performance,* New York: Cambridge University Press.

Teece, D. J. and Coleman, M. 1998. "The Meaning of Monopoly: Antitrust Analysis in High-Technology Industries," *The Antitrust Bulletin,* Fall–Winter: 801–857.

Yamada, H. 1980. "A Historical Study of Typewriters and Typing Methods from the Position of Planning Japanese Parallels," *Journal of Information Processing,* 2: 175–202.

———— 1983. "Certain Problems Associated with the Design of Input Keyboards for Japanese Writing," in Cooper W. E. (ed.), *Cognitive Aspects of Skilled Typewriting,* New York: Springer.

2 The Fable of the Keys (1990)* **

Introduction

The term "standard" can refer to any social convention (standard of conduct, legal standards), but it most often refers to conventions that require exact uniformity (standards of measurement, computer operating systems). Current efforts to control the development of high-resolution television, multitasking computer-operating systems, and videotaping formats have heightened interest in standards.

The economic literature on standards has focused recently on the possibility of market failure with respect to the choice of a standard. In its strongest form, the argument is essentially this: an established standard can persist over a challenger, even where all users prefer a world dominated by the challenger, if users are unable to coordinate their choices. For example, each of us might prefer to have Beta-format videocassette recorders as long as prerecorded Beta tapes continue to be produced, but individually we do not buy Beta machines because we don't think enough others will buy Beta machines to sustain the prerecorded tape supply. I don't buy a Beta format machine because I think that you won't you don't buy one because you think that I won't. In the end, we both turn out to be correct, but we are both worse off than we might have been. This, of course, is a catch-22 that we might suppose to be common in the economy. There will be no cars until there are gas stations there will be no gas stations until there are cars. Without some way out of this conundrum, joyriding can never become a favorite activity of teenagers.[1]

---

* *Journal of Law and Economics*, 33 (1990): 1–25.

The logic of these economic traps and conundrums is impeccable as far as it goes, but we would do well to consider that these traps are sometimes escaped in the market. Obviously, gas stations and automobiles do exist, so participants in the market must use some technique to unravel such conundrums. If this catch-22 is to warrant our attention as an empirical issue, at a minimum we would hope to see at least one real-world example of it. In the economics literature on standards (see for example Farrell and Saloner 1985, Katz and Shapiro 1985 and Tirole 1988), the popular real-world example of this market failure is the standard QWERTY typewriter keyboard[2] and its competition with the rival Dvorak keyboard.[3] This example is noted frequently in newspaper and magazine reports, seems to be generally accepted as true, and was brought to economists' attention by the papers of Paul David (1985, 1986). According to the popular story, the keyboard invented by August Dvorak, a professor of education at the University of Washington, is vastly superior to the QWERTY keyboard developed by Christopher Sholes that is now in common use. We are to believe that, although the Dvorak keyboard is vastly superior to QWERTY, virtually no one trains on Dvorak because there are too few Dvorak machines, and there are virtually no Dvorak machines because there are too few Dvorak typists.

This chapter examines the history, economics, and ergonomics of the typewriter keyboard. We show that David's version of the history of the market's rejection of Dvorak does not report the true history, and we present evidence that the continued use of QWERTY is efficient given the current understanding of keyboard design. We conclude that the example of the Dvorak keyboard is what beehives and lighthouses were for earlier market-failure fables. It is an example of market failure that will not withstand rigorous examination of the historical record (see Coase 1974 and Cheung 1973).

Some economics of standards

Some standards change over time without being impaired as social conventions. Languages for example, evolve over time, adding words and practices that are useful and winnowing features that have lost their purpose. Other standards are inherently inflexible. Given current technologies, it won't do, for example, for broadcast frequencies to drift the way that orchestral tuning has. A taste for a slightly larger centimeter really can't be accommodated by a sequence of independent decisions the way that increased use of contractions in academic writing can obviously. If standards can evolve at low cost, they would be expected to evolve into the forms that are most efficient (in the eyes of those adopting the standards). Conversely, an inappropriate standard is most likely to have some permanence where evolution is costly.

In their influential article on standards, Joseph Farrell and Garth Saloner (1985) present a formal exploration of the difficulties associated with changing from one standard to another. They construct hypothetical circumstances that might lead to market failure with respect to standards. To refer to the condition in which a superior standard is not adopted, they coin the phrase excess inertia. Excess inertia is a type of externality: each nonadopter of the new standard imposes costs on every other potential user of the new standard. In the case of excess inertia, the new standard can be clearly superior to the old standard, and the sum of the private costs of switching to the new standard can be less than the sum of the private benefits, and yet the switch does not occur. This is to be differentiated from the far more common invention of new standards superior to the old, but for which the costs of switching are too high to make the switch practicable. Users of the old standard may regret their choice of that standard, but their continued use of the old standard is not inefficient: would it not be foolish to lay all regrets at the doorstep of externalities?

Farrell and Saloner's construct is useful because it shows the theoretical possibility of a market failure and also demonstrates the role of information. There is no possibility of excess inertia in their model if all participants can communicate perfectly. In this regard, standards are not unlike other externalities in that costs of transacting are essential. Thus, standards can be understood within the framework that Coase (1960) offered decades ago.[4]

By their nature, this model and others like it must ignore many factors in the markets they explore. Adherence to an inferior standard in the presence of a superior one represents a loss of some sort: such a loss implies a profit opportunity for someone who can figure out a means of internalizing the externality and appropriating some of the value made available from changing to the superior standard. Furthermore, institutional factors such as head starts from being first on the market, patent and copyright law, brand names, tie-in sales, discounts, and so on, can also lead to appropriation possibilities (read "profit opportunities") for entrepreneurs, and with these opportunities we expect to see activity set in motion to internalize the externalities. The greater the gap in performance between two standards, the greater are these profit opportunities, and the more likely that a move to the efficient standard will take place. As a result, a clear example of excess inertia is apt to be very hard to find. Observable instances in which a dramatically inferior standard prevails are likely to be short-lived, imposed by authority, or fictional.

The creator of a standard is a natural candidate to internalize the externality.[5] If a standard can be "owned," the advantage of the standard can be appropriated, at least in part, by the owner. Dvorak, for example, patented his keyboard. An owner with the prospect of appropriating substantial benefits from a new standard would have an incentive to share some of the costs of switching to a new standard. This incentive gives rise to a variety of internalizing tactics. Manufacturers of new products sometimes offer substantial discounts to early adopters, offer guarantees of satisfaction or make products available on a rental basis. Sometimes manufacturers offer rebates to buyers who turn in equipment based on old standards, thus discriminating in price between those who have already made investments in a standard and those who have not. Internalizing tactics can be very simple: some public utilities once supplied light bulbs. and some UHF television stations still offer free UHF indoor antennas. In many industries firms provide subsidized or free training to assure an adequate supply of operators. Typewriter manufacturers were an important source of trained typists for at least the first fifty years of that technology (David 1985, 5).[6]

Another internalizing tactic is convertibility. Suppliers of new-generation computers occasionally offer a service to convert files to new formats. Cable-television companies have offered hardware and services to adapt old televisions to new antenna systems for an interim period. Of interest in the present context for a time before and after the Second World War typewriter manufacturers offered to convert QWERTY typewriters to Dvorak for a very small fee (Foulke 1961).[7]

All of these tactics tend to unravel the apparent trap of an inefficient standard but there are additional conditions that can contribute to the ascendancy of the efficient standard. An important one is the growth of the activity that uses the standard. If a market is growing rapidly the number of users who have made commitments to any standard is small relative to the number of future users. Sales of audiocassette players were barely hindered by their incompatibility with the reel-to-reel or eight-track players that preceded them. Sales of sixteen-bit computers were scarcely hampered by their incompatibility with the disks or operating systems of eight-bit computers.

Another factor that must be addressed is the initial competition among rival standards. If standards are chosen largely through the influence of those who are able to internalize the value of standards we would expect in Darwinian fashion the prevailing standard to be the fittest economic competitor. Previous keyboard histories have acknowledged the presence of rivals but they seem to view competition as a process leading to results indistinguishable from pure chance.

Consideration of the many complicating factors present in the market suggests that market failure in standards is not as compelling as many of the abstract models seem to suggest. Theoretical abstraction presents candidates for what might be important, but only empirical verification can determine if these abstract models have anything to do with reality.

The case for the superiority of the Dvorak keyboard

Paul David (1985) introduces economists to the conventional story of the development and persistence of the current standard keyboard, known as the Universal, or QWERTY, keyboard. The key features of that story are as follows. The operative patent for the typewriter was awarded in 1868 to Christopher Latham Sholes, who continued to develop the machine for several years. Among the problems that Sholes and his associates addressed was the jamming of the type bars when certain combinations of keys were struck in very close succession. As a partial solution to this problem, Sholes arranged his keyboard so that the keys most likely to be struck in close succession were approaching the type point from opposite sides of the machine. Since QWERTY was designed to accomplish this now obsolete mechanical requirement, maximizing speed was not an explicit objective. Some authors even claim that the keyboard is actually configured to minimize speed since decreasing speed would have been one way to avoid the jamming of the typewriter. At the time, however, a two-finger hunt-and-peck method was contemplated, so the keyboard speed envisioned was quite different from touch-typing speeds.

The rights to the Sholes patent were sold to E. Remington & Sons in early 1873. The Remingtons added further mechanical improvements and began commercial production in late 1873.

A watershed event in the received version of the QWERTY story is a typing contest held in Cincinnati on July 25, 1888. Frank McGurrin, a court stenographer from Salt Lake City, who was apparently the first to memorize the keyboard and use touch-typing, won a decisive victory over Louis Taub. Taub used the hunt-and-peck method on a Caligraph, a machine that used seventy-two keys to provide upper- and lower-case letters. According to popular history, the event established once and for all that the Remington typewriter, with its QWERTY keyboard, was technically superior. More important, the contest created an interest in touch-typing, an interest directed at the QWERTY arrangement. Reportedly, no one else at that time had skills that could even approach McGurrin's, so there was no possibility of countering the claim that the Remington keyboard arrangement was efficient. McGurrin participated in typing contests and demonstrations throughout the country and became something of a celebrity. His choice of the Remington keyboard which may well have been arbitrary contributed to the establishment of the standard. So it was, according to the popular telling, that a keyboard designed to solve a short-lived mechanical problem became the standard used daily by millions of typists.[8]

In 1936, August Dvorak patented the Dvorak Simplified Keyboard (DSK) claiming that it dramatically reduced the finger movement necessary for typing by balancing the load between hands and loading the stronger fingers more heavily. Its inventors claimed advantages of greater speed, reduced fatigue and easier learning. These claims have been accepted by most commentators including David who refers, without citation, to experiments done by the US Navy that had shown that the increased efficiency obtained with the DSK would amortize the cost of retraining a group of typists within ten days of their subsequent full-time employment.[9] In spite of its claimed advantages the Dvorak keyboard has never found much acceptance.

This story is the basis of the claim that the current use of the QWERTY keyboard is a market failure. The claim continues that a beginning typist will not choose to train in Dvorak because Dvorak machines are likely to be difficult to find and offices will not equip with Dvorak machines because there is no available pool of typists.

This is an ideal example. The number of dimensions of performance are few and in these dimensions the Dvorak keyboard appears overwhelmingly superior. These very attributes however imply that the forces to adopt this superior standard should also be very strong. It is the failure of these forces to prevail that warrants our critical examination.

The myth of Dvorak

Farrell and Saloner (1985) mention the typewriter keyboard as a clear example of market failure. So too does the textbook by Tirole.[10] Both works cite David's article as the authority on this subject. Yet there are many aspects of the QWERTY-versus-Dvorak fable that do not survive scrutiny. First, the claim that Dvorak is a better keyboard is supported only by evidence that is both scant and suspect. Second, studies in the ergonomics literature find no significant advantage for Dvorak that can be deemed scientifically reliable. Third, the competition among producers of typewriters, out of which the standard emerged, was far more vigorous than is commonly reported. Fourth, there were far more typing contests than just the single Cincinnati contest. These contests provided ample opportunity to demonstrate the superiority of alternative keyboard arrangements. That QWERTY survived significant challenges early in the history of typewriting demonstrates that it is at least among the reasonably fit, even if not the fittest that can be imagined.

Gaps in the evidence for Dvorak

Like most of the historians of the typewriter (for example Beeching 1974 and Foulke 1961) David seems to assume that Dvorak is decisively superior to QWERTY. He never questions this assertion, and he consistently refers to the QWERTY standard as inferior. His most tantalizing evidence is his undocumented account of the US Navy experiments. After recounting the claims of the Navy study, he adds "if as Apple advertising copy says, DSK 'lets you type 20 to 40 percent faster' – why did this superior design meet essentially the same resistance as the previous seven improvements on the QWERTY typewriter keyboard" (David 1985, 34, n.5).

Why indeed? The survival of QWERTY is surprising to economists only in the presence of a demonstrably superior rival. David uses QWERTY's survival to demonstrate the nature of path dependence, the importance of history for economists and the inevitable oversimplification of reality imposed by theory. Several theorists use his historical evidence to claim empirical relevance for their versions of market failure. But on what foundation does all this depend? All we get from David is an undocumented assertion and some advertising copy.

The view that Dvorak is superior is widely held. This view can be traced to a few key sources. A book published by Dvorak and several co-authors in 1936 included some of Dvorak's own scientific inquiry (Dvorak *et al.* 1936). Dvorak and his co-authors compared the typing speeds achieved in four different and completely separate experiments conducted by various researchers for various purposes (Dvorak *et al.*, 1936, 226).

One of these experiments examined the typing speed on the Dvorak keyboard and three examined typing speed on the QWERTY keyboard. The authors claimed that these studies established that students learn Dvorak faster than they learn QWERTY. A serious criticism of their methodology is that the various studies that they compared used students of different ages and abilities (for example students learning Dvorak in grades 7 and 8 at the University of Chicago Lab School were compared with students in conventional high schools), in different school systems taking different tests and in classes that met for different periods of time. Still more serious is that they did not stipulate whether their choice of studies was a random sample or the full population of available studies. So their study really establishes only that it is possible to find studies in which students learning to type on QWERTY keyboards appear to have progressed less rapidly in terms of calendar time than Dvorak's students did on his keyboard. Even in this Dvorak study however the evidence is mixed as to whether students, as they progress, retain an advantage when using the Dvorak keyboard, since the differences seem to diminish as typing speed increases.

In general it is desirable to have independent evaluation and here the objectivity of Dvorak and his co-authors seems particularly open to question. Their book is more in the vein of an inspirational tract than a scientific work. Consider the following taken from their chapter about relative keyboard performances):

> The bare recital to you of a few simple facts should suffice to indict the available spatial pattern that is so complacently entitled the universal [QWERTY] keyboard. Since when was the universe lopsided? The facts will not be stressed, since you may finally surmount most of the ensuing handicaps of this [QWERTY] keyboard. Just enough facts will be paraded to lend you double assurance that for many of the errors that you will inevitably make and for much of the discouraging delay you will experience in longed-for speed gains, you are not to blame. If you grow indignant over the beginner's role of innocent victim remember that a little emotion heightens determination. (Dvorak *et al.* 1936, 210)
>
> Analysis of the present keyboard is so destructive that an improved arrangement is a modern imperative. Isn't it obvious that faster, more accurate, less fatiguing typing can be attained in much less learning time provided a simplified keyboard is taught. (Dvorak *et al.* 1936, 221).

The Navy study, which seems to have been the basis for some of the more extravagant claims of Dvorak advocates, is also flawed. Arthur Foulke, Sholes' biographer, and a believer in the superiority of the Dvorak keyboard, points out several discrepancies in the reports coming out of the Navy studies. He cites an Associated Press report of October 7, 1943, to the effect that a new typewriter keyboard allowed typists to "zip along at 180 words per minute" but then adds "However, the Navy Department, in a letter to the author October I4, 1943 by Lieutenant Commander W. Marvin McCarthy said that it had no record of and did not conduct such a speed test, and denied having made an official announcement to that effect" (Foulke 1961 103). Foulke also reports a *Business Week* story of October 16, 1943, that reports a speed of 108, not 180, words per minute.

We were able to obtain, with difficulty, a copy of the 1944 Navy report.[11] The report does not state who conducted the study. It consists of two parts, the first based on an experiment conducted in July of 1944 and the second based on an experiment conducted in October of that year. The report's foreword states that two prior experiments had been conducted but that "the first two groups were not truly fair tests." We are not told the results of the early tests.

The first of the reported experiments consisted of the retraining of fourteen Navy typists on newly overhauled Dvorak keyboards for two hours a day. We are not told how the subjects were chosen, but it does not appear to be based on a random process. At least twelve of these individuals had previously been QWERTY typists with an average speed of thirty-two words per minute although the Navy defined competence as fifty words per minute. The typists had IQs that averaged 98 and dexterity skills with an average percentile of 65. The study reports that it took fifty-two hours for typists to catch up to their old speed. After completing an average of eighty-three hours on the new keyboard, typing speed had increased to an average of fifty-six words per minute compared to their original thirty-two words per minute, a 75 percent increase.

The second experiment consisted of the retraining of eighteen typists on the QWERTY keyboard. It is not clear how these typists were picked or even if members of this group were aware that they were part of an experiment. We are not told whether this training was performed in the same manner as the first experiment (the Navy retrained people from time to time and this may just have been one of these groups). The participants' IQs and dexterity skills are not reported. It is difficult to have any sense whether this group is a reasonable control for the first group. The initial typing scores for this group averaged twenty-nine words per minute but these scores were not measured identically to those from the first experiment. The report states that because three typists had net scores of zero words per minute initially the beginning and ending speeds were calculated as the average of the first four typing tests and the average of the last four typing tests. In contrast, the initial experiment using Dvorak simply used the first and last test scores. This truncation of the reported values reduced the measured increase in typing speed on the QWERTY keyboard by a substantial margin.[12]

The measured increase in net typing speed for QWERTY retraining was from twenty-nine to thirty-seven words per minute (28 percent) after an average of 158 hours of training, considerably less than the increase that occurred with the Dvorak keyboard.

The Navy study concludes that training in Dvorak is much more effective than retraining in QWERTY. But the experimental design leaves too many questions for this to be an acceptable finding. Do these results hold for typists with normal typing skills or only for those far below average? Were the results for the first group just a regression to the mean for a group of underperforming typists? How much did the Navy studies underestimate the value of increased QWERTY retraining due to the inconsistent measurement? Were the two groups given similar training? Were the QWERTY typewriters overhauled, as were the Dvorak typewriters? There are many possible biases in this study. All, suspiciously, seem to be in favor of the Dvorak design.

The authors of the Navy study do seem to have their minds made up concerning the superiority of Dvorak. In discussing the background of the Dvorak keyboard and prior to introducing the results of the study, the report claims: "Indisputably, it is obvious that the Simplified Keyboard is easier to master than the Standard Keyboard" (Navy 1944, 2, n.24). Later they refer to QWERTY as an "ox" and Dvorak as a "jeep" and add: "no amount of goading the oxen can materially change the end result" (Navy 1994, 23).

There are other problems of credibility with these Navy studies having to do with potential conflicts of interest. Foulke (1961, 103) identifies Dvorak as Lieutenant Commander August Dvorak, the Navy's top expert in the analysis of time and motion studies during World War II. Earle Strong, a professor at Pennsylvania State University and a one-time chairman of the Office Machine Section of the American Standards Association, reports that the 1944 Navy experiment and some Treasury department experiments performed in 1946 were conducted by none other than Dr. Dvorak (Strong 1956).[13] We also know that Dvorak had a financial stake in this keyboard. He owned the patent on the keyboard and had received at least $130 000 from the Carnegie Commission for Education for the studies performed while he was at the University of Washington (Yamada 1980).

But there is more to this story than the weakness of the evidence reported by the Navy, or Dvorak, or his followers. A 1956 General Services Administration study by Earle Strong, which was influential in its time, provides the most compelling evidence against the Dvorak keyboard (Strong 1956). This study is ignored in David's history for economists and is similarly ignored in other histories directed at general audiences. Strong conducted a carefully controlled experiment designed to examine the costs and benefits of switching to Dvorak. He concluded that retraining typists on Dvorak had no advantages over retraining on QWERTY.

In the first phase of Strong's experiment ten government typists were retrained on the Dvorak keyboard. It took well over twenty-five days of four-hour-a-day training for these typists to catch up to their old QWERTY speed. (Compare this to the claim David makes about the Navy study's results that the full retraining costs were *recovered* in ten days.) When the typists had finally caught up to their old speed Strong began the second phase of the experiment. The newly trained Dvorak typists continued training and a group of ten QWERTY typists began a parallel program to improve their skills. In this second phase the Dvorak typists progressed less quickly with further Dvorak training than did QWERTY typists training on QWERTY keyboards. Thus Strong concluded that Dvorak training would never be able to amortize its costs. He recommended that the government provide further training in the QWERTY keyboard for QWERTY typists. The information provided by this study was largely responsible for putting Dvorak to rest as a serious alternative to QWERTY for those firms and government agencies responsible for choosing typewriters.[14]

Strong's study does leave some questions unanswered. Because it uses experienced typists it cannot tell us whether beginning Dvorak typists could be trained more quickly than beginning QWERTY typists. Further, although one implication of Strong's study is that the ultimate speed achieved would be greater for QWERTY typists than for Dvorak typists (since the QWERTY group was increasing the gap over the Dvorak group in the second phase of the experiment), we cannot be sure that an experiment with beginning typists would provide the same results.[15]

Nevertheless, Strong's study must be taken seriously. It attempts to control the quality of the two groups of typists and the instruction they receive. It directly addresses the claims that came out of the Navy studies, which consider the costs and benefits of retraining. It directly parallels the decision that a real firm or a real government agency might face: is it worthwhile to retrain its present typists? The alleged market failure of the QWERTY keyboard as represented by Farrell and Saloner's excess inertia is that all firms would change to a new standard if only they could each be assured that the others would change. If we accept Strong's findings, it is not a failure to communicate that keeps firms from retraining its typists or keeps typists from incurring their own retraining costs. If Strong's study is correct, it is efficient for current typists not to switch to Dvorak.

Current proponents of Dvorak have a different view when they assess why the keyboard has not been more successful. Hisao Yamada, an advocate of Dvorak who is attempting to influence Japanese keyboard development, gives a wide-ranging interpretation to the Dvorak keyboard's failure. He blames the Depression, bad business decisions by Dvorak, World War II, and the Strong report. He goes on to say:

> There were always those who questioned the claims made by DSK followers. Their reasons are also manifold. Some suspected the superiority of the instructions by DSK advocates to be responsible (because they were all holders of advanced degrees); such a credential of instructors is also apt to cause the Hawthorne effect. Others maintain that all training experiments, except the GSA one as noted, were conducted by the DSK followers, and that the statistical control of experiments was not well exercised. This may be a valid point. It does not take too long to realize, however, that it is a major financial undertaking to organize such an experiment to the satisfaction of statisticians ... The fact that those critics were also reluctant to come forth in support of such experiments ... may indicate that the true reason of their criticism lies elsewhere. (Yamada 1980, 189)

This is one nasty disagreement.[16]

Nevertheless, Yamada as much as admits that experimental findings reported by Dvorak and his supporters cannot be assigned much credibility and that the most compelling claims cited by Yamada for DSK's superiority come from Dvorak's own work. Much of the other evidence Yamada uses to support his views of DSK's superiority actually can be used to make a case against Dvorak. Yamada refers to a 1952 Australian post office study that showed no advantages for DSK when it was first conducted. It was only after adjustments were made in the test procedure (to remove psychological impediments to superior performance) that DSK did better (Yamada 1980, 185). He cites a 1973 study based on six typists at Western Electric where after 104 hours of training on DSK, typists were 2.6 percent faster than they had been on QWERTY (Yamada 1980, 188). Similarly Yamada reports that in a 1978 study at Oregon State University after 100 hours of training typists were up to 97.6 percent of their old QWERTY speed (1980, 188). Both of these retraining times are similar to those reported by Strong and not to those in the Navy study. Yamada however thinks the studies themselves support Dvorak.[17] But unlike the Strong study neither of these studies included parallel retraining on QWERTY keyboards. As the Strong study points out even experienced QWERTY typists increase their speed on QWERTY if they are given additional training. Even if that problem is ignored the possible advantages of Dvorak are all much weaker than those reported from the Navy study.

Evidence from the ergonomics literature

The most recent studies of the relative merits of keyboards are found in the ergonomics literature. These studies provide evidence that the advantages of the Dvorak is either small or nonexistent. For example A. Miller and J. C. Thomas conclude that "the fact remains however that no alternative has shown a realistically significant advantage over the QWERTY for general purpose typing" (Miller and Thomas 1977, 509). In two studies based on analysis of hand-and-finger motions R. F. Nickells Jr. finds that Dvorak is 6.2 percent faster than QWERTY (Yamada 1983, 336), and R. Kinkhead (1975) finds only a 2.3 percent advantage for Dvorak (cited in Yamada 1983, 365). Simulation studies by Donald Norman and David Rumelhart find similar results:

> In our studies ... we examined novices typing on several different arrangements of alphabetically organized keyboards, the Sholes (QWERTY) keyboard, and a randomly organized keyboard to control against prior knowledge of Sholes. There were essentially no differences among the alphabetic and random keyboards. Novices type slightly faster on the Sholes keyboard, probably reflecting prior experience with it. We studied expert typists by using our simulation model. Here, we looked at the Sholes and Dvorak layouts, as well as several alphabetically arranged keyboards. The simulation

> showed that the alphabetically organized keyboards were between 2 percent and 9 percent slower than the Sholes keyboard, and the Dvorak keyboard was only about 5 percent faster than the Sholes. These figures correspond well to other experimental studies that compared the Dvorak and Sholes keyboards and to the computations of Card, Moran, and Newell ... for comparing these keyboards ... For the expert typist, the layout of keys makes surprisingly little difference. There seems no reason to choose Sholes, Dvorak. or alphabetically organized keyboards over one another on the basis of typing speed. It is possible to make a bad keyboard layout, however, and two of the arrangements that we studied can be ruled out. (Norman and Rumelhart 1983, 45)

These ergonomic studies are particularly interesting because the claimed advantage of the Dvorak keyboard has been based historically on the claimed ergonomic advantages in reduced finger movement. Norman and Rumelhart's discussion offers clues to why Dvorak does not provide as much of an advantage as its proponents have claimed. They argue,

> For optimal typing speed. keyboards should be designed so that:
> A. The loads on the right and left hands are equalized.
> B. The load on the home (middle) row is maximized.
> C. The frequency of alternating hand sequences is maximized and the frequency of same-finger typing is minimized.
>
> The Dvorak keyboard does a good job on these variables, especially A and B: 67 percent of the typing is done on the home row and the left–right hand balance is 47–53 percent. Although the Sholes (QWERTY) keyboard fails at conditions A and B (most typing is done on the top row and the balance between the two hands is 57 percent and 43 percent), the policy to put successively typed keys as far apart as possible favors factor C, thus leading to relatively rapid typing. (Mares 1909)

The explanation for Norman and Rumelhart's factor C is that during a keystroke, the idle hand prepares for its next keystroke. Thus Sholes' decision to solve a mechanical problem through careful keyboard arrangement may have inadvertently satisfied a fairly important requirement for efficient typing.

The consistent finding in the ergonomic studies is that the results imply no clear advantage for Dvorak. These studies are not explicitly statistical, yet their negative claim seems analogous to the scientific caution that one exercises when measured differences are small relative to unexplained variance. We read these authors as saying that, in light of the imprecision of method, scientific caution precludes rejection of the hypothesis that Dvorak and QWERTY are equivalent. At the very least, the studies indicate that the speed advantage of Dvorak is not anything like the 20–40 percent that is claimed in the Apple advertising copy that David cites. Moreover, the studies suggest that there may be no advantage with the Dvorak keyboard for ordinary typing by skilled typists. It appears that the principles by which Dvorak "rationalized" the keyboard may not have fully captured the actions of experienced typists largely because typing appears to be a fairly complex activity.

A final word on all of this comes from Frank McGurrin, the world's first known touch-typist:

> Let an operator take a new sentence and see how fast he can write it. Then, after practicing the sentence, time himself again, and he will find he can write it much faster: and further practice on the particular sentence will increase the speed on it to nearly or quite double that on the new matter. Now let the operator take another new sentence, and he will find his speed has dropped back to about what it was before he commenced practicing the first sentence. Why is this? The fingers are capable of the same rapidity. It is because the mind is not so familiar with the keys. (Mares 1909)

Of course, performance in any physical activity can presumably be improved with practice. But the limitations of typing speed, in McGurrin's experiment, appear to have something to do with a mental or, at least, neurological skill and fairly little to do with the limitations on the speeds at which the fingers can complete their required motions.

Typewriter competition

The Sholes typewriter was not invented from whole cloth. Yamada reports that there were fifty-one inventors of prior typewriters, including some earlier commercially produced typewriters. He states: "Examination of these materials reveals that almost all ideas incorporated into Sholes' machines, if not all, were at one time or another already used by his predecessors" (Yamada 1983, 177, n.41).

Remington's early commercial rivals were numerous, offered substantial variations on the typewriter, and in some cases enjoyed moderate success. There were plenty of competitors after the Sholes machine came to market. The largest and most important of these rivals were the Hall, Caligraph, and Crandall machines. The Yost, another double-keyboard machine, manufactured by an early collaborator of Sholes, used a different inking system and was known particularly for its attractive type. According to production data assembled by Yamada, the machines were close rivals, and they each sold in large numbers (Yamada 1983, 181). Xavier Wagner, who also worked on the 1873 Remington typewriter, developed a machine that made the type fully visible as it was being typed. This machine was offered to, but rejected by, the Union Typewriter Company, the company formed by the 1893 merger of Remington with six other typewriter manufacturers (Beeching 1974, 165, n.13). In 1895, Wagner joined John T. Underwood to produce his machine. Their company, which later became Underwood, enjoyed rapid growth, producing two hundred typewriters per week by 1898 (Yamada 1983, 214). Wagner's offer to Union also resulted in the spin-off from Union of L. C. Smith, who introduced a visible-type machine in 1904 (Yamada 1983, 165). This firm was the forerunner of the Smith-Corona company.

Two manufacturers offered their own versions of an ideal keyboard: Hammond in 1893 and Blickensderfer in 1889 (David 1986, 38).[18] Each of these machines survived for a time, and each had certain mechanical advantages. Blickensderfer later produced what may have been the first portable and the first electric typewriters. Hammond later produced the Varityper, a standard office type-composing machine that was the antecedent of today's desktop publishing. The alternative keyboard machines produced by these manufacturers came early enough that typewriters and, more important, touch-typing were still not very popular. The Blickensderfer appeared within a year of the famous Cincinnati contest that first publicized touch-typing.

In the 1880s and 1890s typewriters were generally sold to offices not already staffed with typists or into markets in which typists were not readily available. Since the sale of a new machine usually meant training a new typist, a manufacturer that chose to compete using an alternative keyboard had an opportunity. As late as 1923, typewriter manufacturers operated placement services for typists and were an important source of operators. In the earliest days, typewriter salesmen provided much of the limited training available to typists (Herkimer County Historical Society 1923). Since almost every sale required the training of a typist, a typewriter manufacturer that offered a different keyboard was not particularly disadvantaged. Manufacturers internalized training costs in such an environment, so a keyboard that allowed more rapid training might have been particularly attractive.

Offering alternative keyboards was not a terribly expensive tactic. The Blickensderfer used a type-bar configuration similar in principle to the IBM Selectric type ball and, so, could easily offer many different configurations. The others could create alternative keyboard arrangements by simply soldering the type to different bars and attaching the keys to different levers. So apparently the problem of implementing the conversion was not what kept the manufacturers from changing keyboards.

The rival keyboards did ultimately fail, of course.[19] But the QWERTY keyboard cannot have been so well established at the time the rival keyboards were first offered that they were rejected because they were nonstandard. Manufacturers of typewriters sought and promoted any technical feature that might give them an advantage in the market. Certainly shorter training and greater speed would have been an attractive selling point for a typewriter with an alternative keyboard. Neither can it be said that the rival keyboards were doomed by inferior mechanical characteristics because these companies went on to produce successful and innovative, though QWERTY-based, typing machines. Thus we cannot attribute our inheritance of the QWERTY keyboard to a lack of alternative keyboards or the chance association of this keyboard arrangement with the only mechanically adequate typewriter.

Typing competitions

Typing competitions provided another test of the QWERTY keyboard. These competitions are somewhat underplayed in the conventional history. David's history mentions only the Cincinnati contest. Wilfred Beeching's history, which has been very influential, also mentions only the Cincinnati contest and attaches great importance to it: "Suddenly, to their horror, it dawned upon both the Remington Company and the Caligraph company officials, torn between pride and despair, that whoever won was likely to put the other out of business!" Beeching refers to the contest as having established the four-bank keyboard of the Remington machine "once and for all" (Beeching 1974, 41).

In fact, typing contests and demonstrations of speed were fairly common during this period. They involved many different machines, with various manufacturers claiming to hold the speed record.

Under the headline "Wonderful Typing," the *New York Times* (1889b) reported on a typing demonstration given the previous day in

Brooklyn by a Mr. Thomas Osborne of Rochester, New York. The *Times* reported that Mr. Osborne "holds the championship for fast typing, having accomplished 126 words a minute at Toronto, August 13 last." In the Brooklyn demonstration he typed 142 words per minute in a five-minute test, 179 words per minute in a single minute and 198 words per minute for 30 seconds. He was accompanied by a Mr. George McBride, who typed 129 words per minute blindfolded. Both men used the non-QWERTY Caligraph machine. The *Times* offered that "the Caligraph people have chosen a very pleasant and effective way of proving not only the superior speed of their machine, but the falsity of reports widely published that writing blindfolded was not feasible on that instrument." Note that this was just months after McGurrin's Cincinnati victory.

There were other contests and a good number of victories for McGurrin and Remington. On August 2, 1888, the *Times* reported a New York contest won by McGurrin with a speed of 95.8 words per minute in a five-minute dictation (*New York Times* 1888). In light of the received history, according to which McGurrin is the only person to have memorized the keyboard, it is interesting to note the strong performance of his rivals. Miss May Orr typed 95.2 words per minute, and M. C. Grant typed 93.8 words per minute. Again, on January 9, 1889, the *Times* reported a McGurrin victory under the headline "Remington Still Leads the List" (*New York Times* 1889a).

We should probably avoid the temptation to compare the Caligraph speed with the Remington speeds, given the likely absence of any serious attempts at standardizing the tests. Nevertheless, it appears that the issue of speed was not so readily conceded as is reported in Beeching's history. Typists other than McGurrin could touch-type, and machines other than Remington were competitive. History has largely ignored events that did not build toward the eventual domination by QWERTY. This focus may be reasonable for the history of the Remington Company or the QWERTY keyboard. But if we are interested in whether the QWERTY keyboard's existence can be attributed to more than happenstance or an inventor's whim, these events do matter.

Conclusions

The trap constituted by an obsolete standard may be quite fragile. Because real-world situations present opportunities for agents to profit from changing to a superior standard, we cannot simply rely on an abstract model to conclude that an inferior standard has persisted. Such a claim demands empirical examination.

As an empirical example of market failure, the typewriter keyboard has much appeal. The objective of the keyboard is fairly straightforward: to get words onto the recording medium. There are no conflicting objectives to complicate the interpretation of performance. But the evidence in the standard history of QWERTY versus Dvorak is flawed and incomplete. First, the claims for the superiority of the Dvorak keyboard are suspect. The most dramatic claims are traceable to Dvorak himself, and the best-documented experiments, as well as recent ergonomic studies, suggest little or no advantage for the Dvorak keyboard.[20]

Second, by ignoring the vitality and variety of the rivals to the Remington machine with its QWERTY keyboard, the received history implies that Sholes' and McGurrin's choices, made largely as matters of immediate expediency, established the standard without ever being tested. More careful reading of historical accounts and checks of original sources reveal a different picture. There were touch-typists other than McGurrin, there were competing claims of speed records, and Remington was not so well established that a keyboard offering significant advantages could not have gained a foothold. If the fable is to carry lessons about the workings of markets, we need to know more than just who won. The victory of the tortoise is a different story without the hare.

There is more to this disagreement than a difference in the evidence that was revealed by our search of the historical record. Our reading of this history reflects a more fundamental difference in views of how markets, and social systems more generally, function. David's overriding point is that economic theory must be informed by events in the world. On that we could not agree more strongly. But ironically, or perhaps inevitably, David's interpretation of the historical record is dominated by his own implicit model of markets, a model that seems to underlie much economic thinking. In that model an exogenous set of goods is offered for sale at a price, take it or leave it. There is little or no role for entrepreneurs. There generally are no guarantees, no rental markets, no mergers, no loss-leader pricing, no advertising, no marketing research. When such complicating institutions are acknowledged, they are incorporated into the model piecemeal. And they are most often introduced to show their potential to create inefficiencies, not to show how an excess of benefit over cost may constitute an opportunity for private gain.

In the world created by such a sterile model of competition, it is not surprising that accidents have considerable permanence. In such a world, embarking on some wrong path provides little chance to jump to an alternative path. The individual benefits of correcting a mistake are too small to make correction worthwhile, and there are no agents who might profit by devising some means of capturing a part of the aggregate benefits of correction.

It is also not surprising that in such a world there are a lot of accidents. Consumers are given very little discretion to avoid starts down wrong paths. A model may assume that consumers have foresight or even that they are perfectly rational, but always in a very limited sense. For example, in the model of Farrell and Saloner, consumers can predict very well the equilibrium among the two candidate standards. But they are attributed no ability to anticipate the existence of some future, better standard. We are not led to ask how the incumbent standard achieved its status as in David's telling, "It jes' growed."

But at some moment, users must commit resources to a standard or wait. At this moment, they have clear incentives to examine the characteristics of competing standards. They must suffer the consequences of a decision to wait, to discard obsolete equipment or skills, or to continue to function with an inferior standard. Thus, they have a clear incentive to consider what lies down alternative paths. Though their ability to anticipate future events may not be perfect, there is no reason to assume that it is bad relative to any other observers.

Finally, it is consistent that, in a world in which mistakes are frequent and permanent, "scientific approaches" cannot help but make big improvements to market outcomes. In such a world, there is ample room for enlightened reasoning, personified by university professors, to improve on the consequences of myriad independent decisions. What credence can possibly be given to a keyboard that has nothing to accredit it but the trials of a group of mechanics and its adoption by millions of typists? If we use only sterilized models of markets, or ignore the vitality of the rivalry that confronts institutions, we should not be surprised that the historical interpretations that result are not graced with the truth that Cicero asks of historians.

Notes

** Earlier drafts benefited from seminars at Clemson University and North Carolina State University, and we would like to thank the participants at those seminars We would also like to thank James Buchanan, Dan Klein, Bill Landes, Nancy Margolis, Craig Newmark, John Palmer, Gregory Rehmke. George Stigler, and Wally Thurman for their suggestions.

1. This trap is treated more seriously in the literature on standards than in other economics literature. This reflects a supposition that foresight, integration, or appropriation are more difficult in the case of standards. The current literature fails to explain why these "externalities" are particularly relevant for standards. we will have more to say about this in forthcoming work [Chapters 3–10 in this volume].
2. "QWERTY" stands for arrangement of letters in the upper left-hand portion of the keyboard below the numbers This keyboard is also known as the Sholes, or Universal, keyboard.
3. This is also sometimes known as the DSK keyboard for Dvorak Simplified Keyboard (or the simplified keyboard). As explained below, the keys are arranged in a different order.
4. Of course. inertia is not necessarily inefficient Some delay in settling on a standard will mean that relatively more is known about the associated technology and the standards themselves by the time most users commit to a technology. Recall the well-known discussion of Harold Demsetz (1969) on the nature of efficiency. If a God can costlessly cause the adoption of the correct standard any inertia is excessive (inefficient) in comparison. But it seems ill advised to hold this up as a serious benchmark. Excessive inertia should be defined relative to some achievable result. Further, some reservation in committing to standards will allow their creators to optimize standards rather than rushing them to the market to be first. If the first available standard were always adopted, then standards, like patents, might generate losses from the rush to be first. Creators might rush their standards to market, even where waiting would produce a better and more profitable product.
5. We may ask ourselves why new standards are created if not with the idea of some pecuniary reward. One would hardly expect nonobvious and costly standards to proliferate like manna from heaven.
6. Herkimer County Historical Society (1923, 173–192) notes that in the early 1920s a single typewriter company was producing 100,000 typists a year.
7. Foulke (1961, 106) notes: "Present day keyboard machines may be converted to the simplified Dvorak keyboard in local typewriter shops, is now available on any typewriter and it costs as little as $5 to convert a Standard to a simplified keyboard."
8. This history follows David (1985), but also see Wilfred Beeching (1974) as an example of an account with the features and emphasis described here.
9. David (1985, 332). If true, this would be quite remarkable. A converted Sholes typist will be typing so much faster that whatever the training cost it is repaid every ten days. Counting only working days this would imply that the investment in retraining repays itself approximately twenty-three times in a year. Does this seem even remotely possible? Do firms typically ignore investments with returns in the range of 2200 percent?
10. Tirole (1988, 405 n.2) states: "Many observers believe that the Dvorak keyboard is superior to this QWERTY standard even when retraining costs are taken into account. However it would be foolish for a firm to build this alternative keyboard and for secretaries to switch to it individually." Under

some circumstances it might have been foolish for secretaries and firms to act in this manner but this type of behavior hardly seems foolish in many real-world situations. For example, large organizations (federal. state. and local governments, Fortune 500 companies, etc.) often have tens of thousands of employees. And these organizations could undertake the training if the costs really are compensated in a short time.

11. We tried to have the Navy supply us with a copy when our own research librarians could not find it. The Navy research librarian had no more success even though she checked the Navy records, the Martin Luther King Library, the Library of Congress, the National Archives, the National Technical Communication service, etc. We were finally able to locate a copy held by an organization, Dvorak International. We would like to thank, its director, Virginia Russell for her assistance. She believes that they obtained their copy from the Underwood Company. We would be more sanguine about the question of the document's history had it been available in a public archive. The copy we received was Navy Department, July and October 1944 (see the references below).
12. It is not an innocuous change. We are told that three QWERTY typists initially scored zero on the typing test but that their scores rose to twenty-nine, thirteen, and sixteen within four days (Dvorak *et al.* 1936, 20). We are also told that several other typists had similar improvements in the first four days. These improvements are dismissed as mere testing effects that the researchers wish to eliminate. But the researchers made no effort to eliminate the analogous testing effect for the Dvorak typists. Truncating the measurements to the average of the first four days reduces the reported speed increases for the three typists with zero initial speed by at least thirteen, twelve, and fourteen. Assuming the existence of two other typists with similar size testing effects, removing this testing effect would reduce the reported speed improvements by 3.6 words per minute lowering the gain from 46 percent to 28 percent. The effect of the truncation at the end of the measuring period cannot be determined with any accuracy but there is no testing effect to be removed at this stage of the experiment after many tests have been taken. While the apparent effect of these measurement techniques is significant, the indisputable problem is that they were not applied equally to the QWERTY and Dvorak typists.
13. However, Yamada, trying to refute criticisms of Dvorak's keyboard, claims that Dvorak did not conduct these studies, he only provided the typewriters (see Yamada 1980). He admits that Dvorak was in the Navy and in Washington when the studies were conducted but denies any linkage. We do not know whom to believe, but we are skeptical that Dvorak would not have had a large influence on these tests, based on the strong circumstantial evidence and given Foulke's identification of Dvorak as the Navy's top expert on such matters. Interestingly, Yamada accuses Strong of being biased against the Dvorak keyboard (1980, 188). He also impugns Strong's character. He accuses Strong of refusing to provide other (unnamed) researchers with his data. He also implies that Strong stole money from Dvorak because in 1941, when Strong was a supporter of Dvorak's keyboard, he supposedly accepted payment from Dvorak to conduct a study of the DSK keyboard without ever reporting his results to him.

14. At the time of Strong's experiment Dvorak had attracted a good deal of attention. At least one trade group had taken the position that pending confirmation from the Strong study, it would adopt Dvorak as its new standard. See *New York Times* (1955a; 1955b; 1956a; 1956b; 1956c).
15. In fact, both the Navy and General Service Administration studies found that the best typists take the longest time to catch up to their old speed and showed the smallest percentage improvement with retraining.
16. Also see n. 13 above.
17. Yamada interprets the Oregon study to support the Dvorak keyboard. To do so he fits an exponential function to the Oregon data and notes that the limit of the function as hours of training goes to infinity is 17 percent greater than the typist's initial QWERTY speed. This function is extremely flat, however, and even modest gains appear well outside the range of the data. A 10 percent gain, for example, would be projected to occur only after 165 hours of training .
18. Also see Beeching (1974, 40 n.13 and 199) Yamada (1980, 184) in discussing the Hammond keyboard arrangement states: "This 'ideal' arrangement was far better than QWERTY but it did not take root because by then Remington Schools were already turning out a large number of QWERTY typists every year." In 1893, Blickensderfer offered a portable typewriter with the Hammond keyboard.
19. We should also take note of the fact that the QWERTY keyboard, although invented in the United States, has become the dominant keyboard throughout the world. Foreign countries, when introduced to typewriters, need not have adopted this keyboard if superior alternatives existed since there would not yet have been any typists trained on QWERTY. Yet all other keyboard designs fell before the QWERTY juggernaut. In France and some other countries, the keyboard is slightly different than the QWERTY keyboard used in the United States The major difference is that the top left-hand keys are Azerty (that is also what these keyboard designs are called) and several letters are transposed, but most of the keys are identical
20. There are several versions of the claim that a switch to Dvorak would not be worthwhile. The strongest. which we do not make. is that QWERTY is proven to be the best imaginable keyboard. Neither can we claim that Dvorak is proven to be inferior to QWERTY. Our claim is that there is no scientifically acceptable evidence that Dvorak offers any real advantage over QWERTY. Because of this claim, our assessment of a market failure in this case is rather simple. It might have been more complicated. For example, if Dvorak were found to be superior, it might still be the case that the total social benefits are less than the cost of switching. In that case, we could look for market failure only in the process that started us on the QWERTY keyboard (if the alternative were available at the beginning). Or we might have concluded that Dvorak is better and that all parties could be made better off if we could costlessly command both a switch and any necessary redistribution. Such a finding would constitute a market failure in the sense of mainstream welfare economics. Of course, this circumstance still might not constitute a market failure in the sense of Demsetz, which requires consideration of the costs of feasible institutions that could effect the change (see Demsetz 1969).

References

Beeching, W. 1974. *A Century of the Typewriter*, New York: St. Martin's Press.

Cheung, S. N. S. 1973. "The Fable of the Bees: An Economic Investigation," *Journal of Law and Economics*, 16: 11–33.

Coase, R. H. 1960. "The Problem of Social Cost," *Journal of Law and Economics*, 3: 1–44.

———— 1974. "The Lighthouse in Economics," *Journal of Law and Economics*, 17: 357–376.

David, P. A. 1985. "Clio and the Economics of QWERTY," *American Economic Review*, 75: 332–337.

———— 1986. "Understanding the Economics of QWERTY: The Necessity of History," in Parker, W. N. (ed.), *Economic History and the Modern Economist*, New York: Basil Blackwell.

Demsetz, H. 1969. "Information and Efficiency: Another Viewpoint," *Journal of Law and Economics*, 10: 1–22.

Dvorak, A. Merrick, N. L., Dealey, W. L. and Ford, G. C. 1936. *Typewriting Behavior*, New York: American Book Co.

Farrell J. and Saloner, G. 1985. "Standardization, Compatibility, and Innovation," *Rand Journal of Economics*, 16: 70–83.

Foulke, A. 1961. *Mr. Typewriter: A Biography of Christopher Latham Sholes*, Boston: Christopher Publishing.

Herkimer County Historical Society 1923. *The Story of the Typewriter*, New York: Andrew H. Kellogg.

Katz M. L. and Shapiro, C. 1985. "Network Externalities, Competition, and Compatibility," *American Economic Review*, 75(3): 425–440.

Kinkhead R. 1975. "Typing Speed, Keying Rates and Optimal Keyboard Layouts," *Proceedings of the Human Factors Society*, 19: 159–161.

———— 1985. "Copying and Indirect Appropriability: Photocopying of Journals," *Journal of Political Economy*, 93: 945–957.

Mandeville, B. M. 1962. *The Fable of The Bees*, New York: Capricorn Books.

Mares, G. C. 1909. *The History of The Typewriter*, London: Guilbert Pitman.

Margolis, S. E. 1987. "Two Definitions of Efficiency in Law and Economics," *Journal of Legal Studies*, 16: 471–482.

Miller, L. A. and Thomas, J. C. 1977. "Behavioral Issues in the Use of Interactive Systems," *International Journal of Man-Machine Studies*, 9: 509–536.

Navy Department 1944. *A Practical Experiment in Simplified Keyboard Retraining – a Report on the retraining of fourteen standard Keyboard Typists on the Simplified Keyboard and a Comparison of Typist Improvement from Training on the Standard Keyboard and retraining on the Simplified Keyboard*, Department of Services, Training Section, Washington DC, Navy Department, Division of Shore Establishments and Civilian Personnel (July and October).

New York Times 1888. "Typewriters Contest for a Prize," August 2.

———— 1889a. "Remington Still Leads the List," January 9.

———— 1889b. "Wonderful Typing," February 28.

———— 1955a. "Revolution in the Office," November 11.

———— 1955b. "US Plans to Test New Typewriter," November 30.

———— 1956a. "Pyfgcrl vs. QWERTYuiop," January 22.

———— 1956b. "Key Changes Debated," June 18.

———— 1956c. "US Balks at Teaching Old Typists New Keys," July 2.

Norman, D. A. and Rumelhart, D. E. 1983. "Studies of Typing from the LNR Research Group," in Cooper W. E. (ed.), *Cognitive Aspects of Skilled Typewriting*, New York: Springer-Verlag.

Strong E. P. 1956. *A Comparative Experiment in Simplified Keyboard Retraining and Standard Keyboard supplementary Training*, Washington, DC: US General Services Administration.

Tirole J. 1988. *The Theory of Industrial Organization*, Cambridge, MA: MIT Press.

Yamada H. 1980. "A Historical Study of Typewriters and Typing Methods from the position of planning Japanese Parallels," *Journal of Information Processing*, 2: 175–202

———— 1983. "Certain Problems Associated with the Design of Input Keyboards for Japanese Writing," in Cooper, W. E. (ed.), *Cognitive Aspects of Skilled Typewriting*, New York: Springer-Verlag.

3

Network Externality: An Uncommon Tragedy (1994)*

In recent years many of us have faced choices regarding how and whether to participate in such interactions as computer networks and telecommunications systems. When making such choices, one consideration is inevitably how our participation will affect others and how the participation of others will affect us. For example, in making the choice between DOS and Macintosh operating systems, most of us naturally considered what the people around us were choosing or were likely to choose. Since so many choices seem to have some network dimension, it is no surprise that economists have taken up these ideas and that they have coined a term to connote these network elements. This term is "network externality."

Among the most influential statements on network externality have been those by Michael Katz and Carl Shapiro. Their 1985 paper in the *American Economic Review* defines the concept: "There are many products for which the utility that a user derives from consumption of the good increases with the number of other agents consuming the good." Elaborating they add, "[T]he utility that a given user derives from a good depends upon the number of other users who are in the same network." This idea of a network embraces far more than the physically connected examples of computer networks and telecommunications systems. They also mention goods, such as computer software, automobile repair, and video games as exhibiting positive consumption externalities. These are just a few examples from what we believe would be a very large set. It is easy to come up with many more examples illustrating the concept of a network as they have defined it.

---

* *Journal of Economic Perspectives,* 8 (1994): 133–150.

When gourmet cooks find it easier to find preferred ingredients because more people are taking up their avocation, this would be a gourmet-network externality. When fans of live entertainment prefer big cities because the large market for entertainment assures a full variety of acts, this would be an audience-network externality. Indeed, we can say that the urban amenities and agglomeration economies that we associate with urban life are urban precisely because some activities function best, if at all, where large numbers of participants can be involved.

Nor is there any reason that a network externality should necessarily be limited to positive effects, although positive effects have been the main focus in this literature. If, for example, a telephone or computer network becomes overloaded, the effect on an individual subscriber will be negative. When we admit the possibility of a negative network externality, the set of goods that exhibit network externalities expands strikingly. As members of a network of highway users, we suffer from a negative network externality because freeways are subject to crowding. And although a larger installed base of computer users might lower the price of computer software, there are many goods, such as housing and filet mignon, where larger networks of users appears to increase the price.

According to the received definition, then, goods exhibit network externality wherever the consumer enjoys benefits or suffers costs from changes in the size of an associated network, that is, changes in quantities demanded. These benefits and costs result from such considerations as compatibility, brand familiarity, product information, status, service availability or the prices of network related goods. This almost perfect generality should sound an alert: what we have here is either much bigger or much smaller than its current position in the literature would indicate. It is either the case that most goods exhibit network externalities, and the unique insights of this literature are of far broader consequence than is currently understood, or it is the case that network externalities are limited in ways not yet specified.

As the reader will likely suspect, we believe the concept of network externalities must be limited. A classic network like CompuServe does represent an interesting class of economic phenomena, but the definition of that class must be considerably refined if it is to support fruitful analysis. The purpose of this paper, then, is to elucidate, refine, and ultimately limit the implied scope of network externality.[1] Our concern is not merely semantic. The application of the concept of network externality has been broad and rapid. Further, both by name and by some of the explicit results of the network literature, network externalities are asserted to constitute market failure.[2] If almost every aspect of the economy exhibits network externality, and if externalities presumptively are market failures, then our most basic results about the efficiency of markets may be in error and dramatic policy changes might be warranted.

We believe such changes would be misguided. While network effects are common and important, network externalities as market failures, we will argue, are theoretically fragile and empirically undocumented.

Definitions and clarification

In what follows we will introduce a number of distinctions, the most important of which is this: The circumstance in which the net value of an action (consuming a good, subscribing to telephone service) is affected by the number of agents taking equivalent actions will be called a *network effect*. Broadly defined, network effects are indeed pervasive. However, we reserve the term "network externality" for a specific kind of network effect in which the equilibrium exhibits unexploited gains from trade regarding network participation. The advantage of this definition over other possible definitions is that it corresponds with the common understanding of externality as an instance of market failure.

Katz and Shapiro draw a distinction between direct and indirect network externalities. Direct network externalities are those generated "through a direct physical effect of the number of purchasers on the quality of the product," as in the attachment of homes to a telephone network. Indirect network externalities, on the other hand, involve instances that lack that direct physical effect; for example, software being more plentiful and lower in price as the number of computer users increases. Katz and Shapiro also note another instance of indirect network externality, the availability of post-purchase service for durable goods, such as automobiles.[3] In general, they ascribe indirect network externalities to any situation where complementary goods become more plentiful and lower in price as the number of users of the good increases.

A related distinction has been made between networks that are (or can) be owned and networks that are not (or cannot) be owned. This distinction is partly a function of the legal structure and partly a result of physical characteristics of networks. In some networks, participants are literally connected to each other in some fashion. The telephone system is one such network, as are pipeline, telex, electrical, and cable television systems. These *literal networks* require an investment of capital, and there is a physical manifestation of the network in the form of pipelines, cables, transmitters, and so on. It is not only feasible but almost inevitable for property rights to be established for these types of networks. Those who attach to such networks without permission from the owner, or who attach without adhering to the rules may be disconnected, a characteristic that removes the problem of nonexclusion.[4]

In contrast, other networks, which we might refer to as "metaphorical networks," such as the network of speakers of English, provide interrelationships in which there are no physical connections (though there may be direct interaction). The network of Chevrolet owners, whose relationship to each other is that they draw on common repair expertise, is such a network. So is the network of recreational fishermen, who enjoy exchanging stories and who may provide assistance to each other in emergencies. While the ownership of such a metaphorical network is possible, it may be difficult. Unlike the telephone company, which can monitor uninvited users because they must all hook up to the same electronic circuits, an owner of a language would have great difficulty monitoring illicit use, even if he were legally empowered to prevent it.[5] Thus metaphorical networks are less likely to be owned, and in some instances may not be ownable.

As we discuss below, the recognition that some networks can be owned solves many of the problems that might be thought to occur when network participants create what have been called direct network externalities. First, however, we examine the efficiency consequences of indirect network externalities.

Indirect network externalities

In the 1920s economists debated the efficiency implications of increasing- and decreasing-cost industries. Pigou argued that all industries, except those with constant costs, required taxes or subsidies to attain the efficient level of output. In Pigou's view, the industry marginal factor cost curve represents the true social cost of production. The impact of one firm's actions on competing firms is just another externality that distorted market mechanisms away from the ideal. This of course is false, since the additional payments going to inframarginal inputs as industry output increases (assuming upward-sloping supply) are rents, which are not part of the social cost of providing additional output, as pointed out by Knight (1924) and others (Ellis and Fellner,

1943). In order to make these points clear, Pigou's critics introduced a distinction between pecuniary and technological externalities, a distinction that was once a common feature in microeconomics textbooks.

Pecuniary externalities are external effects that work through the price system. When firm A produces one more unit of output, marginally lowering price, that increased production harms rival firms B and C. Indeed, the *sine qua non* of competition is each firm's indifference to the impact of its actions on other firms in the industry. Each firm acts in a way that harms the other firms in the industry, but that harm is offset by a transfer of wealth to consumers.

Technological externalities, on the other hand, comprise the class of externalities that economists have focused on in recent decades as market failures: pollution, congestion, and so on. Although technological externalities are often thought to be market failures, some interactions that have been identified by economists as externalities have in fact been internalized by markets. For example, while economists were writing of the positive externality brought to apple growers by the pollination activities of bees, beekeepers were internalizing this activity (and consequently invalidating the arguments of economists) by contracting with owners of apple orchards.[6] Economists have demonstrated great resourcefulness in reconstructing reality to fit economic theory (as documented by Coase 1960; Cheung 1973; Cowen 1988).

But at least in principle, the difference between technological and pecuniary externalities is clear. With technological externalities, actual benefits or costs are imposed outside of market mechanisms. Resolution of such problems may occur through property rights, private negotiations, or government interventions that allow the externalities to be internalized. However, in the case of pecuniary externalities, those on one side of the market (say, buyers) benefit, while those on the other side of the market (say, sellers) suffer. Here, the market outcome is the one that would be reached if all these external effects were internalized; piecemeal internalization is harmful. If firms in an otherwise competitive industry were to internalize their impacts on each other, the industry would be a monopoly or a cartel and the internalization would cause inefficiency.

Today this distinction between technological and pecuniary externalities has largely been forgotten, perhaps because it is no longer needed to correct Pigou. But the trap that caught Pigou is still set, ready to spring on the unwary analyst. In fact, the pecuniary externalities that so perplexed Pigou walk and quack very much like the indirect network externalities that are waddling through the literature today. As an example, listen to Farrell and Saloner (1985, 70) discussing indirect network externalities: "There may be a market-mediated effect, as when a complementary good (spare parts, servicing, software) becomes cheaper and more available the greater the extent of the (compatible) market." These "market-mediated" (read price) effects are likely pecuniary.

For a negative indirect network externality, the analogy is obvious: if a group of breakfast-eaters joins the network of orange juice drinkers, their increased demand raises the price of orange juice concentrate, and thus most commonly effects a transfer of wealth from their fellow network members to the network of orange growers.[7] Certainly, the breakfast-eaters have affected the orange juice drinkers. Just as certainly, they have not compensated the orange juice drinkers for the harm they have caused them. And most assuredly, we would not want them to make such recompense. This is a pecuniary externality.

The positive indirect network externality is a bit more complicated, but it amounts to largely the same thing. We consider these situations in much greater detail in Liebowitz and Margolis (1995a) [reprinted as Chapter 4 in this volume]. The gist of our argument is that if price falls as a network gets larger, that fall in price could be due to one of three factors: a positive technological externality across producers; an input that decreases in cost; or a decrease in rents to some (perhaps specialized) agents as the industry grows. If outside observers can only see that price decreases as output increases, they will be unable to distinguish among these cases. Without some additional information to differentiate between pecuniary effects (including redistributions in rents) and genuine externalities, it is impossible to prescribe appropriate public policy.

As an example, consider the oft-cited case of the "network" of computer users. Suppose that personal computer prices fall as the number of users increases. If this is a true externality, say because there are positive technological externalities between computer producers, there would be a justification for some sort of subsidy to the industry. However, a second possibility for declining computer prices could be declining costs of an input, such as microprocessors. In this case, a subsidy to the computer industry will be a poorly directed, and perhaps counterproductive policy tool. If a subsidy is required anywhere, it would be in the microprocessor industry, since a subsidy to the computer industry will not optimally address the number of processors per computer, or the use of processors in noncomputer applications. And without further investigation into the cause of the declining microprocessor price, we can not know whether a subsidy is warranted in the microprocessor market. Clearly, treating as network externalities all cases where price and quantity move inversely can easily lead both to bad economics and to bad policy.

There is yet an additional problem with indirect network effects. Again, consider the common modern experience that rapidly declining prices of many activities are associated with dramatic increases in participation in those activities. So, for example, the costs of videocassette recorders, computers, and fax machines have declined rapidly at the same time that use of these machines has increased. (The association is not confined to contemporary new technologies: automobiles, electrical power generation equipment, refrigeration, and other "old tech" items experienced the same pattern in their day.) The problem is that this simple observation of rapidly declining prices does not distinguish between economies of scale and ordinary technological progress.[8] Is the equilibrium moving along a downward-sloping supply function as demand increases, or is it moving down a demand curve as changes in technology move the supply curve? This distinction is critical to whether the phenomenon exhibits a network externality. The choice among networks, which is so central to this literature, is only central if there are economies of scale in particular networks.[9] Where observed cost reductions are due to general advances in technology, rather than network size *per se*, then there is no network effect and no necessity to a collective choice of a particular network. To the extent that the observed association of cost decreases and output increases is the result of improved technology and not economies to scale for particular networks, the implied scope for the concept of network externality is smaller than is currently understood. Again, theory, empirics, and policy require that we note a distinction that the mainstream literature ignores.

The concept of indirect network externalities, therefore, suffers from two main weaknesses. First, it is not an externality in the modern sense since it often describes nothing more than welfare neutral interactions that occur in properly functioning markets. Second, the implied scope of positive network externalities is likely misunderstood where analysis fails to identify properly the cause of a declining price.

Direct network externalities

Unlike indirect network effects, direct network effects at least present us with some explicit interaction that may occur outside of markets.

The paradigmatic case for a direct network effect, if not an externality, is the network of telephone users. Clearly it is reasonable to expect that the value of a telephone to one person depends upon others' being connected to it. But even for this example, there is reason to call for greater conceptual precision than has commonly been offered. In what follows we consider a number of reasons that the direct network effects that so easily come to mind may not in fact qualify as network externalities.

Inframarginal externalities

Perhaps the feature that most distinguishes network externalities from that of ordinary externalities has to do with the kind of market failure that the network externality literature has contemplated. The focus in the literature overwhelmingly addresses the question, "Do we get the right network?" as opposed to "Is the network the right size?" The question of the "right" network does not involve the marginal impacts of network size, but rather the consequences of what can be called inframarginal externality.

The idea of an *inframarginal externality* was introduced thirty years ago by Buchanan and Stubblebine (1962). In their very general definition of externality, one party's activity level shows up as an argument in another's utility function. For inframarginal externality, the marginal utility of the external activity is zero. Very simply, the affected party is not affected by marginal changes in the externality-causing activity. To find the optimum, we can no longer look at the marginal conditions, but must examine the total benefits and costs. The concept has been neglected, perhaps because the usual interest on external harms (like those of pollution) offers no natural analog to satiation, since we are usually comfortable assuming increasing marginal damage in those cases. Consideration of network externality, however, prompts renewed attention to this idea.

Many activities require a critical mass but are not much helped by participation beyond that level. City size is limited because urban agglomeration economies are exhausted, at the margin, where crowding offsets the benefits of additional interaction.[10] Similarly, the fact that other people use the same sort of VCR that we use makes a tape rental market available to us, but the marginal benefits of increasing the number of households that use our kind of VCR are likely exhausted now that businesses that rent video tapes are just about as prevalent as ones that sell milk.

Attention to inframarginal externality alters the problem in several ways. First, where marginal benefits of network size are exhausted there are no unexploited gains from trade regarding network size. Further, where marginal gains of network size are exhaustible at network sizes that are small relative to the market, there is no impediment to the coexistence of multiple networks. The choice of the "best" network becomes one of choosing the best set of networks. Finally, the infra-marginal externality that may afflict the discrete choice of a network is not different from other coordination problems that exist in many other market choices, as we discuss later in this paper.

Internalizing through ownership

It might reasonably be expected that an owned or sponsored network would not be subject to market failure. After all, a network owner would be motivated to make investments or provide incentives to increase the net value of the network by internalizing any network effects. It has been argued, however, that ownership does not necessarily offer a solution to the problem of network externalities because a network owner cannot credibly commit to charging prices below marginal cost, as might be required to induce optimal participation.[11]

To analyze this situation, we begin with a conventional representation of the incentives of an owned network in which ownership solves the network problem. The model is neither original nor complicated: It is the tragedy-of-the-commons problem turned on its head.

In Figure 3.1, B(N) is the benefit that any participant (all individuals are assumed identical) derives from participation in the network. As such, it is both the marginal private benefit and the average social benefit, and it increases with N, the number of participants in the

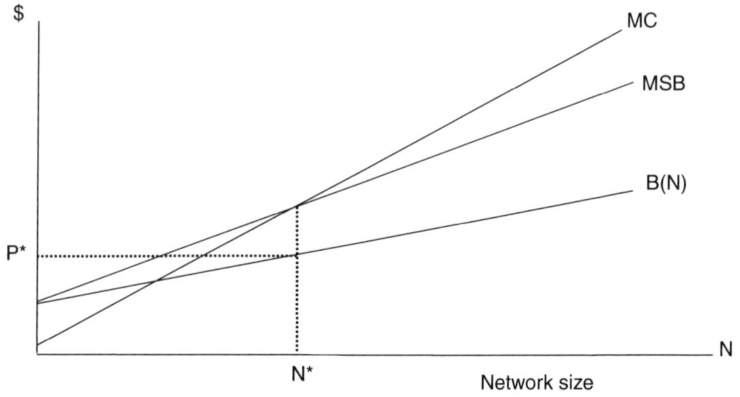

Figure 3.1 An owned network

network. To the owner of the network, it represents the average revenue (demand) curve. The marginal social benefit (MSB) lies above B(N), because MSB includes the positive impact of an additional participant on the other network participants. The MSB, being the first derivative of NB(N), is also the marginal revenue available to the network owner. (Marginal revenue here is the price paid by the marginal participant plus the effect of the marginal participant on the willingness to pay of all participants.) The marginal cost of serving another network participant is also shown (MC), and it is assumed to increase with network size. The profit-maximizing behavior for the network owner will be to charge the price P*, and accommodate N* participants on the network, since this equates marginal revenue with marginal cost. In this case, the network owner does charge a price that is below marginal cost, and there is no problem with the credibility of this action.

The model illustrated in the diagram has a number of special assumptions, but these assumptions are the exact analogs to those used in the simple models of the tragedy of the commons, frequently illustrated as the fisheries problem. And although the model certainly cannot claim to be perfectly general, it does counter the impression of the inevitability of a sub-optimal network.

There is nothing in this model that denies the possibility of competition in networks, just as there is nothing in the fisheries model that dictates that a single owner of a lake becomes a monopolist in fish. In the perfectly competitive case, competition shifts the B(N) curve down until P* will just cover the costs of operating the network. For example, when America On-line enters the market with lower prices, the willingness to pay for the Prodigy network falls. Thus, while the network owner can be said to capture the participant's full value from the use of the particular network, the value captured is not the value of network participation in general.[12]

One assumption embodied in the model is increasing marginal cost of serving a network participant. This assumption is conventional in most of economics, but it is possible to offer specific support for its application to networks. For literal networks, where addition of customers ordinarily means connecting to subsequently more distant or otherwise more costly participants, the assumption seems particularly compelling, and there is some empirical support for it (see Kahn 1988, 1, 124, 2, 123). Even for metaphorical networks, it is reasonable that the first participants will be those most suited to use the network, requiring the least support for their participation. As examples of each effect: Cable television reaches the boondocks only after the more urban areas are covered, and the Internet was first used by UNIX wizards, not computer neophytes.

Of course, other cost conditions are possible. Constant or decreasing marginal cost, which is the assumption that has most commonly been made in the network externality literature, converts the problem to one of natural monopoly. If MC were constant in Figure 3.1, the optimal size of the network would be infinite (or the entire population). The existence of multiple networks competing with each other would now be inconsistent with efficiency. But although it is possible to impose on networks the natural monopoly problem (and some networks have provided some of the best examples of natural monopoly), this is not a new or different problem, but only a familiar problem with a new name. Note also that if the "externality" were internalized by network users, the MSB curve would now represent behavior of network users. Yet this would not solve the natural monopoly problem (choosing the best network), although it would lead to the proper size for any given network. Thus it is not clear that the externality framework is useful in resolving problems of network choice.

Difficulties arise when the problem is configured such that willingness to pay in an initial period is contingent on the expected network size in a second period. Katz and Shapiro (1986) present a case in which a firm with lower costs in period two has an advantage over a firm with lower costs in period one because the former can credibly commit to lowering price in the first period, but the later can not commit to lowering prices in the second period. This result is fairly specialized, however, arising in a particular context that gives rise to a time-inconsistency problem. Certainly the commitment problem would not apply to those networks where participants make a payment each period for their place in the network (or rentals for durable goods), since in this case first period consumers need not fear getting "stuck" with the wrong product in period two. By assuming that consumers' contractual obligations span multiple periods, and stipulating a difficulty of contracting to constrain actions across these periods, we can, of course, construct problems for this market.

While it may be of interest to note that contracting costs or time inconsistencies affect networks in the same ways that they affect other economic relationships, it is misleading to present these difficulties as fundamental economic characteristics of *networks*. Our argument here and elsewhere is that networks that are owned are no more (or less) afflicted by market pathologies than are other economic relationships.

While ownership would seem straightforward for most literal networks, it is not impossible for the kinds of networks that we have called metaphorical. Franchise systems of various sorts are mechanisms for introducing ownership to networks of restaurants, retailers, or other service firms. And less obvious networks can be owned: bars, country clubs, and private schools can all be thought of as facilitating networks – internalizing network effects. They are valued both for the services that they provide and also for the social networks that they support. You can drink alone for less, but you pay a barkeeper for the service of creating a network. Such network services will not come free, given that there are real costs of creating them, but they needn't carry a monopoly price. Competition among such networks is certainly possible.

Internalizing through transactions

Even if ownership over some networks may not be possible, many network effects might nonetheless be internalized by the direct interaction of participants. A group of programmers who are working on a software project can capture all of the potential benefits of a network by adopting a common language for the group. Although other programmers outside the group may use the same language, the network effects will be limited to those who ultimately interact. The same analysis applies to the exchange of video tapes or computer-data-storage media. In such instances, which we suspect are very common, it is not important how large the compatible network is, only that all individuals who would interact are compatible.

Interactions of this sort involve transactions. Although we may not be able to transact with every motorist who fouls the air that we breathe, we can advise our parents to buy a VHS video cassette recorder if they want to see home movies of their grandchildren; and we can negotiate with a co-author regarding which word-processing software to use. Since the exchange of such materials is itself a transaction, it seems unreasonable to assume that in such cases transactions costs are prohibitive. But if transactions are relatively easy, then the existence of an externality is unlikely.

Black boxes and the market failure of discrete choices

The literature of conventional externality is largely about the level of externality-bearing activities – too much pollution or congestion, too few Good Samaritans. The network externality literature, on the other hand, is rarely concerned with determining optimal network size, but often concerned with the choice among possible networks, i.e. discrete choices.[13] The representative network externality problem is this: some action would be socially wealth increasing if enough people joined in, but each agent finds that independent action is unattractive. The familiar tax-and-subsidy solution to externality problems (a solution based on altering marginal magnitudes), although suited to changing the scale of externality-generating activities, is not in general appropriate for discrete choices (inframarginal problems). Instead, the network effects diagnosed in this literature pose problems of transition, a problem of coordinating movement from one equilibrium to another.

Economics has not generally done well in explaining transition (Fisher, 1983). Speaking metaphorically, neoclassical economics has put transition into black boxes, assuming that an unknown process is responsible for costless and timeless movement. This might be thought of as a Panglossian view of market transitions. But the analysis of discrete choice problems in the network externality literature goes to the opposite extreme, assuming that something which has not been modeled does not exist. Proponents of network externalities have attempted to fill these black boxes, but do so with restrictive models in which these transitions often do not occur. A clear implication of the network externalities literature is that often we cannot move from one technology to a superior one, from one standard to a better one, from one kind of network to a better one. This view might be thought of as the Chicken-Little view of market transitions. While it is inevitable and probably desirable that we work with restricted models, we should avoid the presumption that the things that are excluded from these models are unimportant or nonexistent.

Of course, potential problems with transitions afflict all components of the economy. For example, imagine that a new automobile manufacturer, Superior Motors, devises a new automobile design that lowers the cost of producing automobiles. The common assumption in economics is that information is not prohibitively costly, that consumers will soon find out about this new option, and that the new lower-cost automobile will soon come to dominate the market. Those less sanguine about this result might point out that building a better mousetrap is not enough to ensure success, that the mousetrap needs to be properly marketed, financed, and so on. But the usual reply would be that since Superior Motors has lower costs, it can profitably invest at least as much in marketing as its rivals, and thus would come to dominate its market.

It is nevertheless possible to construct out of these circumstances a coordination problem. Although Superior Motors has a lower cost curve, it has to overcome diseconomies of small scale. Will the innovation prevail in the face of lagged consumer response and these diseconomies? One argument is that the firm (and capital markets) knows its cost curve, can anticipate the consequences of operation at a particular scale, and will proceed to maximize profits. But by installing a kind of myopia in the problem, and focusing on the time lag between first operation and attaining efficient scale, the problem of implementing the new technology can appear fraught with pitfalls.

Indeed, with this Chicken-Little perspective on the world, we will find it remarkable that even the most ordinary new technology or action is ever implemented. It will seem remarkable that gasoline stations ever became available because, after all, at one time there were no cars. It will seem just as remarkable that cars ever became available because, after all, at one time there were no gas stations. We wonder at farmers' willingness to plant seeds and wait the months necessary for the crop to mature. Life is fraught with uncertainty.

Clearly, even the simplest act of production requires the capacity to form an expectation of the outcome and to take the risk that what is produced today can be sold tomorrow. It can be argued that the whole area of entrepreneurship continues to reside in those black boxes that contain the subject of economic transition. A transition to a standard or technology that offers benefits greater than costs will constitute a profit opportunity for entrepreneurial activities that can arrange the transition and appropriate some of the benefits. Granted, modeling these activities is difficult. Many topics have resisted successful modeling. But if science is unable to explain how bees fly, it is science that needs to be amended, not our acknowledgment that bees, in fact, manage to stay aloft. Similarly, the fact that current economic models of transition indicate that worthwhile transitions may not occur is not sufficient reason to abandon the presumption that they usually do occur. Economies do, in fact, seem to move from one state to another. This is not to say that mistakes are never made, in markets or elsewhere. But we have overwhelming evidence that markets do make transitions to superior products and standards – from horses and buggies to automobiles, from typewriters to computers, from mail to fax. Given the march of technological progress, claims that wrong choices were made, or that superior options were not implemented in a timely fashion require a fairly high standard of countervailing evidence. We turn now to some consideration of evidence.

Empirical support for network failures

Although the theoretical papers in the network externality literature frequently cite particular examples to illustrate their points, the examples are often a combination of anecdotes and speculation. There is really very little detailed and careful empirical support for the view that there are important network externalities that remain uninternalized. We are aware of *no* compelling examples of markets' failing in the sense that the "wrong" choice of network, among feasible alternatives, was made. Nor are we aware of any effort to examine whether the scale of the networks that do exist is economically efficient. To back up this claim, we discuss a few of the leading examples. Given the constraints of space, we necessarily use broad strokes.

Probably the most frequently cited example of market failure due to network externalities is the design of the typewriter keyboard (David, 1985).[14] The beguiling and often told story is that the strike mechanism of the earliest mechanical typewriters was prone to jamming, so the typewriter's inventors designed the (now standard) QWERTY keyboard in order to slow down typing speed. This arrangement became the market leader, largely by accident, because it became associated with the world's only touch typist. Typists remain burdened by this speed-reducing design today, even though there exists a competing Dvorak keyboard – scientifically designed to be easier to learn and to allow greater speed. Nevertheless, we all learn touch typing on the QWERTY design because there are so few Dvorak typewriters, and there are so few Dvorak keyboard typewriters because almost no one knows how to type on them. This vicious cycle keeps us stuck on the wrong standard. The empirical support for the story is a US Navy study conducted during the World War II. Purportedly, that study conclusively demonstrates the superiority of the Dvorak design, determining that the costs of retraining QWERTY typists on the Dvorak design will be recouped within ten days from the start of training.

Alas, almost every element of this tale is false, as we show in Liebowitz and Margolis (1990) [Chapter 2 in this volume]. The QWERTY keyboard was not created to slow down typing speed. Early on, there were other publicized touch typists using other keyboards. The Navy study was very poorly documented and designed, and appears to have been conducted by Navy Lieutenant Commander August Dvorak, creator and patent holder on the keyboard bearing his name. A later, carefully constructed and controlled study, performed for the General Services Administration in the 1950s, demonstrated quite the opposite results from the Navy study. More recent studies indicate that there is practically no difference in typing speed between the two keyboard designs. The Dvorak typewriter keyboard, it turns out, is a rather poor empirical base upon which to support a theory.

Probably the second most popular example is the claim that the Beta videotaping format is superior to VHS. This claim may achieve much of its popularity because the competition between these formats is so widely known, because so many of us have firsthand experience with this choice, and because a significant number of the people who chose the Beta format did so because they believed it to perform better than VHS.[15] Although it is a common belief that Beta was better in some way, the evidence does not support the view that Beta was better in any way that counted to the bulk of consumers. For example, Klopfenstein (1989 28) writes:

> Although many held the perception that the Beta VCR produced a better picture than VHS, technical experts such as Weinstein (1984) and Prentis (1981) have concluded that this was, in fact, not the case; periodic reviews in Consumers Reports found VHS picture quality superior twice, found Beta superior once, and found no difference in a fourth review. In conclusion, the Beta format appeared to hold no advantages over VHS other than being the first on the market, and this may be a lesson for future marketers of new media products.

Lardner's history of the videorecorder market (1987) provides additional support for this conclusion. There were no real technical differences initially between Beta and VHS. The major differences were the size of the cassette, the threading of the tape, and the tape speed. This similarity in technical specification was due a prior patent-licensing agreement between Sony and Matsushita (creators of Beta and VHS respectively), who had previously cooperated in selling a professional videorecorder called the U-matic. Sony offered its Beta technology and design to Matsushita, but the latter decided to pursue its own machine (produced by JVC). Matsushita's decision was partly based on its different perception of consumer desires. Sony management believed the paramount concern to the consumer would be transportability of the cassette, so they produced a paperback-sized cassette even though this limited recording time to one hour. Matsushita management believed that consumers would be more concerned with the capacity of the tape, so they opted for a larger cassette that allowed a two-hour recording time, making the taping of a complete movie or sports event possible. Sony's headstart gave Beta the entire market for several years. But within two years of VHS's introduction, thanks to its lower price and longer playing time, VHS had surpassed Beta and soon after came to dominate the market.

The typewriter keyboard and VCR format are not the only claims of market failure in the network externalities literature, but these are the claims most often repeated [for a more detailed discussion of the VCR case see Chapter 5 in this volume]. Many of the other claims are of a highly conjectural nature, based on hypothetical technological developments that might have borne extraordinary fruit if only they had been more thoroughly explored. An example is the claim (reported in Arthur 1989) that the internal combustion engine might have been the wrong choice of automobile engine (vis-à-vis steam). Though our skepticism about the validity of this claim is apparently not universal, we find this particular example difficult to take seriously.

All of this points to a challenge to those claiming that network externalities are important in the economy. The theoretical literature establishes only that within models that incorporate particular abstractions, market failure of the type that causes the wrong network to be chosen, is possible. Given these abstractions, it is essential that the literature present real examples of demonstrable market failure if the concept of network externality is to have any relevance.

Conclusion

Although *network effects* are pervasive in the economy, we see scant evidence of the existence of *network externalities*. Many of the external effects of network size are merely pecuniary. Some phenomena that look like they are network effects are simply manifestations of technological progress. Some network effects that constitute real interaction are nevertheless exhausted, at the margin. These occurrences carry no special likelihood of market failure, or externality. For networks where some ownership is inevitable, efficient internalization of the network effect can readily occur. For unownable networks that exist by virtue of exchange of materials among individuals, negotiated transactions can still offer a solution to market problems. Finally, where there are real network effects that are not internalized, these problems are perhaps best understood as garden variety externalities; too much or too little of the activity. Those network effects that have been modeled as transition problems may be coordination problems only within the abstract settings in which they are presented, and these theoretical problems are, as yet, without empirical support.

The debate over network externalities is a reminder of more general methodological concerns. It demonstrates that rigor comes in small and incomplete packages. The models of network externality proceed with great rigor from a simple and plausible assumption – that the benefits of an activity depend upon the number of participants – to a variety of conclusions. But these models can not tell whether such a problem is important. After we economists have had our fun, thinking about network effects and considering how social interactions have a similarity to networks, we need to acknowledge that the *a priori* case for network externalities is treacherous and the empirical case is yet to be presented. Most constructs in economics find their way only very slowly into either public policy or established theory. The construct of network externalities should be one of them.

Notes

1. This paper touches on the results of several papers that we have written on standards (1990, 1994), network externalities (1995), and path dependence (1995b).
2. Two seminal articles, Katz and Shapiro (1986) and Farrell and Saloner (1985) address market failures, as does some of the most recent work in this area (for example, see Church and Gandal 1992). David (1985) and Arthur (1989) also address inefficiencies.
3. We should note that although we cite Katz and Shapiro in the text, we do not wish to diminish the importance of the work of Farrell and Saloner (1985), who presented similar ideas at about the same time, with almost identical discussions of the concept of network externalities.
4. Many of these networks have limited bandwidth for which users must compete. This implies that these networks are not public goods since consumption is *rivalrous*, and that these networks do not suffer from the inefficiencies associated with public goods.
5. One individual's use of a language does not impede anyone else's use of the same language. So languages and similar metaphorical networks have non-rivalrous consumption, leading to the inefficiencies associated with public goods. We acknowledge that there are two textbook definitions of public goods, with one consisting solely of nonrivalrous consumption, and the other adding the condition of nonexcludability. But we note that nonrivalrous consumption, by itself, is sufficient to lead to deviations from textbook efficiency.
6. We of course do not know that markets address each of these difficulties optimally. But since the evidence for inefficiency in these cases appears to be largely fictional, there is no reason to presume that these markets work particularly badly.
7. We have simplified the story a bit here by assuming that costs rise as output increases, without giving an explanation. The simplest explanation is that

there are orange groves of differing quality, and lower quality groves are brought on line as demand increases. For the full story see Liebowitz and Margolis (1995a) [Chapter 4 in this volume].

8. This is a problem that has a long history in economics going back at least to Marshall. He believed that most nonagricultural industries were competitive but also had decreasing costs. This led to his construct of external economies, which allowed the coexistence of the otherwise incompatible concepts of competition and declining cost curves. He was chastised for being empirically confused about movements of the cost curves downward over time and movements along a downward-sloping cost curve, by later generations of economists such as Stigler (1941), and Ellis and Fellner (1943). Some recent economists (e.g. Arthur) seem to believe that Marshall was right all along.
9. If the size of the market is thought to influence technological progress, a seemingly reasonable assumption, then a new type of network effect could be examined. But this is a very different problem. Network externalities have not been defined as changes in technological progress brought about by changes in the sizes of networks.
10. It is interesting to note that models of urban agglomeration economies, which predate the current literature of network externality, nevertheless deal with a kind of network effect. What is particularly interesting about this literature is that it highlights the forces that bring about equilibrium, that act to limit city size. In those models, congestion and limitations on substitutability of capital for land ultimately act to offset, at the margin, the agglomeration economy. See Henderson (1977) and Mills (1967).
11. Katz and Shapiro (1986, 825) conclude that market failures due to network externalities are not resolved by ownership sponsorship. "Sponsorship can internalize some of the externalities through below cost pricing at the beginning of a technology's life. But sponsorship can create problems of its own."
12. This just restates the perfectly competitive result that consumers appear to generate no surplus when they purchase products from individual competitive firms, but they do earn surplus in the overall market.
13. It is, in fact, precisely because network externality models seem to require discrete choices that these models are so appealing for those writing on standards, or for those concerned with path dependence. We discuss standards in our 1994 paper. Path dependence (largely the focus of work by Brian Arthur and Paul David) is based on several ideas, among them that the path of economic change influences the outcome, and that the economy might not be able to escape from an inefficient path. In other writing (1990, 1995b) we have considered these problems, including different possible meanings of the term "path dependence."
14. Besides its use in the literature on standards and network externalities, the keyboard example has been used (and continues to be used!) by various other researchers, usually in fields with very weak empirical support. Thus it can be found in recent game theory textbooks. It also plays a role in the literature of path dependence (but see our 1995a paper). We have also come across it in the strategy literature and in biologically based economics. The citations are too numerous to mention.

15. Arthur's telling (1990, 92) is typical of this literature, with its innuendo of market failure and hazy facts: "The history of the videocassette recorder furnishes a simple example of positive feedback. The VCR market started out with two competing formats selling at about the same price: VHS and Beta ... Both systems were introduced at about the same time and so began with roughly equal market shares; those shares fluctuated early on because of external circumstance, "luck" and corporate maneuvering. Increasing returns on early gains eventually tilted the competition toward VHS: it accumulated enough of an advantage to take virtually the entire VCR market. Yet it would have been impossible at the outset of the competition to say which system would win, which of the two possible equilibria would be selected. Furthermore, if the claim that Beta was technically superior is true, then the market's choice did not represent the best outcome."

References

Arthur, W. B. 1989. "Competing Technologies, Increasing Returns, and Lock-in by Historical Events," *Economic Journal*, 99: 116–131.

———— 1990. "Positive Feedbacks in the Economy," *Scientific American*, 262: 92–99.

Buchanan, J. and Stubblebine, W. 1962. "Externality," *Economica*, 29 (November): 371–384.

Cheung, S. N. S. 1973. "The Fable of the Bees: An Economic Investigation," *Journal of Law and Economics*, 16: 11–33.

Church, J. and Gandal, N. 1992. "Network Effects, Software Provision, and Standardization," *Journal of Industrial Economics*, 60: 85–104

Coase, R. 1960. "The Problem of Social Cost," *Journal of Law and Economics*, 3: 1–44.

Cowen, T. (ed.) 1988. *The Theory of Market Failure*, Fairfax VA: George Mason Press.

David, P. A. 1985. "Clio and the Economics of QWERTY," *American Economic Review*, 75: 332–337.

Ellis, H. S. and Fellner, W. 1943. "External Economies and Diseconomies," *American Economic Review*, 33: 493–511.

Farrell, J. and Saloner, G. 1985. "Standardization, Compatibility, and Innovation," *Rand Journal of Economics*, 16,1: 70–83.

———— 1986. "Installed Base and Compatibility: Innovation, Product Preannouncements, and Predation," *American Economic Review*, 76: 940–955.

Fisher, F. M. 1983. *Disequilibrium Foundations of Equilibrium Economics*, Cambridge: Cambridge University Press.

Henderson, J. V. 1977. *Economic Theory and the Cities*, New York: Academic Press.

Kahn, A. E. 1988. *The Economics Of Regulation: Principles and Institutions*, Cambridge, MA: MIT Press, 2 vols.

Katz M. L. and Shapiro, C. 1985. "Network Externalities, Competition, and Compatibility", *American Economic Review*, 75(3): 425–440.

———— 1986. "Technology Adoption in the Presence of Network Externalities," *Journal of Political Economy*, 94(4): 822–841.

Klopfenstein, B. C. 1989. "The Diffusion of the VCR in the United States," in Levy, M. R. (ed.) *The VCR Age*, Newbury Park, CA, Sage.

Knight, F. H. 1924. "Some Fallacies in the Interpretation of Social Cost," *Quarterly Journal of Economics*, 38: 582–606.
Lardner, J. 1987. *Fast Forward: Hollywood, the Japanese, and the onslaught of the VCR*, New York: W. W. Norton.
Levinson, R. J. and Coleman, M. T. 1992. "Economic Analysis of Compatibility Standards: How Useful is It?," *FTC Working Paper.*
Liebowitz, S. J. and Margolis, S. E. 1990. "The Fable of the Keys," *Journal of Law and Economics*, 33: 1–25; reprinted as Chapter 2 in this volume.
———— 1994. "Market Processes and the Selection of Standards," *UTD Working Paper.*
———— 1995a. "Are Network Externalities a New Source of Market Failure?," *Research in Law and Economics*, 17, 1–22; reprinted as Chapter 4 in this volume.
———— 1995b. "Path Dependence, Lock-in, and History," *Journal of Law, Economics and Organization*, 11: 205–226; reprinted as Chapter 5 in this volume.
Mills, E. 1967. "An Aggregative Model of Resource Allocation in a Metropolitan Area," *American Economic Review*, 57: 197–210.
Stigler, G. J. 1941. *Production and Distribution Theories*, New York: Macmillan.

4

Are Network Externalities a New Source of Market Failure? (1995)* **

Every new age is enamored of its own advances. In this "age of technology," our focus is on such highly visible technologies as computers, fax machines, and new methods of communication. So taken are we with these new technologies that we tend to treat these new inventions as *sui generis*, so different in essentials that we cannot even speak of them in the same terms as we have used in the past. To discuss the advances of this age of technology, the economist has invented a new concept: network externality. Network externality has been defined as the change in the benefit, or surplus, that an agent derives from a good when the number of other agents consuming the same kind of good changes. It is argued that network externality is endemic to new, high-tech industries, and that such industries experience problems that are different in character from the problems that have, for more ordinary commodities, been solved by markets (Katz and Shapiro 1985; Farrell and Saloner 1985).

The concept of network externality has been applied in the literature on standards, in which a primary concern is the choice of a correct standard (Farrell and Saloner 1985, Katz and Shapiro 1985, Liebowitz and Margolis 1994). The concept has also played a role in the developing literature of path dependence, which maintains that the explanation for many market outcomes is mere happenstance (Arthur 1989; David 1985).[1] While the path dependence literature has focused on technologies, the reasoning of path dependence arguments has also been extended to the choice of social institutions (Binger and Hoffman 1989, North 1990).

---

* *Research in Law and Economics*, 17 (1995): 1–22.

These literatures treat the concept of network externality uncritically. Thus it is natural for a reader encountering a paper discussing network externality to look for the association most commonly made with externalities: that the market fails.[2] And the reader is not disappointed: papers in this literature have found market failure. As we will show below, this argument, *carried to its logical conclusion,* would indicate that most markets fail standard economic tests of efficiency, and thus might be thought to call for government intervention into most markets. This conclusion is too important to pass without careful scrutiny.

This paper elaborates a claim that network externalities are not well understood. We demonstrate that one class of phenomena identified as network externalities is actually pecuniary in nature, and not a cause of welfare loss. We also argue that many of the remaining network externalities are not externalities at all, but are better thought of as *network effects* that are resolvable by the familiar mechanisms of ownership and contract that internalize these effects. Further, we discuss the mischaracterization of technology that has been offered to justify network externalities and we elaborate upon the technical features of models that have led other authors to conclusions that differ from ours. In sum, it is our argument that, notwithstanding the enthusiasm that has greeted this literature, the concept of network externality has, in important respects, been improperly modeled, incorrectly supported, and inappropriately applied.

Two types of network externalities

Katz and Shapiro (1985) consider two types of positive network externalities. First, they consider direct externalities – those generated "through a direct physical effect of the number of purchasers on the quality of the product." Their example of direct externality is the number of homes attached to a telephone network. Second, they consider "indirect effects" such as complementary goods being more plentiful and lower in price as the number of users of the good increases.[3] Their example here is better software as the number of computers of a particular type increases. They go on to consider another source of indirect network externality, the availability of post-purchase service for durable goods, such as automobiles.

In a similar vein, Farrell and Saloner (1985, 70) observe: "There may be direct 'network externality' in the sense that one consumer's value for a good increases when another consumer has a compatible good, as in the case of telephones or personal computer software. There may be a market-mediated effect, as when a complementary good (spare parts, servicing, software ...) becomes cheaper and more readily available the greater the extent of the (compatible) market."

Although these writers and others observe a distinction between direct and indirect externalities, this distinction does not figure into the existing theoretical analyses. In the theoretical treatments, both types of network externalities are assumed to have the same consequences: direct and indirect interactions alike are embodied in payoff functions, regardless of their source. Farrell and Saloner, for example, postulate a benefits function Bj(S,Y) in which j denotes the firm, Y denotes the firm's technology choice, and S denotes the size of the network (number of firms choosing Y). Katz and Shapiro (1986) specify that a consumer's net benefits are $v(x_1 + x_2) - p$, where x_1 and x_2 are the sizes of the network in time period one and two and p is the price of a unit of the technology. We argue below that direct and indirect network externalities are fundamentally different and should not be modeled as equivalent. In the next section, we discuss the problems of drawing welfare conclusions regarding indirect network externalities. After that, we consider direct effects, arguing that the mere fact of a network *effect* does not necessarily imply a network externality.

Indirect network externalities

The past as prologue

Economists once argued that increasing cost industries require a tax, and decreasing cost industries require a bounty. Marshall appears to have originated these propositions, and Pigou seems to get most of the blame.[4] From the modern perspective, the early twentieth-century debate on the nature of externalities may appear rather quaint, due to the nonmathematical apparatus that it used. However, this quaint apparatus did ultimately manage to distinguish between technological and pecuniary externalities.

The economic foundation for the belief that all nonconstant costs lead to market failures focused on the impact of additional output on the price of the product. Pigou argued that the change in expenditure on the inframarginal units that accompanied a change in output was a social cost, and that to reach an efficient solution, this cost should be internalized. In other words, for Pigou, the marginal expenditure curve associated with the supply curve was the social marginal cost curve.

Some economists quickly understood and agreed that external pecuniary diseconomies simply involve transfers from buyers to producers: They are not instances of market failure. Though economists have not generally recognized that external pecuniary economies have the same attribute, modern interest in all pecuniary effects has waned; textbook discussions of externality barely mention them.[5] The current pedagogy calls attention only to nonpecuniary externalities, and associates all externalities with market failure.

This bit of history of thought is very closely related to the literature on network externality. Almost any product with increasing or decreasing costs can be considered a network, as network is being used in the current literature: Additional consumption may raise or lower the cost of a product to other consumers and it may raise or lower the cost of substitutes and complements. Since such effects are practically universal in the economy, if network externalities are taken seriously as externalities, almost all markets must be candidates for either taxes or bounties. This, of course, is a reincarnation of the Marshall–Pigou concern that competitive market solutions would be in need of repair unless costs were constant. Any network externality that is "market mediated," meaning that the size of the network influences the price of inputs to a firm, or goods and services to a consumer, is the same as the pecuniary external economies and diseconomies that so perplexed Marshall, Pigou and at least some in the generations of economists that followed. For this reason we turn to a more detailed examination of these arguments. We consider first the familiar pecuniary external diseconomies to set the stage and establish terminology for the less familiar pecuniary external economies.

Pecuniary external diseconomies

In Figure 4.1, let C_1 represent the conventional long-run industry supply function for a ordinary commodity, such as shoes. Assume for the moment that there are no external effects (price of inputs assumed constant). Assume also that the industry supply function is increasing because, say, there are limited locations for producers or an unequal distribution of shoemaking skills. The competitive equilibrium is at J. With each firm producing on its marginal cost curve, the associated price, P_1 is equal to the marginal cost of shoes. We can imagine having a "network" of shoe buyers, where each buyer's purchase has an impact on other shoe buyers. If someone elects to buy one more pair of shoes, the expenditures of the network of shoe buyers will go up by more than P_1, the price of a pair of shoes. The incremental expendi-

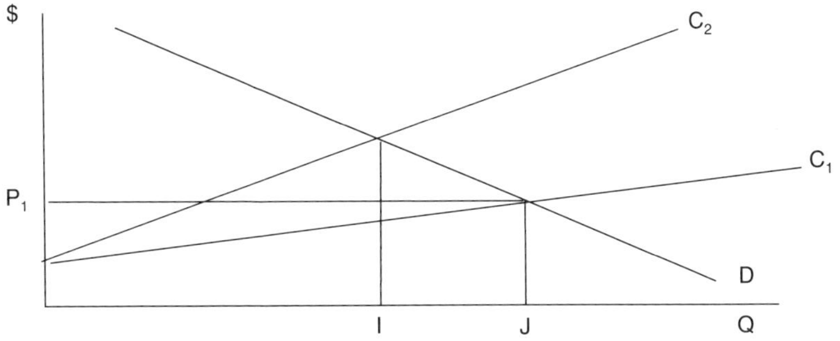

Figure 4.1 Pecuniary external diseconomies

tures are shown as C_2. This is analogous to the MFC curve that is used in the context of factor demand.

The puzzle to Pigou and some others of his generation was whether this marginal expenditure curve, C_2, is the socially relevant cost curve. Pigou originally wrote that it was, and suggested taxes to move market outcomes to I. The answer of the profession was, and is, that if the difference between C_2 and C_1 occurs as rents to the producers of inframarginal shoes, then C_2 does not represent the marginal social cost of shoes. Instead, this component of the increased expenditure of shoe buyers is merely a transfer from the consumers of inframarginal shoes to the producers of inframarginal shoes. This transfer (rent) to producers has no impact on efficiency. This is the simplest example supporting the interpretation of the industry supply curve as marginal social cost, the interpretation put forward by Young, Knight, and others, as a counter to Pigou's claim.

If each shoe producer's costs are affected by industry expansion the analysis becomes more involved and it becomes crucial how and why costs are affected. One possibility is a real interaction among shoe producers that affects their costs, a technological externality within the shoe industry (congestion) that would make C_2 the social marginal cost curve. Another possibility is that costs change because the price of some input increases as the shoe industry expands.

Assume, for example, that the external diseconomies are caused by increases in the price of leather as shoe output increases. In this case, the issues we raise are just kicked one market upstream. After all, as we move up the supply curve, the increased revenue per shoe, when an additional shoe is produced, does not now go to the inframarginal shoe producers, since these shoe producers all must pay an equivalently higher price for leather. Here the extra payment made by shoe consumers is not a rent going to shoe producers, but must go somewhere else.

We now must ask why the price of leather is rising. If it is due to some limited locational or other element, so that consumers' increased expenditure on inframarginal shoes is found to be a rent to inframarginal leather suppliers, then C_1 is the social marginal cost curve for shoes. An alternative is that the upstream (leather) industry faces technological diseconomies external to its component firms (e.g. congestion).[6] In this case, leather is not sold at social marginal cost, and C_2 is the social marginal cost of shoes.

It should be clear that the issues considered in regard to the input market are an exact echo of the issues considered for the primary (shoe) market. Every industry can be thought inefficient if its inputs are mispriced. To halt an unstoppable recursion through suppliers, then suppliers' suppliers, and so on, we will assume that input prices represent marginal social costs and confront these issues but once, in the primary market, as is normally done. Assuming that inputs are efficiently priced, and assuming no technological externality among shoe producers, C_1 is the marginal social cost of shoes.

Restating these old results in terms of the current terminology, we note one immediate qualification for indirect network externalities. Those negative network externalities that are "market mediated," as when an input or complementary good becomes more expensive, and that do not reflect some upstream market imperfection, are irrelevant as externalities. Indeed, if we are consistent in our treatment of network externalities, and treat increasing costs industries as networks, we ought to conclude that most forms of consumption and production involve "negative indirect network externalities." Pecuniary external diseconomies, however, involve no inefficiency. Internalizing these externalities is harmful: such internalization merely mimics monopsony power.

Pecuniary external economies

Models of network externalities are concerned primarily with positive network externalities. Thus with regard to indirect effects they are concerned with decreasing prices for goods or their complements. For example, the price of DOS compatible software falls as the number of DOS users increases. For decreasing costs, the nature of pecuniary externalities is less familiar so we consider their sources and consequences here.

Decreasing-cost industries have not been treated as symmetric with increasing-cost industries.[7] As we have just demonstrated, for increasing-cost industries, if there are no input price effects, and no real technical effects of industry expansion, the increased expenditure for inframarginal goods is just a transfer. Inframarginal units of production capacity, capable of producing at relatively low cost, remain in the industry and earn rents as price and output increase. For the case of decreasing costs the analogous explanation is not generally taken to be available. The decrease in expenditure on inframarginal units is generally not recognized as a loss in rents to producers. Downward-sloping supply is not the result of low-cost units being held off the market until prices fall, and being supplied only to "take advantage" of low prices. So it is most often argued that downward-sloping supply must be a consequence of some real externality or economy of scale, rather than a bidding down of producers' rents that would be the exact analog of the external diseconomies case.

But, of course, downward-sloping supply could also be caused by decreasing input prices. This would seem to be the case that most closely represents actual examples of indirect network externalities. We take up that case now, using computers and integrated circuits (chips), instead of shoes and leather, to aid intuition and exposition. As in the foregoing, we maintain that the input (chips) is sold at marginal cost. Without a technological externality or simple economy of scale in the computer industry, downward-sloping supply for computers will require that the price of chips falls as the computer industry expands. In order to avoid indefinite recursion up the supply chain, we consider the case in which downward-sloping supply is the result of economic factors in the chip industry.

We make the common assumption that the decrease in the cost of chips is external to any computer firm. Computer producers then can have upward-sloping or horizontal cost curves in the usual manner, with each firm's cost curves being a function of industry output. The industry supply curve is rotated clockwise, relative to the summation of firm supply curves, by external cost effects. In Figure 4.2, C_1 is the supply and C_2 is the marginal expenditure curve associated with C_1.

The downward-sloping supply curves imply that the marginal expenditure by consumers on computers lies below the supply curve. This is because the marginal cost of an additional computer is the cost of the last unit plus the (negative) effect on cost for all other units that are now made less costly by the decreased price of chips.

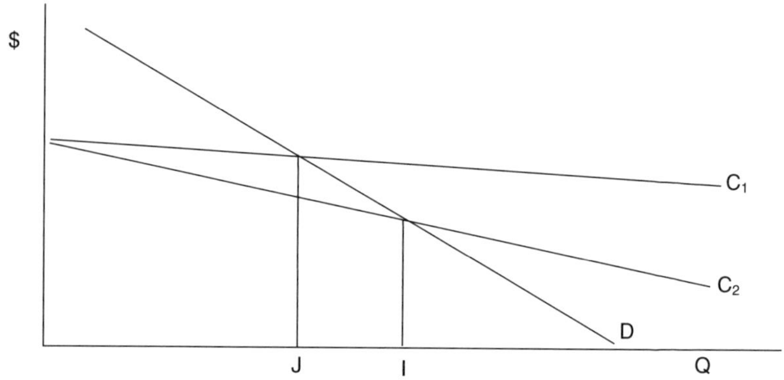

Figure 4.2 Pecuniary external economies

In the case of upward-sloping supply, the increase in expenditure on the inframarginal computers was considered a rent going from consumers to producers. Here, the decrease in expenditures on the inframarginal computers is passed from producers to the consumers of computers (the shaded area in Figure 4.3). But since the costs to the computer producers go down due to the decreased price of chips, the producers of inframarginal computers are merely passing on lower costs. Thus the benefits to computer users actually come from the producers of inframarginal chips.

If we are to treat this example consistently with the case of upward-sloping supply, we must assume that all markets other than the computer market are producing at P = MC. With that assumption,

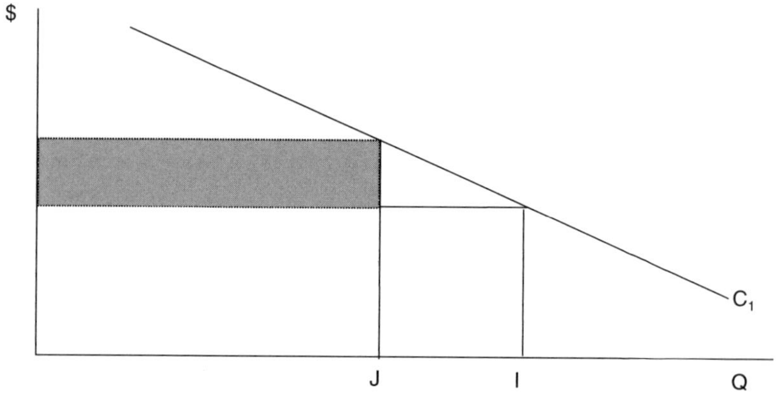

Figure 4.3 Consumer benefits from pecuniary external economies

downward-sloping supply for chips implies that marginal costs fall as chip output increases. One possible explanation for this is that the chip industry is a natural monopoly. In that case, marginal cost pricing cannot cover total costs. This is equivalent to the familiar example of a perfectly regulated (single-priced) natural monopoly that requires a subsidy from some source to cover its unavoidable operating loss. When output increases in the computer industry, causing the price of chips to fall (increasing the absolute value of the negative producer surplus), the chip industry experiences a larger loss, requiring a larger subsidy by the regulator. Thus the transfer goes from the source of subsidy to the computer-chip industry to the computer consumer. Under these circumstances, the case of downward-sloping supply is symmetric with upward-sloping supply. All of this is to say that downward-sloping supply may correctly represent decreasing cost, presenting no externality to be internalized.

Alternatively, the downward-sloping supply of chips could be the result of technological economies that are external to individual firms in the chip industry.[8] In that case, the marginal social cost of chips does lie below the supply curve. Of course, to retain our assumption that inputs are bought at a price equal to social marginal cost, we must assume that the externality in the chip industry is internalized in some way, for example, by a Pigouvian subsidy system. This subsidy must increase as the production of computers increases, and it is the increase in subsidy that is transferred, in the end, to consumers of computers. Once again, the analysis is fully symmetrical. This is to say that if a technological externality upstream (chips) is correctly internalized, the downward-sloping supply in the downstream (computer) industry involves no additional externality to be internalized.

Implications

Indirect network externalities thus appear to be either pecuniary externalities, which require no remediation, or the reflection of conventional market failures in upstream markets. Introduction of the concept of indirect network externalities takes something that has long been recognized and (to some degree) understood and presents it as something new and unfamiliar.

There exists a casual empiricism that suggests that computer users are better off when there are more of their like. But if computer users are better off because of an external economy or natural monopoly in the chip industry, misdiagnosing this phenomenon as an externality pertaining to the number or type of computer users will prompt incorrect policy responses. Internalizing such an indirect network externality will not, for example, move us toward the correct number of chips per computer, or computers per user. It will not prompt efficient expansion into other uses of chips outside of the computer "network." Thus the labeling of an upstream market problem as a downstream "indirect network externality" is not a harmless semantic shift. It interferes with understanding and would prompt, if taken seriously, improper policy responses.

The reader may note that this analysis has been couched in terms of changes in input prices. Although the network externality literature is often couched in terms of price changes for complementary products, such as computers and software, this is not really an important distinction. The complement is really an input in the creation of a product or service jointly provided by the two goods. A computer producer, who buys the software and bundles it at sale, fits the description above, with software replacing computer chips. Even if a customer buys both the computer and the software from separate vendors, the costs of the joint services are the same as if the customer had bought both from a single firm (if both markets are competitive). As in the above, misdiagnosing the externality as one pertaining to the number of computer users misdirects our attention and prompts policy measures directed at the wrong margin of adjustment.

Direct network externalities

There are many activities in which the phrase "the more the merrier" applies. It is this simple interaction that we have termed a network effect. But network externality – unexploited gain from trade regarding network effects – is not an inevitable consequence of network effects. Nor is it a consequence that is escaped only by coincidence. Network effects may be shown to be more like other social interactions than has previously been supposed. Accordingly, theoretical cases of network externalities may be shown to be consequences of particular assumptions of about technologies, tastes and markets. With that, market failure in this context may be understood as arising not from networks effects *per se*, but rather from conditions that economics associates (rightly or wrongly) with inefficiencies for goods in general. It is also of note that the restrictions invoked in some cases to construct a network externality preclude consideration of network size, an important margin on which network effects might operate.

Is there a market failure?

Many of the most conventional externalities studied by economists can be eliminated by some configuration of ownership. For example, if exterior maintenance of apartment buildings creates external benefits for proximate units, common ownership of nearby units should have survival value. The tragedy of the commons has a solution in property rights to the commons. We might well expect that ownership of a network would resolve these externalities as well. Such a conclusion would be important, because many network activities are "owned" or, in the terminology offered by Katz and Shapiro, "sponsored." Some networks are owned by their very nature: They are literal physical networks, such as telephone or power grids that must be constructed as networks through coordinated action. Figurative networks, such as the "network" of Apple computer users, or of Airstream trailer owners can also be owned through patent, copyright, or trademark protection. Of course, some networks, such as the network of English speakers, seemingly cannot be owned.

A prior expectation that ownership solves network externality problems encounters dissonance in the network externality literature. Katz and Shapiro conclude that market failures due to network externalities are not resolved by sponsorship. "Sponsorship can internalize some of the externalities through below cost pricing at the beginning of a technology's life. But sponsorship can create problems of its own" (1986, 825).

We begin an alternative examination of these issues by offering a simple model, a variant of the well-known fishing-on-the-lake model. Although this model captures many fundamental features of the costs and benefits of networks, it clearly cannot cover every case. But the cases its does not cover are, we will argue, special cases. In particular, they are special cases that we encounter elsewhere in economics and treat (elsewhere) as special cases.

In Figure 4.4, the horizontal axis denotes the number of participants in some network. It can be the number of telephones, computer users, or fishermen on a lake. Assume that participation in the network consists of buying one unit of some basic element of the network: telephone service, a computer, a day on the lake. As is fundamental to positive network externalities (and in contrast to our usual fish stories), we assume that the private benefit of each network participant increases as the number of participants increases. We assume that network participants are identical. This assumption is the familiar one

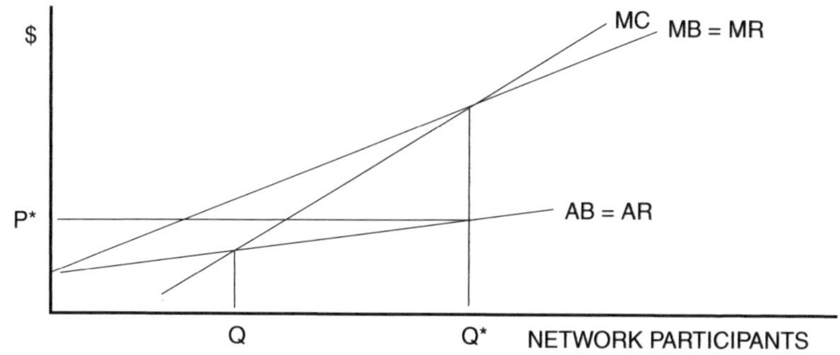

Figure 4.4 Positive network externalities

in the fisheries example: We seldom take note of differences in fishing ability. Analogously, homogeneity is a fairly common assumption in the contemporary network literature. (See, for examples, Church and Gandal 1993, 243; Katz and Shapiro 1986, 826.) Figure 4.4 shows a relationship between average benefit, AB, and the number of network participants. The height of AB represents each participant's willingness to pay for one unit of network participation; willingness to pay that rises as the number of network participants increases. (Note that absent a network effect, AB would be horizontal, at the common benefit received by all participants.) MB, the marginal network benefit, represents the change in total benefits to network members when an additional member joins. MB lies above AB since an additional member raises the benefits for all network participants.

For the moment, we assume that the marginal cost of the network commodity increases with output. This is a conventional assumption about cost, and it has intuitive appeal for many networks. For example, literal networks, like cable television, connect the closest customers first, and expand by connecting ever-more-distant customers at ever-increasing costs. Kahn (1988 1 124, 2 123) provides empirical support for this pattern in public utilities networks. For figurative networks, such as a network of computer users, additional marketing effort may be required to reach customers less familiar with the product. Finally, network participation frequently requires the use of some "entry" commodity (for example, a telephone or computer), and that commodity may be subject to ordinary production costs.

Since AB represents the willingness of participants to pay for network participation, it is the highest price that the network owner can charge. Thus, it is the average revenue function for the network owner as well as the average benefit function for network participants. The marginal revenue captured by the network owner when an additional participant joins the network is equal to the price paid by the marginal participant, plus the increase in price that can be charged to all network participants. In this example, MB is also the marginal revenue function associated with AB. The network owner maximizes profit, equating marginal revenue with marginal cost. Q* is the network size, and P* is the price. P* obviously is less than marginal cost.

Because the return to the network owner of serving a participant is greater than price, there is no credibility problem with sub-marginal cost pricing. A problem that can be constructed in network settings, in which a sponsor could not credibly commit to sub-marginal cost pricing (Katz and Shapiro 1986, 834, 838) does not necessarily arise for networks. It does arise, as it does for many allocation problems, where an enforceable contract is unavailable, and where a potential transaction would span more than one time period.

It is fairly trivial to relate this outcome to the social wealth-maximizing optimum. The optimum conditions are the familiar equivalence of marginal social cost and marginal social benefits. Since the change in benefits to society when a consumer joins the network is represented by the MB curve, the marginal social benefit thus coincides with the network owner's marginal revenue function, and Q* is the optimal network size for both society and the network owner.

An upward-sloping benefits function does introduce some unfamiliar features to this analysis. In Figure 4.4, while P*, Q* does clear the market, stability will not originate on the demand side. In the more familiar fishing problem, with optimal pricing of participation (the right to fish), the implicit dynamic story is that if too many fishermen show up to fish, they will find the optimal price of fishing to be unattractive, given the expected catch, and fishermen will leave until fishing on the lake is as good as anything else. If too few fisherman show up, again at the optimal price, fishing is too good a deal, and more fishermen will arrive. In contrast, for the positive-effects network, stability must originate with the supplier. The network owner would announce P* and provide Q* positions in the network. Here, if more than Q* seek to participate, the network owner could ration demand, or alternatively, the network owner could offer to accommodate all participants, but would optimally charge a price equal to average benefit, plus the difference between marginal benefit and marginal cost. (That price equals the net marginal cost of an additional network participant.) Such a price is above average benefit, so network participants would depart, moving the equilibrium to Q*. Similarly, at participation levels below Q*, the profit-maximizing price is marginal cost less the difference between marginal and average benefit; again the net cost imposed on the network. Such a price is below average benefit, and so would attract additional participants. Stability thus originates on the supply side, so in still another respect, the model is a mirror image of the usual fisheries problem.

It is possible to construct a "chattering disequilibrium" model. No one joins the network, then everyone joins, etc. But the same can be done for the ordinary fisheries problem: If too many fishermen show up, they all go home, If no fishermen show up, they all want to fish. Ordinarily these knife edge problems are ignored.

A network market failure can be found, however, when the network is not owned. If we reinterpret MC as the supply function of a group of atomistic suppliers of the basic network commodity, rather than the marginal cost of a single producer, then equilibrium occurs at Q. Notice here, however, that the manifestation of the market failure is the size of the network. It is not in the choice of networks.

This analysis of the operation of an owned network is an exact analog of the standard example of overfishing a lake. That particular network externality is a negative one, but the analysis is the same. Replacing common ownership of a lake with a single owner results in efficiency precisely because the owner takes into account of the interactions of the fishermen in order to maximize the surplus, which, of course, he appropriates. In the fishing example, without network ownership, the network is too big; but for the case of positive network externalities, the network is too small. Of course, if the lake is the only source of fish, we might have to worry about monopoly in the output market, or if the lake is the only use of labor, we might worry about monopsony in the labor market. Similarly the owner of a network may or may not be a monopolist in the supply of network services. But monopoly is monopoly, and monopsony is monopsony, and either are only coincidentally associated with network problems.

Why the difference?

A number of other writers emphasize the likelihood of market failure where there are network effects. Two seminal articles, Katz and Shapiro (1986) and Farrell and Saloner (1985) find these problems, as does some of the most recent work on the subject (for example, see Church and Gandal 1993). The many models of network externality differ in particulars, and our problem is not to reconstruct each of them here. There are, however, structural features that are common to many of the models of network externality, and these structural features can be shown to support particular outcomes that are consistent with market failure.

One important feature of many network externalities models is the assumption of constant marginal cost. See, for example, Chou and Shy (1990, 260), Church and Gandal (1993, 246), Katz and Shapiro (1986, 829) and Farrell and Saloner (1992, 16). This assumption is common in economics, and commonly results only in reduced complexity, as in classical duopoly models. (For an example related to compatibility, see Matutes and Regibeau 1992.) But the assumption is decisive in network externality models for this reason: The assumption of some fixed costs, together with constant marginal cost, installs an inexhaustible economy of large scale operation. This, in turn, installs an externality if goods are priced at average cost.

Another structural feature is an assumed limitation, or predetermination, of the total number of network participants. Typically it is assumed that there are N consumers (or users, or participants, or adopters, etc.) who all adopt some product, network, or technology. For example, Katz and Shapiro specify, "each consumer is infinitely lived and has inelastic demand for a single unit of infinitely durable hardware" (1992, 58). Their 1986 paper specifies N_t identical consumers in each period. Either all of these consumers adopt a particular technology, or none of them do. In Farrell and Saloner (1985), N firms adopt or don't adopt a new standard.

As we will see, what is dispositive is that the models are constructed so that posited economies to scale are not exhausted when all potential participants are served by a network. So long as the stipulated technology is characterized by inexhaustible economies to scale, it does not particularly matter what the number of potential consumers is, so long as it is finite.

Figure 4.5 reproduces our model with a fixed number of participants and constant marginal cost. Again the average benefit is upward-sloping, and marginal benefit lies above the average private benefit. Since marginal cost is constant, however, marginal cost must intersect the benefits curves from above. With this, the optimum must lie at infinity, or at some other maximal boundary. That boundary is, of course, the predetermined full set of demanders, each of whom demands the good with zero elasticity. Thus both the limitation on demanders and the restriction on marginal cost play a role. In this setting, the nature of the problem cannot be the number of network participants: that is established by assumption.

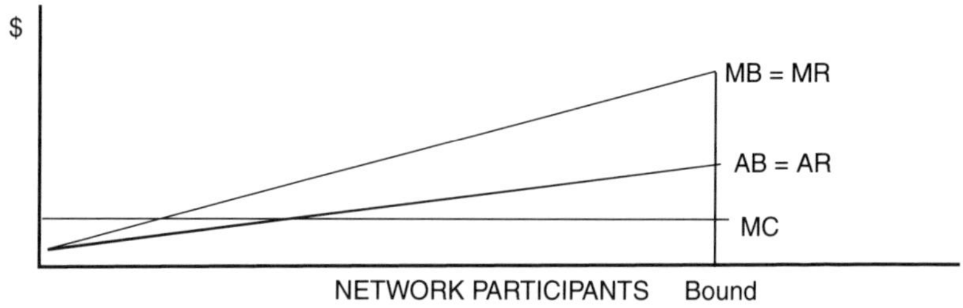

Figure 4.5 Positive network externalities – fixed number of participants

The contrast between the results shown in Figures 4.4 and 4.5 illustrates the importance of the assumptions on cost and participation. Our point here is not that there cannot be economies to scale, but rather that many of the results associated with network externalities are anchored in the assumption of inexhaustible scale economies. This is important in two regards. The first is that for many of network commodities, economies to scale *are* exhaustible. The second is that the cause of some of the putative problems with networks would also result in problems for ordinary goods, and thus the apparent network problems have less to do with networks *per se* and more to do with economies to scale.

Because these models suggest that only a single network (or standard, or technology, etc.) will survive, the network externality literature implies a possible coordination problem: Which network gets the franchise? Natural monopoly does raise legitimate questions, but these questions are not well addressed as externalities. As we demonstrate in our (1994) paper, the coordination problem is not removed by internalization, strictly defined as allowing consumers to take account of the effects of their behavior on others. To remove all coordination problems, consumers would also need to take account of the behavior of all coalitions on everyone else in the economy, which is a far greater task than can be accomplished by mere internalization of network externalities. Other models (Economides 1989; Chou and Shy 1990) have demonstrated this coordination problem without network externalities.

The future is not what it used to be

The literature on network externalities challenges economists' traditional use of decreasing returns and grants a fundamental role to economies to scale. Though economists have long accepted the possibility of increasing returns, they have generally judged that except in fairly rare instances, the economy operates in a range of decreasing returns. The literature on network externalities has attained some of its influence by choosing as its examples some new-technology products that appear to exhibit increasing returns. Following the lead of futurists, writers in this field predict that as modern technologies take over a larger share of the economy, the share of the economy described by increasing returns will increase. Brian Arthur has emphasized these points to a general audience: "[T]he prevalent view is still that things happen in equilibrium and that there are constant or diminishing return ... A high-tech, high value-added world calls for a new kind of economics" (Arthur, quoted in Wysocki 1990).

Arthur approvingly cites Marshall for an early emphasis on the importance of increasing returns. But Arthur appears to be unaware of the intervening criticism of Marshall's view. Marshall's views on increasing returns were largely erroneous, a confusion of movements along cost curves and movements of cost curves (see Stigler 1941, 68–76; Ellis and Fellner, 1943, 243). Our criticism of the current view of increasing returns expands on these early criticisms of Marshall.

The support for a belief in increasing returns is based largely on anecdotes and casual characterizations of technology. The past decades have evidenced a number of technologies that have experienced two correlated phenomena: First, enormous declines in price; second, tremendous growth in sales. In recent years the prices of VCRs have declined remarkably, and at the same time, there has been an incredible increase in their use. The same story applies to computers, lasers, and cellular phones. The simple explanation is that these technologies are subject to increasing returns. Since bigger has been cheaper, it has been assumed that bigger causes cheaper. But an available alternative is that as the technology has advanced with time, the average cost curves are shifting down. Consider for example, the history of old technologies, such as refrigerators and automobiles. These industries, currently thought to exhibit conventional decreasing returns, experienced tremendous cost decreases early in their history.[9] Thus the currently popular association of new technology with increasing returns may well be treacherous.

The casual argument for the association of new technology with increasing returns imposes a very restricted structure on production. Products are argued to be knowledge based, and the knowledge costs of a product are generally argued to be associated entirely with fixed costs. For example, the programming costs of a new piece of software

are large, and the costs of copying disks are very small and constant. This leads to the conclusion that average costs will fall indefinitely as output increases. But this argument fails on several grounds. First, the knowledge-based part of costs are not all fixed. Support services and sales services, for example, are knowledge based, but are variable costs. Goods that are sold to a broader market generally must accommodate more diverse requirements than products that are sold to a smaller and more specialized group. Second, this characterization of production leaves other conventional components of cost out of the picture. Conventional variable costs easily coexist with fixed cost components in common textbook examples of U-shaped cost curves. As output increases, the decrease in average fixed costs must itself eventually decrease, and is more than offset by increases in average variable costs. Without investigation, it is unreasonable to accept that the law of diminishing marginal product somehow takes a vacation in new-technology industries. While the scale properties of a technology pertain to the simultaneous expansion of all inputs, it seems evident that resource limitations do ultimately restrain firm size. Economists have long supposed that limitations of management play a role in this, a relationship formalized in Radner (1992).

It is arresting, at first glance, to observe that the disks and paper that constitute a software product are worth only a few dollars. Observations like that appear to support the view that such products are unlike older, more familiar products. But we might as well observe that the ingredients in a nouvelle cuisine meal are worth only a few dollars or that the constituent items in sneakers, automobiles or Corn Flakes are only a small percent of their final price. That observation does not lead us to conclude that efficiency requires us to dine at the same restaurant, or wear the same kind of shoes, etc. The additional costs involved with catering to slightly different tastes, or transporting consumers to products, or vice-versa, are the types of costs that are easily overlooked in simple models. These other costs are exactly the type of costs that can cause average cost to rise even though average fixed costs fall as output increases. Thus the observation that disks and paper are of trivial cost is insufficient to allow the conclusion that we will and should all compute with the same spreadsheet. This caution is reinforced by the observation that software markets are not monopolized, and in fact seem to accommodate numbers of firms comparable to numbers in such "old-technology" industries as steel or automobiles.

It is also far from clear that current high-tech items have a greater knowledge-based component than previous incarnations of high-tech items. For example, it is not clear that creating a spreadsheet is a more challenging conceptual enterprise than inventing the Bessemer process. For most new products, the costs of "figuring it out" are fairly significant. And once the technology is figured out, additional units of the good, embodying the solutions developed, will come cheap. Once a caveman had discovered the technology to get one fire started, he could easily make many fires. The producer who has figured well will have an advantage for a time, and will, for that time, dominate the market. RCA, Ampex, and Ford serve as examples of pioneering firms that engineered downward shifts of their cost functions. If these firms merely moved down fixed average cost functions, they would today still be the leaders in televisions, video recorders, and automobiles.

We don't deny the importance of progress. Certainly the state of knowledge is changing. We don't even make a claim about changes in the rate of progress (whatever that might be). Our claim is only that knowledge is always a component of goods, that the knowledge share of total cost is not necessarily greater now than it was in the past, and that the fixed-cost attribute of knowledge need not overwhelm other cost components.

Transactions among network participants

It is generally considered infeasible for consumers to transact with one another to internalize an externality such as air pollution, since consumers are many, transactions are costly, free riding is possible, etc. Along similar lines, it seems unlikely that network participants would be able to internalize indirect network externalities, since such interactions involve large numbers of participants. In contrast, direct network externalities involve direct interaction of individuals, so the number of people who affect each other may well be a reasonable few. Thus transactions to resolve an inefficiency cannot be ruled out.

Take the example of a telephone network. It is often observed that each additional phone attached to the network enhances the value of the network to other users of the network. But most users make most of their calls to only a small number of phones. The Smith family, for example, may frequently call friends or parents on the phone. Each call is a transaction of sorts. The Smith family will derive the greatest value from those network participants they intend to call most frequently. But it is not difficult for the Smith family to transact with their parents or friends to get them to install a phone on a common network. A similar story applies to video recording. If Smith's parents are thinking of getting a Beta format machine, and the Smiths already have VHS, Smith might remind his parents that he can provide videotapes of the grandchildren only on VHS, and thus help to internalize the joint value in tape exchange between parents and children. And it is not only family relationships that allow this internalization. Companies that do significant business with one another will try to standardize on similar products, in order to allow greater interaction. It is not terribly difficult to negotiate over the terms of enhancing this interaction. Since the very nature of these networks is interaction among individuals, it is unreasonable to invoke the usual condemnation of transacted solutions, which is that individuals are unable to interact. Transactions to resolve these direct network effects tend toward desirable outcomes. It is fortunate that indirect network effects are unlikely to be addressed in this way, since any such transactions would tend to emulate monopsony outcomes.

Conclusions

The reception given to the idea of network externalities is based in large part on the general impression that there are a large and increasing number of activities in which costs or benefits rise or fall as the number of participants increases. And this impression seems to apply particularly to new, high-tech industries.

Network externality has been promoted as a new concept that deals with new technologies. Such a new concept would seem to require models that are new as well. But as we have seen, some of what is new here is mistaken. In some instances, the focus on the network itself merely prevents proper diagnoses of more familiar problems in related markets, conventional problems such as natural monopoly and ordinary production externality. In other instances, special cases are too readily taken for the general network problem. Finally, these new models have detached the analysis from an important body of understanding. In this regard we note that the problems with pecuniary externalities were noticed almost immediately upon publication of Pigou's book in 1912, while the modern version of the error has remained in the literature for quite some time.

We may often find that we are better off when more people make the same choice that we make. Who has not considered a party invitation without wondering who else will be there? But that behavior does not imply that all guest lists are wrong. It is a grand conceptual leap from observing a network effect to concluding the existence of a socially relevant externality. So long as we have only the vague impression that "bigger is better" (or "smaller is better"), we should be slow to conclude that there are externalities of the sort that suggest the need for social remedy.

Notes

** The authors thank Lee Craig, Neil Gandal, Craig Newmark, Pierre Regibeau, George Stigler, Richard Zerbe and workshop participants at North Carolina State University. Errors are our own.

1. But see Liebowitz and Margolis (1990, 1995) [Chapters 2 and 5 this volume] for a critical examination of the empirical and theoretical support for the view that happenstance is a controlling factor in market outcomes.
2. The market failure, however, is somewhat unusual in that the choice of a network, or type of product, is the dimension in which the market fails. Discrete failure contrasts with conventional externalities, in which the problem is a matter of degree – too much pollution, too little gardening.
3. Having a larger market will increase the supply of auxiliary goods, but it will also increase the demand. Whether the prices will go down is another question entirely. These papers may have in mind that the auxiliary market is more competitive when it is bigger, which would tend to lower price. But it also seems to imply that production of the complementary products embody economies of scale, which need not lower price, even though costs would be lowered.
4. Pigou first made these statements in his text *Wealth and Welfare*, published in 1912. Allyn Young criticized these conclusions in a 1913 review of the book. With the publication of the revised text in 1920, renamed *The Economics of Welfare*, Pigou took back these statements in cases where the increase in cost was due to rising factor prices, but clung to the general arguments. He was then subject to further criticism, and in 1924 revised his doctrine once more, still clinging to a narrow version related to international trade, which was then shown to be deficient by Knight in 1924. According to Ellis and Fellner (1943), Graham and Hicks were among the more notable economists to embrace Pigou's vision.
5. Not only do they receive merely cursory treatment in most textbooks, but the entry in Palgrave's *Dictionary* (Eatwell *et al.* 1987) under "external economies" states: "At an earlier stage, external economies in the meaning now given were called technological external economies ... During the early part of the 20th century, external economies were defined so as to include beneficial price effects of producer activity ... termed pecuniary external economies. ... When the debate had arrived at this point, pecuniary external economies could be dropped as a cause of market failure and hence, the concept lost its specific economic interest" (Bohm 1987, 262). In the discussion of "externality" from the same source, J. J. Laffont states: "A quite general consensus was that pecuniary externalities are irrelevant for welfare economics" (Laffont 1957, 264). See also Farrell (1988) who presents pecuniary externalities, and a version of Pigou's reasoning, as a puzzle to modern economists.
6. There are important instances in which the prices in upstream industries do not reflect social marginal cost. First, it may be that the upstream industry

consists of firms facing economies of scale. This situation is likely to lead to monopoly, or oligopoly at least, and the price charged will not reflect the marginal production costs. Even when there are constant returns to scale and competition, it is possible that the price will not reflect social marginal cost. Such an outcome would occur, for example, where industries used some common, but unpriced, input, or where firms simply got in each other's way. One example is the well known congestion externality.

7. Worcester deals with this case. Interestingly, this 1969 paper anticipates some of the recent interest. To exemplify pecuniary economy he offers "increased specialization via purchased inputs or subcontracting with expansion of industry output: clothing , aircraft." (1969, 884).
8. This opens up a whole new problem that was of interest to Pigou and his compatriots: Is it possible to have a technological external effect? Knight (1924) and Sraffa (1926) are notable in their view that a firm could grow and emulate any economy that was available to the industry as a whole, thus negating the possibility of a technological external effect.
9. For example, Sloan (1972) tells us that the real price of refrigeration services dropped by 77 percent from 1931–1955 (1972, 422) and that the Frigidaire 0.50-caliber aircraft machine gun dropped from $689.95 in 1941, to $169 by 1944 (1972, 449). Rae (1965) tells us that the price of the Model T dropped from $950 in 1909 to $360 in 1916 (1965, 61).

References

Arthur, W. B. 1989. "Competing Technologies, Increasing Returns, and Lock-In by Historical Events," *Economic Journal*, 99: 116–131.

Binger, B. R. and Hoffman, E. 1989. "Institutional Persistence and Change: The Question of Efficiency," *Journal of Institutional and Theoretical Economics*, 145: 67–84.

Bohm, P. 1987. "External Economies," in Eatwell *et al.* 1987, 262–263.

Chou, D. and Shy, O. 1990. "Network Effects Without Network Externalities," *International Journal of Industrial Organization*, 8: 259–270.

Church, J. and Gandal, N. 1993. "Complementary Network Externalities and Technological Adoption," *International Journal of Industrial Organization*, 11: 239–260.

David, P. A. 1985 "Clio and the Economics of QWERTY," *American Economic Review*, 75: 332–337.

Eatwell J., Milgate, M. and Newman, P. (eds.) 1987. *The New Palgrave: A Dictionary of Economics*, New York: Stockton Press.

Economides, N. 1989. "Desirability of Compatibility in the Absence of Network Externalities," *American Economic Review*, 79: 1165–1181.

Ellis H. S. and Fellner, W. 1943. "External Economies and Diseconomies," *American Economic Review*, 33: 493–511.

Farrell, J. 1988. "Sylvia, Ice Cream and More," *Journal of Economic Perspectives*, 2: 175–182.

Farrell J. and Saloner, G. 1985. "Standardization, Compatibility, and Innovation," *Rand Journal of Economics*, 16: 70–83.

——— 1992. "Converters, Compatibility and Control of Interfaces," *The Journal of Industrial Economics*, 40: 9–36.

Kahn, A. E. 1988. *The Economics of Regulation: Principles and Institutions*, Cambridge, MA: MIT Press, 2 vols.
Katz M. L. and Shapiro, C. 1985. "Network Externalities, Competition, and Compatibility," *American Economic Review*, 75(3): 425–440.
——— 1986. "Technology Adoption in the Presence of Network Externalities," *Journal of Political Economy*, 94(4): 822–841.
——— 1992. "Product Introduction and Network Externalities," *The Journal of Industrial Economics*, 40: 55–84.
Knight, F. H. 1924. "Some Fallacies in the Interpretation of Social Cost," *Quarterly Journal of Economics*, 38: 582–606.
Laffont, J. J. 1987. "Externalities," in Eatwell *et al.* 1987, 264–267.
Liebowitz, S. J. and Margolis, S. E. 1990. "The Fable of the Keys," *Journal of Law and Economics*, 33, 1–25; reprinted as Chapter 2 in this volume.
——— 1994. "Market Processes and the Selection of Standards," *UTD Working Paper*.
——— 1995. "Path Dependence, Lock-in, and History," *Journal of Law, Economics and Organization*, 11: 205–226; reprinted as Chapter 5 in this volume.
Matutes, C. and Regibeau, P. 1992. "Compatibility and Bundling of Complementary Goods in a Duopoly," *The Journal of Industrial Economics*, 40: 37–54.
North, D. C. 1990 *Institutions, Institutional Change and Economic Performance*, New York: Cambridge University Press.
Pigou, A. C. 1912. *Wealth and Welfare*, London: Macmillan.
——— 1920. *The Economics of Welfare*, London: Macmillan.
——— 1924. "Comment," *Economic Journal*, 34: 31.
Radner, R. 1992. "Hierarchy: the Economics of Managing,"*Journal Of Economic Literature*, 30: 1382–1415.
Rae, J. B. 1965. *The American Automobile*, Chicago: University of Chicago Press.
Sloan, A. P. 1972. *My Years with General Motors*, New York: Anchor Books.
Sraffa, P. 1926. "The Laws of Returns under Competitive Conditions," *Economic Journal*, 36: 535–550.
Stigler, G. J. 1941. *Production and Distribution Theories*, New York: Macmillan.
Worcester, D. A. 1969. "Pecuniary and Technological Externality, Factor Rents and Social Costs," *American Economic Review*, 59: 873–885.
Wysocki, B. 1990. "Santa Fe Institute Engages in Research with Profit Potential," *Wall Street Journal*, May 8: 13.
Young, A. A. 1913. "Pigou's Wealth and Welfare," *Quarterly Journal of Economics*, 27: 672–686.

5

Path Dependence, Lock-in, and History (1995)*

Path dependence has been offered as an alternative analytical perspective for economics, a revolutionary reformulation of the neoclassical paradigm. Brian Arthur, a leading figure in this literature, distinguishes between "conventional economics," which largely avoids increasing returns or path dependence, and the "new" "positive feedback economics," which embraces them (Arthur, 1990,99). Before we stroll too far along the path dependence path, however, it makes sense to stop, take stock, and figure out where that path is leading us.

The claim for path dependence is that a minor or fleeting advantage or a seemingly inconsequential lead for some technology, product or standard can have important and irreversible influences on the ultimate market allocation of resources, even in a world characterized by voluntary decisions and individually maximizing behavior. The path dependence literature comes to us accompanied and motivated by a mathematical literature of nonlinear dynamic models, known as chaos or complexity models, for which a key finding is "sensitive dependence on initial conditions." Analogously, a key finding of path dependence is a property of "lock-in by historical events" (to echo the title of Brian Arthur's influential 1989 paper), especially where those historical events are "insignificant." If such path dependence does occur, it means that marginal adjustments of individual agents may not offer the assurance of optimization or the revision of sub-optimal outcomes. In turn, this implies that markets fail. Although not all phenomena that have been described as path dependence imply market failure, these normative concerns have been a prominent part of the path dependence literature.[1]

* *Journal of Law, Economics and Organization,* 11 (1995): 205–226.

In this chapter we identify three distinct forms of path dependence. Two of these forms – which we define as first- and second-degree path dependence – are commonplace, and they offer little in the way of an objection to the neoclassical paradigm. Only the third and strongest form of path dependence significantly challenges the neoclassical paradigm, and as this paper shows, the theoretical arguments for this form require important restrictions on prices, institutions, or foresight.[2]

Unfortunately, the three discrete forms of path dependence are often conflated in the literature. When things that are different are grouped together and treated as things that are similar, error is assured. In this case, the error is transferring the plausibility of the empirical and logical support for the two weaker forms of path dependence (first- and second-degree) to the strongest implications of third-degree path dependence. In fact, although it is fairly easy to identify allocations, technologies, or institutions that are path dependent in some form, it is very difficult to establish the theoretical case or empirical grounding for path-dependent inefficiency.

Defining path dependence

There are three possible efficiency outcomes where a dynamic process exhibits sensitive dependence on initial conditions. First, this sensitivity might do no harm. That is to say, initial actions, perhaps insignificant ones, do put us on a path that cannot be left without some cost, but that path happens to be optimal (although not necessarily uniquely optimal). For example, a capricious decision to part one's hair on the left may lead to a lifetime of left-side parting, but the initial urge to part on the left might capture all there is to be taken into account. On a grander scale, a decision to use a particular system for powering the machinery in a plant may be a controlling influence for decades, but the long-term effects of the decision may be fully appreciated by the initial decision-maker and fully taken into account. We will call instances in which sensitivity to starting points exists, but with no implied inefficiency *first-degree path dependence.*

Where information is imperfect, a second possibility arises. Where this is the case, it is possible that efficient decisions may not always appear to be efficient in retrospect. Here the inferiority of a chosen path is unknowable at the time a choice was made, but we later recognize that some alternative path would have yielded greater wealth. In such a situation, which we will call *second-degree path dependence,* sensitive dependence on initial conditions leads to outcomes that are regrettable and costly to change. They are not, however, inefficient in any meaningful sense, given the assumed limitations on knowledge.

Related to this second type of path dependence is *third-degree path dependence*. In third-degree path dependence, sensitive dependence on initial conditions leads to an outcome that is inefficient – but in this case the outcome is also "remediable."[3] That is, there exists or existed some feasible arrangement for recognizing and achieving a preferred outcome, but that outcome is not obtained.

The three types of path dependence make progressively stronger claims. First-degree path dependence is a simple assertion of an intertemporal relationship, with no implied claim of inefficiency. Second-degree path dependence stipulates that intertemporal effects propagate error. Third-degree path dependence requires not only that the intertemporal effects propagate error, but also that the error was avoidable.

The essence of the distinction between third-degree path dependence and the weaker forms is the availability of feasible, wealth-increasing alternatives to actual allocations, now or at some time in the past. The paths taken under first- and second-degree path dependence cannot be improved upon, given the available alternatives and the state of knowledge. Third-degree path dependence, on the other hand, supposes the feasibility, in principle, of improvements in the path.

Third-degree path dependence is the only form of path dependence that conflicts with the neoclassical model of relentlessly rational behavior leading to efficient, and therefore predictable, outcomes.[4] In instances of third-degree path dependence, outcomes cannot be predicted even with a knowledge of both starting positions and the desirability of alternative outcomes. In a world where efficiency cannot successfully predict outcomes, some (most?) outcomes must be inefficient.

Illustrating the concepts of path dependence

One story that has been put forward in casual discussions of path dependence is the competition between Beta and VHS. There is a common perception, repeated in several papers (e.g. Arthur 1990, 92) that Beta was superior to VHS, and the market's choice did not represent the best economic outcome. We can use this story to illustrate how these forms of path dependence might be associated with a real case. Below we will return to this case, presenting its actual history as an application of several of the ideas presented in this paper.

Home users of video recorders benefit from compatibility with other home users. Compatibility allows them to exchange recorded materials with other people and allows participation in the rental market for prerecorded movies. VHS is now the dominant format for home video recording. Thus consumers' choices of video-recorder formats may exhibit path dependence: decisions by earlier adopters can be expected to have some effect on the decisions of later adopters.

Different constructions of this case would lead to different claims of path dependence. The first is to assume that VHS and Beta were basically identical and that the eventual market choice of VHS was arbitrary. One thing led to another – the network effects of video recorders implied that some format would gain control of the market. This claim's relevance to economics is only that an initial arbitrary choice led to something significant and durable, and that if we were to look to our efficiency models alone we would not be able to explain the choice of VHS over such alternatives as Beta. Efficiency models cannot be expected to predict which of several equally efficient possibilities will be chosen. If this randomness is the full claim that is made for this case, the choice of VHS would be an instance of first-degree path dependence.

If, however, we go further, to claim (counterfactually, as we show later) that VHS was notably inferior as a videotaping format, we make a case for one of the stronger forms of path dependence. We might claim, for example, that Beta was revealed over time to have been a far better format for special effects and quality of picture, that when the initial consumers made their choices they did not realize that Beta would soon allow 5 hour tapes. That is to say, during the time that VHS came to dominate the market it was not known that Beta would be better in the future. After the fact, it may appear that choosing VHS was a mistake, although it was not a mistake given the information that was available at the time. This is second-degree path dependence.

If we go still further, and claim that at the beginning, sufficient information existed to determine that Beta was superior, then we make a claim of third-degree path dependence. Such a thing might have occurred if, at the time that VHS came to dominate the market, most consumers had a preference for Beta, but each consumer was unaware that others had similar preferences. In that case, a slim lead for an inferior VHS format might have been propagated into eventual market dominance. Alternatively, if it were widely understood today that switching to Beta has a benefit greater than the cost, but we remain mired in the VHS standard, we would have another instance of third-degree path dependence.

Third-degree path dependence is a dynamic market failure that is brought about by the persistence of certain choices. Of course, market failure in this guise would raise all the questions that it raises in static contexts. We would have to ask why no arrangement was made to bring about consideration of all costs and benefits. If our only answer were that such arrangements are too costly – perhaps requiring a determination of the plans of all possible VCR consumers – then we would not really have a feasible alternative allocation. Since the costs of making these arrangements are not different from any other costs, we would conclude that the costs of switching formats exceed the benefits.[5]

Where does this leave the third-degree form? If we were presently using the wrong format, a possible claim is that we should now switch to Beta, that there is a feasible arrangement that would make everyone better off if everyone did so. The move has yet to occur, perhaps because each consumer prefers VHS, given that all other users have VHS. Here we would have a coordination problem of the sort that has been identified in a number of different circumstances.[6] Alternatively, the third-degree form would apply if there had been a feasible improvement available at some time in the past, even if none exists today.

Mathematical counterparts, memory, and definition

One confounding feature of discussions of path dependence is that the term has established meanings in branches of mathematics that some economists have encountered. The meanings are all related to each other, however, and the construction of path dependence from probability theory is analogous to uses that relate to lock-in.

Economists usually first encounter the term path dependence as it relates to integrability conditions. That use is somewhat removed from our present concern, but even there path dependence may be understood as irreversibility, which is not unrelated. A closely related development is the literature of hysteresis in economic variables.[7] The meaning closest to the current use in economics is that of stochastic processes that incorporate some concept of memory, as in the following:[8] Consider a sequence of binomial choices between two mutually exclusive outcomes A_1 and A_2. The probabilities of each [either] occurring on the nth trial are P_n and $(1 - P_n)$ respectively. Writing the event in the ith trial as E_i, the probabilities may be written $P_{n+1} = f(P_n, E_n, E_{n-1}, \ldots, E_1)$. The response probability is said to be "d-trial path dependent" where the probability function can be written $f = f(P_n, E_n, E_{n-1}, \ldots, E_{n-d})$. In the special case where $d = 0$, the process is "path independent".

The use of path dependence in economics is, for the most part, loosely analogous to this mathematical construction: Allocations chosen today exhibit memory; they are conditioned on past decisions. It is where such a mathematical process exhibits "sensitive dependence on initial conditions," where past allocations exhibit a controlling influence, that it corresponds most closely to the concerns that economists and others have raised as problems of path dependence. In such a case, "insignificant events" or very small differences among conditions are magnified, bringing about very different outcomes. It is that circumstance that yields both the "nonpredictability" and "potential inefficiency" that Arthur (1989, 116) posits as important properties of increasing returns systems, suggesting both the positive and normative research programs associated with path dependence.

We turn now to a statement of path dependence for economic allocations that exhibit this characteristic of memory and then consider the associated meanings of any potential inefficiencies that may be implied.[9] An allocation process exhibits path dependence if an action a_0 from the set A_0 taken at some time t_0 affects the set of choices A_n that are available at some later time t_n. We define *first-degree path dependence* as the simple assertion that this intertemporal relationship exists. First-degree path dependence carries no implication that the dependence on initial conditions results in any inefficiency. Action a_0 can be said to be *path efficient* where there is no alternative action $a_1 \in A_0$ such that the discounted present value of the total net benefits of selecting a_1 are greater than the discounted present value of net benefits from a_0.

Any economy with durable characteristics exhibits path dependence in at least this form. What we have today is in part a consequence of what we had and what we did yesterday. We inherit a capital stock. We also inherit language, customs, laws, grudges, skills – the wealth of nations. Such a concept is as old as economics. All dynamic models that specify a capital stock that is constrained to change according to a continuous differential equation use this notion of path dependence. So too does the short run concept of variable costs: A firm with fixed assets will continue to use an inferior technology where the average variable costs of the old technology are lower than the average total costs of the new. Under such circumstances, the old firm might be considered "locked-in" to this inferior but still more profitable technology, exhibiting a first-degree form of path dependence.

Second-degree path dependence occurs where an action is taken that subsequent events reveal to be inferior to some alternative. Where information is imperfect, it is inevitable that some durable commitments are shown to be inferior as information is revealed with the passage of time. This problem of imperfect knowledge is present with any action, but it is highlighted by attention to intertemporal paths, especially under conditions of sensitive dependence on initial conditions. The choice of a_0 is ex ante path efficient if at each time t_0 there is no known alternative action $a_1 \in A_0$ that would provide a greater discounted social benefit than a_0. In contrast to simple path efficiency, this leaves open the possibility that at some $t > t_0$ it is revealed that there was some action $a_1 \in A_0$ that could have been undertaken at t_0 which would have provided greater discounted social benefits than a_0. Second-degree path dependence then would be said to occur where actions are only ex ante efficient. While actual outcomes under second-degree path dependence may prompt some (naive) regret, seeming inefficiencies are not remediable; the existence or superiority of alternative paths are not known at the time that initial decisions are made.

Second-degree path dependence may occur as the consequence of imperfect foresight. Everyone maximizes, individually and collectively, given their current knowledge, but current knowledge is deficient. Values of state variables cannot be predicted solely from information regarding an initial endowment, preferences, and the state of knowledge. To explain or predict where we are today, we would have to know what was incorrectly "known," or at least anticipated, in the past – i.e. the history of our ignorance.[10]

Second-degree path dependence may also have its origins in the real limitations of institutional arrangements. In some instances the costs of institutional change will preclude adjustment even where experience reveals preferable alternatives.[11]

Third-degree path dependence occurs if an action is ex ante path inefficient, which means that at some time t_0 there is an alternative action $a_1 \in A_0$ such that the discounted present value of the total social benefit of selecting a_1 instead of a_0 are known to be greater than the discounted present value of costs, yet the action a_0 is taken.[12]

There may be good reasons to suppose that inefficiencies would occur where there is this condition of sensitive dependence on initial conditions. After all, in these cases agents are making seemingly minor decisions that have major consequences. The path dependence literature puts forward several reasons that might explain why, even when all relevant costs and benefits are recognizable, the wealth-maximizing path might not be chosen. In one way or another, these reasons are all related to market failures: Some markets do not exist; some of the affected parties are not yet born; some economic actors cannot coordinate.

There are, however, important reasons why the simple condition of sensitive dependence on initial conditions does not make the case for market failure. First, agents making "small decisions" may well be confronted with all the consequences of their action, as we will consider below. Second, the losses implicit in any path inefficiency may prompt individuals to seek better arrangements. Finally, the trouble caused by sensitive dependence that is not remediable by private action may not be remediable in any other way.

What forms of path dependence are implicit in the literature?

Brian Arthur's (1989) consideration of path dependence is couched in terms of "lock-in by historical events." In his examples of the workings of positive-feedback models, which we examine in detail below, he finds that path inefficiency is possible where there are increasing returns. In this regard, Arthur's version of path dependence is the third-degree form – as long as the information regarding payoffs is available to relevant decisionmakers.

The state of knowledge plays an explicit role in Robin Cowan's (1991) consideration of competition between "technologies of unknown merit." In his model, private agents or social planners try alternative technologies. Lock-in is fostered by two effects: Each trial of a technology provides experience in that technology, increasing the payoffs to that technology in subsequent trials; and each trial of a technology decreases uncertainty about its merits. In this context, it is possible that the technology that is adopted is the one that, according to the hypothetical "true" densities of the performance distributions, is inferior.[13]

The situation that Cowan describes would appear to be a case of third-degree path dependence. Cowan's hypothetical social planner internalizes the benefits of experimentation, possibly avoiding undesirable lock-in. Thus Cowan's model specifies a failing of decentralized markets that is, in principle, remediable.

In recent years, examples and discussions of path dependence have proliferated in the literature. Mokyr (1991) discusses the connection between biological contingency and path dependence in economics, presenting instances that appear ex post to be mistakes, instances of second-degree path dependence.[14] Roland's (1991) conclusions that the economic institutions likely to evolve in the Soviet Union will be influenced by the set of preexisting institutions are at their most basic level of the first-degree type, sometimes of the second-degree (should Russia emulate Japan or the US?) and sometimes of the third-degree (keeping a large state sector as a "very inefficient form of social security").

Although he did not use the current terminology, Schelling anticipated some of the kinds of problems that are considered in the path dependence literature. He discusses as "interactive behaviors" problems in which outcomes depend heavily on the order in which actions occur. Inferior outcomes may prevail in these cases, even in the face of known preferred alternatives, illustrating the third-degree form (1978, 36–38). Shelling offers these cases, however, as examples of non-market behavior, and he also notes that market institutions often arise as remedies for these problems (1978, 33). Elsewhere he acknowledges the unfeasibility of some hypothetical improvements (1978, 132).

The archetypal case of path dependence has been, of course, the configuration of the typewriter keyboard. As Paul David (1985) presented this history, the standard "QWERTY" keyboard arrangement is dramatically inferior to an arrangement offered by August Dvorak, but we are locked into the inferior arrangement by a coordination failure: No one trains on the Dvorak keyboard because Dvorak machines are hard to find, and Dvorak machines are hard to find because no one trains on Dvorak keyboards. The process is said to be path dependent in that the timing of the adoption of QWERTY, and not its efficiency, explains its survival.

Our 1990 paper [Chapter 2 in this volume] demonstrates that the QWERTY case is highly problematic, but our concern here is with the rhetoric of this case. Some of David's claims for this case do not go beyond first-degree path dependence. His observation that "One damn thing leads to another" (David 1985, 332), is readily acceptable because it claims no more than first-degree path dependence. But David makes stronger claims. In accepting and repeating the claim that the cost of retraining in Dvorak is recovered ten days after the start of training (1985, 332), for example, he positions the QWERTY case as an active example of third-degree path dependence. David's 1985 paper concludes: "Competition in the absence of perfect futures markets drove the industry prematurely into standardization *on the wrong system* where decentralized decision making subsequently has sufficed to hold it" (1985, 336, emphasis in original). We stay with the wrong keyboard, according to David, not because sunk investments in QWERTY make the switch to the Dvorak arrangement an inferior choice, but because of "decentralized decision making." This attribution of the error to decentralized decision making clearly suggests that alternative, presumably centralized, decision mechanisms would correct this error. This is a third-degree claim. As is often the case, David's reader is likely to find the claim of path dependence in the third-degree form to be more palatable because of his earlier establishment of weaker forms of path dependence.

The impact of increasing returns

The importance of path dependence would appear to reside in the third-degree form. While there will be occasional and interesting instances in which analysis reveals an unexpected intertemporal effect, the overwhelming share of first- and second-degree dependencies will be garden variety durabilities that are well incorporated into economics. But if it is third-degree path dependence that offers a "new economics," the question arises: Does such a phenomenon exist, and if so, what conditions bring it about? The answer offered by Arthur and others is that undesirable lock-in is a likely consequence of increasing returns. We turn now to that proposition.

We base our discussion on an example provided by Arthur (1989) that has the advantages of simplicity, clarity, and concreteness. This example deals with a choice of technologies, but it really is quite general. It could, for example, describe a choice between alternative locations where there is a spatial agglomeration economy. Though very simple, this table illustrates the paradigmatic case for the impact of increasing returns. Table 5.1 reproduces Arthur's Table 2, showing the adoption payoffs for agents from adopting one of two available technologies.

In this example, an initial adopter is presumed to know that he will receive a payoff of 10 if he adopts technology A, versus a payoff of 4 if he adopts technology B. In such circumstances, Arthur claims, the

Table 5.1 Adoption payoffs

Number of previous adoptions	0	10	20	30	40	50	60	70	80	90	100
Technology A	10	11	12	13	14	15	16	17	18	19	20
Technology B	4	7	10	13	16	19	22	25	28	31	34

initial adopter will chose A. Subsequent adopters are still more likely to adopt technology A, since the advantage of being a subsequent adopter of A over being the first adopter of B only increases. So A is chosen, and its dominance is stable: There is no tendency for the choice of technology to shift to B.

The example illustrates undesirable lock-in because A is *not* the better choice if the eventual number of adopters is large.[15] Depending upon assumptions about the state of knowledge, this path inefficiency may exhibit third-degree path dependence. Lock-in to A would exemplify third-degree path dependence if the information in Table 5.1 were known. On the other hand, the choice of A is not an instance of third-degree path dependence if no one in society has the information that is in the table.

Arthur does not specify what agents know or how agents might determine their payoffs. We might construe them as knowing the whole table, or parts of it, or none of it. But the existence of this information is crucial for the determination of the eventual choice of technology, and also for the type of path dependence implied.

We consider two distinct interpretations of the payoffs in the table.[16] In the first, the numbers in the table are taken to represent equal payoffs to each adopter, given the ultimate number of adopters, regardless of when each adopter makes his decision. That is to say, the payoff for early adopters changes as the number of later adopters changes. In this case, B becomes the superior technology when more than thirty adoptions occur. In the second case, the numbers represent the payoffs only to the marginal adopter, with all inframarginal adopters forever receiving the payoffs available at the moment of their adoption, in which case B becomes the superior choice only when more than fifty adoptions have occurred.

All payoffs depend on the ultimate number of adopters

For now, assume that at any moment all the adopters enjoy the same payoff, that is, the values in the table represent the surpluses that are available to all adopters when any given number of adoptions have taken place. Although Arthur has stated that this is not his view of the table, it is an assumption that fits in best with many supposed instances of path dependence. For example, in the selection of a standard, an adopter benefits if he is later joined by other adopters. Agglomeration economies tell a similar story – one's payoff depends on the final number of adopters.

Given this interpretation and the numbers in the table, can it be concluded that technology A, the "wrong" technology is chosen? In general, it cannot. For example, if the information in the table is known to adopters (as they are to Arthur's hypothetical outside observer), each adopter would attempt to forecast the eventual number of adopters and the resulting best technology. In this instance, we cannot assert how agents will behave without specific assumptions about the role of expectations. Where agents have full information, there is no problem of lock-in to inappropriate technologies. Where the number of prospective adopters is greater than thirty, all agents can see that B will eventually offer greater rewards, and everybody knows what everybody knows. It is a Nash equilibrium that agents pick the solution that is optimal, given the number of adopters. For instance, suppose everyone knows that VHS is better when there are a large number of VCRs sold, and everyone knows there will be a large number of VCRs sold. Everyone would choose VHS. There is no lock-in to an inferior technology.

Some deficiency in information is required for lock-in to an inferior technology to occur. Yet that deficiency must not be complete if the lock-in is remediable. If no one knows the payoffs to the technologies except for hypothetical omniscient observers, at most we have an instance of second-degree path dependence. (Similarly, it might be argued that if no one in the economy is aware of the potential returns to a technology, it cannot be argued that the technology has been discovered in any meaningful sense.) Remediable lock-in to the wrong technology, or third-degree path dependence, requires that some agent(s) in the economy has, or could obtain, the information required to make a correct choice. And even where that occurs, third-degree lock-in is not assured, since the knowledgeable party(ies) might coordinate the choice of technology, especially since it should be profitable to do so. One likely strategy for such a party would be to acquire the technology at a price that reflects the prevailing expectations and appropriate some of the gain from such coordination.

Thus, in order for third-degree lock-in to occur, there must be agents who know enough to make correct choices but who fail to take advantage of the implied profit opportunities, and at the same time, adopters who generally know nothing more than the payoff going to the next adopter. These are very restrictive conditions.

Individual payoffs depend on the number of prior adopters

The alternative interpretation of this table is that early adopters never come to enjoy the high returns of a later adopter. Under this interpretation, each adopter's payoffs are determined solely by the number of prior adopters, and not at all by the number of later adopters. This interpretation might apply readily to technology choices where early movers have additional costs of developing a technology, or pioneering costs in a geographic area that later movers avoid.

Again, assumptions about what adopters know are crucial. If adopters are aware of the complete table, or even just the general trend of the payoffs in the table, then they must also be aware of a decision that is as fundamental as the choice between A and B: the best *time* to adopt. According to the table, there is a payoff to waiting. Given these payoffs, who would want to be an early adopter? If the table tells the full story of payoffs, there is never an advantage to going first. Some additional structure, or some additional mechanism is needed to explain the adoption of any technology at all. As we discuss in the next section, the very considerations that solve the adoption timing problem also bear on the problem of choosing among technologies.

Of course, it might be that agents are *not* aware of the payoffs in the table, or even of the trend as the number of adopters changes. If no one has any information at all, then the choice of technology is unpredictable, but in this case the "superiority" of a technology is also something of an imaginary notion.

Only when agents know nothing except their current individual payoffs in choosing technology A or B will they unhesitatingly enter the market, and then they will incorrectly choose A. But in order for the choice of A to be an example of third-degree path dependence, it is necessary that someone in the economy knows that B is better. And for such a lock-in to occur, it is also necessary that the knowledgeable party does not manage to turn this knowledge into profit by coordinating buyers (or selling the information to them). These again are very restrictive assumptions.

Market mechanisms and path dependent processes

Where the restrictive informational assumptions required for third-degree path dependence are satisfied, the problems foretold by the table may still be overturned by any number of possible market responses, including investment in brand name, patent, and early market share commitments. Such market responses are, of course, absent from the table, but they nevertheless may constitute a significant rearrangement of incentives.

To see one way that markets address lock-in, in the following assume that payoffs depend on the number of prior adopters (as discussed above), and that adopters have some knowledge of the table of payoffs.

Further, to consider these issues with a more convenient vocabulary, for the moment take Arthur's table to be the payoffs to firms that locate at one of two geographic sites, A or B. As a result of agglomeration economies, payoffs increase with the number of firms that choose each location. These are, of course, the increasing-returns conditions that are held to bring about lock-in. But there are two questions that arise here. First, given the pattern of returns, how does either location attract any firms, given that there appears always to be a return to delay? Second, which location prevails? As is shown in the following, the very same avenues of appropriation that solve the problem of who goes first are the mechanisms that can assure the choice of an efficient path.

The solution to the problem of getting any firms to locate at any location comes fairly readily. It is land ownership. In the familiar Ricardian or Von Thunen framework, any unique advantages of a particular location accrue to the landowner as site rents. Under conditions that are reasonably likely, owners of land can expect to extract the rents created by any locational advantages that eventually attach to the land. Where agglomeration economies are fairly localized, as in the conventional urban model (Mills 1967; Henderson 1977), a "pioneer firm" can appropriate the rents that result from agglomeration economies by acquiring all the land in close proximity to the initial plant. Alternatively, ownership of other unique resources, such as transportation facilities, may constitute opportunities to internalize the agglomeration economies.

Someone must capture and, to some extent, redistribute these rents, or else payoffs like those in the table provide no way of getting started: Everyone wants to go last. Ownership internalizes the externality that is implicit in the table. Land owners have incentives to offer adequate inducements to potential early entrants. They can offer long-term leases at lower rents, or subsidize infrastructure, or even pay direct subsidies to early arrivals. Rewards offered to initial entrants will be recaptured out of the larger surpluses generated by subsequent entrants. The exogenously determined rewards posited in Arthur's table thus can be understood as incorporating artificial rigidity of incentives or inflexible prices of productive inputs and outputs.

The solutions to the starting problem, foresight and ownership, also are involved in the determination of which location prevails. City A and city B are competing with each other. At all times, the rents that can be extracted in one city will be limited by the benefits available in the other. A principal landowner in city B could attract an initial entrant by offering a subsidy, or could undertake the agglomeration economy activity at an initial loss. Similarly, a principal landowner in city A could compete by cutting rents or by providing subsidies to initial entrants. Clearly the landowner in city B will have to discount much further to attract an initial entrant, but just as clearly, the total wealth that can be created by situating the agglomeration-economy activities at B is greater than the wealth created by situating these activities at A. If the ultimate number of entrants were expected to be 100, a monopoly landowner at A could profitably invest no more than 1450 as inducements to entrants, while a monopoly owner at B could profitably invest up to 2090.[17]

As in other circumstances, free rider and holdout problems may be important. But in a circumstance like the one presented in the table, all other things equal, the site that creates more wealth will have an advantage over a site that creates less. Owners at site B can be less perfect at overcoming their appropriation problem than owners at A and still win the competition.

Extending this analysis back to the choice of technologies, networks, or standards requires only that we extend the idea of ownership. Ownership of a technology can take various forms including ownership of critical inputs, patent, copyright, and industrial design. Literal networks such as telephones, pipelines, and computer systems are most often owed by private parties. Standards are often protected by patent or copyright. Resolution of these problems may be an important and as yet not fully recognized function of the patent system[18] and other legal institutions.

An alleged case of path dependence

We used the competition between the VHS and Beta videotaping formats to illustrate the possible types of path dependence claims.[19] We now turn to the actual history of this case, a history that is significant for several reasons. It is a case that is commonly cited to illustrate the claim that theoretical models of path dependence have empirical content. Further, it incorporates structural features found in some of the models discussed here, in particular economies to scale and ownership. Finally the actual history arguably reverses the claim that an inferior format (VHS) dominated as a result of technological interrelatedness and economies to scale.

The first commercially viable video recorder was publicly demonstrated in 1956 by the Ampex Corporation. These machines were sold for several years to professional broadcasters, as Ampex did not perceive a large consumer market. Eventually, Ampex concluded that transistors would replace tubes, and having no experience in transistors, entered into an agreement with Sony. Sony would transistorize the video recorder, and in return would receive the rights to use Ampex's patents for the home-use (nonprofessional) market, which Ampex was willing to cede. This relationship quickly soured, however, and Ampex found that it needed a Japanese partner to sell its recorders to the Japanese broadcast market. This time Ampex entered a partnership with Toshiba. Other Japanese electronics producers then purchased the use of Ampex's patents for their manufacture of video recorders. Eventually various incompatible models of video recorders coexisted in the marketplace, but none of these early machines proved successful in the home-use market.

In 1969 Sony developed a cartridge based system, the U-matic, for the home-use market. Since Matsushita, JVC (an independent subsidiary of Matsushita), Toshiba and Hitachi all had such products in the works, Sony sought to bring in some partners to share the format so as to better establish its format as a standard. Thus Matsushita and JVC were invited to join Sony, and when Sony agreed to make a few changes to the machine, the three companies each agreed to produce machines based on the U-matic specification (although Sony got the bulk of the sales by bringing the machines to market first). These three companies also agreed to share technology and patents. Production of the U-matics began in 1971 but high costs and excessive bulk led to it's failure in the home-use market, although educational and industrial users provided a sustainable customer base.

Attempts to break into the home market continued. In 1972 an American company came out with a product called "Cartrivision", which did many of the things that a Betamax was to later do (although it traded off picture quality for a longer playing time). This machine was sold with a library of prerecorded programs. Cartrivision failed when several technical problems arose, including the decomposition of the prerecorded tapes in a warehouse, leaving the investors unable to overcome negative publicity. Phillips produced a home recorder in 1972, but it never achieved much success. Sanyo and Toshiba joined forces to launch a machine known as the V-Cord, which did poorly in the home-use market. Matsushita produced a machine called the AutoVision, which proved to be a dismal failure. Matsushita's management attributed this failure to the AutoVision's thirty minute tape capacity. Another Matsushita subsidiary, Kotobuki, introduced the

VX-100 to the home-use market. Sony began selling the Betamax in April of 1975, with a tape capacity of one hour. JVC was also working on a machine, known as the Video Home System, or VHS.

As it had done earlier with the U-matic, Sony sought to make Betamax the standard that would cut through the clutter of competing formats. Prior to introducing the Betamax to the market, it once again offered its format to Matsushita and JVC. Sony provided technical details of the Betamax, including an advance in azimuth recording that helped eliminate the problem of crosstalk. After lengthy discussions, dragging on over a year, the three finally agreed to have a meeting where the Betamax, VHS and VX machines would be compared. This meeting took place in April of 1976 (a year after Sony had put the Betamax on the market). Lardner (1987) describes the meeting as follows:

> The first item on the agenda was the simultaneous playing, through all three [machines], of a "Sesame Street" type of children's program ... The Sony contingent's eyes were on the JVC machine ... What they saw was a considerably smaller machine than the Betamax ... Mechanically, too, VHS had a notable distinction: the use of a loading system called M-loading ... The basic concept had been tried in some of the early U-matic prototypes... In other respects, JVC's and Sony's machines were strikingly similar. Both were two-head, helical-scanning machines using half-inch tape in a U-matic type of cassette. Both – unlike the V-cord, The VX, and indeed all the color video recorders to date – used azimuth recording and countered the problem of cross talk by juggling the phase of the color signal. So the Betamax and the VHS were in a class by themselves as far as tape efficiency went. The real difference between them lay in how the two companies had chosen to exploit that advantage: Sony to make the cassette paperback size, and JVC to achieve a two-hour recording capacity ... Eventually one of [the Sony men] said what all of the Sony representatives were thinking: "Its a copy of Betamax." (Lardner 1987, 151–152)

Needless to say, this apparent usurping of the Sony technological advances by JVC created bitterness between the one-time allies, leaving Sony and Matsushita–JVC to go their separate ways.

The only real technical difference between Beta and VHS was the manner in which the tape was threaded and, more importantly, the size of the cassette. A larger cassette allowed more tape to be used, and for any given speed of tape, this implied a greater recording time. For any given recording technique, slowing the tape increases recording time, but it also decreases picture quality. Because of its larger size cassette, VHS could always have an advantageous combination of picture quality and playing time. Otherwise, the differences between Beta and VHS were fairly trivial, from a technical point of view, although both of these formats were clearly superior to many of the alternatives. Memories of the differences between Beta and VHS are likely magnified by the advertising claims of each camp, the passage of time, and possibly by the fact that Beta still survives, reincarnated as a high-end videophile device.

The different choices of cassette size were based on a different perception of consumer desires: Sony believed that a paperback sized cassette, allowing easy transportability (although limiting recording time to one hour), was paramount to the consumer, whereas Matsushita, responding to the failure of its "Autovision" machine, believed that a two hour recording time, allowing the taping of complete movies, was essential.

This difference was to prove crucial. Sony, in an attempt to solidify its dominance of the US market, which it had virtually monopolized for almost two years, allowed its Beta machines to be sold under Zenith's brand name (Zenith being one of the major US television manufacturers). To counter this move, Matsushita set up a meeting with RCA to discuss a similar arrangement. RCA had previously concluded and publicly stated that a two hour recording time was essential for a successful home video recorder. By the time the meeting took place, however, Sony had announced a two hour Betamax, Beta II. RCA proposed to Matsushita that it produce a machine that could record a football game, which implied a three hour recording time. Six weeks later Matsushita had a working four hour machine which used the same techniques to increase recording time that Sony had used in the Beta II.

RCA began selling VHS machines in the summer of 1977 (two years after Sony's introduction of the Betamax), dubbing its machine "SelectaVision." The advertising copy was simple: "Four hours. $1000. SelectaVision." Zenith responded by lowering the price of its Beta machine to $996. But within *months*, VHS was outselling Beta in the United States. A Zenith marketing executive is quoted as saying: "The longer playing time turned out to be very important, and RCA's product was better styled."

Although Sony was able to recruit Toshiba and Sanyo to the Beta format, Matsushita was able to bring Hitachi, Sharp, and Mitsubishi into its camp. Any improvement in one format was soon followed by a similar improvement in the other format. The similarities in the two machines made it unlikely that one format would be able to deliver a technological knockout punch. Similarly, when one group lowered its price, the other soon followed. The two formats proved equally matched in almost all respects save one: VHS's longer playing times. When Beta went to two hours, VHS went to four. When Beta increased to five hours, VHS increased to eight. Of course, consumers wishing higher picture quality would set either machine to shorter playing times.

The market's referendum on playing time versus tape compactness was decisive and immediate. Not just in the United States, but in Europe and Japan as well. By mid 1979 VHS was outselling Beta by more than 2 to 1 in the US. By 1983 Beta's world share was down to 12 percent. By 1984 every VCR manufacturer except Sony had adopted VHS.[20]

Klopfenstein (1989, 28) summarizes (our italics):

> Although many held the perception that the Beta VCR produced a better picture than VHS, technical experts such as Weinstein (1984) and Prentis (1981) have concluded that this was, in fact, not the case; periodic reviews in Consumers Reports found VHS picture quality superior twice, found Beta superior once, and found no difference in a fourth review. *In conclusion, the Beta format appeared to hold no advantages over VHS other than being the first on the market, and this may be a lesson for future marketers of new media products.*

How then does this history address the theory and empiricism around path dependence? First, and most obviously, it contradicts the claim that the Beta format was better and that its demise constitutes evidence of the pernicious workings of "decentralized decision making" or "sensitive dependence on initial conditions." Regarding the one aspect that clearly differentiated the two formats, consumers preferred VHS.

Second, even though the differences between the two formats are small, the advantage of longer recording times was sufficient to allow VHS to overcome Beta's initial lead. There might not have been any great harm had the market stayed with Beta, since its recording time was up to five hours by the early 1980s. But consumers were not willing to wait those few extra years, and the market was supple enough to make the switch to the better path.

Third, the history illustrates the role of ownership, strategy and adopter's foresight in allowing a change in paths. The formats were each owned, and both Sony and JVC–Matsushita expended considerable effort to establish its standard, indicating that they expected to capture some of the benefits of doing so. The ability of VHS to attract partners such as RCA and Matsushita indicates the market participants' ability to recognize the large potential gains from promoting a superior standard. Although it is sometimes argued that the dominance of VHS resulted from the random association of VHS with a more aggressive licensing and pricing strategy, we have shown the pricing and promotion of the two formats to be closely matched. On the other side of the market, consumers could identify a preferred standard and predict that an adequate number of others would do the same. Not only was the switch to VHS rapid, but it was repeated in separate national markets. Thus there is no evidence that the market choice was due to blunders, unlucky promotional choices, or insufficient investment by the owners of the Beta format.

Path dependence and the role of history

Much of the reason for the influence of the literature of path dependence, particularly among economic historians, is the appeal that it makes for the importance of history. If outcomes depend critically upon insignificant and unpredictable events, rather than on underlying conditions such as endowments and technology, then an historical chronicle is elevated in importance relative to other methods of explanation. But this rationale for an interest in history is very limited. In the path dependence literature, the importance of history is related to what have been called the *nonergodic* properties of the economy. Arthur uses this terminology, defining processes to be "nonergodic" if outcomes are affected by the *sequence* of events. Regarding history Arthur notes:

> The argument of this paper suggests that the interpretation of economic history should be different in different returns regimes. Under constant and diminishing returns, the evolution of the market reflects only *a priori* endowments, preferences, and transformation possibilities; small events cannot sway the outcome. But while this is comforting, it reduces history to the status of mere carrier – the deliverer of the inevitable. Under increasing returns, by contrast, many outcomes are possible. Insignificant circumstances become

> magnified by positive feedbacks to "tip" the system into the actual outcome "selected." The small events of history become important. (1989, 127)

In this analysis, history is important only because the sequence of events determines current values. If the sequence does not affect the end result, there is little place for history; it is a "mere carrier – the deliverer of the inevitable."

But surely history should be of interest even when economic processes are ergodic – even when there are decreasing returns. While it may be useful to model supply-and-demand equilibria, no one actually believes that exogenous changes do not occur. There are important and frequent external shocks to the economy, and, at any moment, unknown parameters (such as the importance to consumers of video recorder taping time). So a knowledge of some initial endowment alone could never tell us very much about the eventual path of *real* economies over time. In addition, the endowment of one generation is the bequest of another, and there is value in learning what actions previous generations took that increased or decreased their wealth.

These views of the role of history constitute rival paradigms. One holds that efficiency explanations are important and that economic history, at least, is the search for purpose in past actions. We find, where we can, explanations of events that are based on purposeful behavior: Technology responds to scarcities, technique responds to price, and so on. The other holds that history is important only to the extent that, for one reason or another, agents do not successfully optimize. History then is the tool to understand what rationality and efficiency do not explain, that is, the random sequence of insignificant events that are not addressable by economic theory. We leave it to the reader to decide which paradigm promises greater returns to the study of history.

Conclusion

Anyone would be willing to acknowledge that some of the things people do have durable consequences – which, by definition, is also an acknowledgment of first-degree and second-degree path dependence. Further, it is difficult to deny that if immeasurably small things that we do today lead inexorably to enormous differences in the world we receive tomorrow, our futures are unpredictable and potentially inefficient. The special importance of path dependence, however, is associated with third-degree claims – that is, inherited inefficiencies that purportedly are, or were, remediable. Remediable inefficiency, if it occurred, would be a significant lapse and a demonstrated instance would be an interesting finding worthy of analysis. A pattern of such instances would be of great importance. However, lesser forms of path dependence should not be mistakenly classified as remediable.

Our assertion of the rarity of third-degree path dependence is not simply the result of some Panglossian mysticism. Rather it follows from a rather worldly consideration. Where there is a knowable and feasible improvement from moving onto a better path, those who will benefit from the improvement, and who know it, will be willing to pay to bring the improvement about. Where simple spot market transactions are insufficient to bring these improvements about, institutional or strategic innovation seems a likely response, especially if the improvement is important enough that the innovator is likely to be well paid.

The logic underlying path dependence is seductive but incomplete. Although these simple numerical and algebraic examples appear both logically sound and structurally uncontroversial, these examples actually imbed severe restrictions. The seeming inevitability of third-degree path dependence is overturned, in instances shown here, by rather ordinary and conventional means, as prosaic as the market for land. Given that the theoretical claim that can be made for path dependence should be understood as only a demonstration of possibility, the case for path dependence becomes an empirical one.

The empirical case is on no firmer footing than the theoretical case. To date, convincing documentation of cases in which market activity sustains remediable error remains absent. As we have developed here, the oft cited case of videotaping formats is not a demonstration of third-degree path dependence. Perhaps the best evidence of the empirical shortcomings of path dependence is the continued use of the story of the QWERTY keyboard as support for theoretical models, in spite of our 1990 demonstration that the actual history does not support a claim of deleterious path dependence. This purported example of a market failure has so much appeal that a theoretical literature continues to define and support itself around it. That QWERTY remains the paradigmatic case for path dependence surely says something important about the empirical content of this theory.

Given all this, path dependence would certainly seem to be a poor candidate as the distinguishing implication of a "new economics." But still, there may be something to be learned from what does not happen. The theoretical exercises that are offered by Brian Arthur and others suggest the inevitability of failure under simple assumptions. That these models are not borne out empirically suggests the importance of communication, planning, property, and other market institutions that are absent from these models but which are essential elements in any explanation of the actual workings of the economy.

Notes

1. It has been claimed, for example, that historical accidents may have left us with the wrong types of automobiles, video recorders, nuclear power plants, and typewriter keyboards. These examples are cited by many authors in this literature as well as the literatures on standards (Farrell and Saloner 1985), network externalities (Katz and Shapiro 1986), game theory (Dixit and Nalebuff 1991), and organizational ecology (Carroll and Harrison 1993). See Zerbe (1992) and Levinson and Coleman (1992), in addition to our own earlier work (1990, 1994b, 1995 [Chapters 2, 3, and 4 in this volume], and 1994a) for alternative views to much of this literature.
2. For example, it plays a role in the recent exchange between Bowles and Gintis (1993) and Williamson (1993a) over the value of the neoclassical paradigm.
3. Williamson (1993b, 140 offers the term "remediability" to describe the condition that such feasible alternatives exist, and urges remediability as the appropriate standard for public policy discussion. Similar positions have been argued by Demsetz (1973), Coase (1964), Calebresi (1968) and Dahlman (1979), among others. In the framework that these authors have advocated, market failure is not demonstrated unless a specific policy recommendation can be shown in which the benefits exceed the costs, including all of the administrative costs of the policy. We note that this is not a Panglossian view of the world – the world need not be optimal – but it does alter the burden of proof. Claims of market imperfections cannot be established upon the theoretical possibility of an improved allocation, but require a feasible alternative for a particular case.
4. Further, some of the most prominent examples in this literature feature specific claims of inefficiency. For example, listen to Paul David: "The accretion of technological innovations inherited from the past therefore cannot legitimately be presumed to constitute socially optimal solutions provided for us – either by heroic enterprises or herds of rational managers operating in efficient markets" (1992, 137).
5. These are the dynamic versions of issues raised above; see n. 3
6. For a general statement see Rasmussen (1989, 44).
7. In the physical sciences, hysteresis means that the equilibrium "remembers" all disturbances. Explicit applications in economics have been directed mostly at explaining persistent unemployment, especially regarding recent European experience. A difference is that the hysteresis literature is concerned with the possibility that shocks echo in the data, perhaps permanently whereas the economic literature on path dependence has focused on discrete choices where outcomes are discretely separated. For discussion, see Blanchard and Summers (1987), the mini symposium in the *Journal of Post Keynesian Economics*, especially the paper by Katzner (1993), and the

Symposium in Empirical Economics, especially the overview paper by Franz (1990).

8. Adopted from *Encyclopedic Dictionary of Mathematics*, (1987).
9. In the discussion that follows, we use the Hicks–Kaldor standard as an efficiency norm
10. Second-degree path dependence also is being invoked in the "what if" type of regrets, perhaps better termed "hypothetical path dependence," that one finds in this literature. The key element here is that knowledge is limited but could have been increased through the use of resources. For example, it is sometimes claimed (Arthur, 1990) that it might have been wiser to have used electric cars at the turn of the century, and not the gasoline-powered internal combustion engine. The fact that our current state of knowledge indicates that electric-powered automobiles are less efficient is considered irrelevant, since if we had been producing electric cars since the turn of the century our knowledge about batteries would presumably be advanced far beyond what it currently is, and electric cars under that scenario might be more efficient than are the internal combustion automobiles of today. Of course, it is impossible to refute this claim since it rests on knowing the unknowable: What would we know today if we had invested resources in generating knowledge other than that in which we did invest? Hypothetical path dependence cannot provide real examples, nor can it be disproved.
11. Williamson (1994) notes the possibility that redistributive arrangements may be deliberately constructed to be costly to alter in order to bind parties to political bargains. Interestingly, the resulting inflexibility may be recognized as an unavoidable cost, given the political decision to redistribute wealth.
12. One question that leaps immediately to mind is who it is that possesses this information. We discuss the role of information below.
13. The concept of a superior technology is not unambiguous. The advantage of a technology cannot be defined independently of the state of knowledge, which itself depends on the path taken. Thus superiority can not be defined exogenous to the trials of the technology
14. We should note that both Gould (1991) and Mokyr (1991) warn of misapplication of biological evolution to social systems. Both note that in social systems there is the possibility of returning to once-discarded solutions
15. Actually, Arthur states that this example does not exhibit any "nonergodicity," meaning that it is not path dependent in the sense that small difference in historical sequences of events do not play a role in the final equilibrium. In this example the end result is the same no matter the order of initial participants. But it illustrates "lock-in" very well.
16. Arthur has informed us in correspondence that he intended that the payoffs be based only on the adopter's position in the table, not the eventual number of adopters. We note, however, Arthur's inconsistent usage in the text of his article since under his intended assumption, option B is not preferred until the fifty-first adopter, not the thirtieth mentioned in his text.
17. These calculations assume that the table represents the steps in a step function, so that entrants to A from one to ten get ten, entrants from eleven to twenty get eleven, etc.

18. Though see Kitch (1977) for a related argument
19. This history draws on Lardner (1987, Chapters 3, 4, and 10).
20. Contrast this version with Arthur's (1990) history: "The history of the videocassette recorder furnishes a simple example of positive feedback. The VCR market started out with two competing formats selling at about the same price: VHS and Beta ... Both systems were introduced at about the same time and so began with roughly equal market shares; those shares fluctuated early on because of external circumstance, "luck" and corporate maneuvering. Increasing returns on early gains eventually tilted the competition toward VHS: it accumulated enough of an advantage to take virtually the entire VCR market. Yet it would have been impossible at the outset of the competition to say which system would win, which of the two possible equilibria would be selected. Furthermore, if the claim that Beta was technically superior is true, then the market's choice did not represent the best outcome" (1990, 92).

References

Arthur, W. B. 1989. "Competing Technologies, Increasing Returns, and Lock-in by Historical Events," *Economic Journal*, 99: 116–131.

———— 1990. "Positive Feedbacks in the Economy," *Scientific American*, 262: 92–99.

Blanchard, O. J. and Summers, L. H. 1987. "Hysteresis in Unemployment," *European Economic Review*, 31(2): 288–295.

Bowles, S. and Gintis, H. 1993. "The Revenge of Homo Economicus: Contested Exchange and the Revival of Political Economy," *Journal of Economic Perspectives*, 7: 83–102.

Calebresi, V. 1968. "Transactions Costs, Resource Allocation and Liability Rules: A Comment," *Journal of Law and Economics*, 11: 67–74.

Carroll, G. R. and Harrison, R. 1993. "Evolution among Competing Organizational Forms," *Word Futures: The Journal of General Evolution*, 37: 91–110.

Coase, Ronald. H. 1964. "The Regulated Industries: Discussion," *American Economic Review*, 54: 194–197.

Cowan, R. 1991. "Tortoises and Hares: Choice among Technologies of Unknown Merit," *Economic Journal*, 101: 801–814.

Dahlman, C. 1979. "The Problem of Externality," *Journal of Law and Economics*, 22: 141–163.

David, P. A. 1985. "Clio and the Economics of QWERTY,"*American Economic Review*, 75: 332–337.

David, P. 1992. "Heroes, Herds and Hysteresis in Technological History: The Battle of the System' Reconsidered," *Industrial and Corporate Change*, 1: 129–180.

Demsetz, H. 1973. "Information and Efficiency: Another Viewpoint," *Journal of Law and Economics*, 10: 1–22.

Dixit, A. and Nalebuff, B. 1991. *Thinking Strategically*, New York: W. W. Norton.

Encyclopedic Dictionary of Mathematics 1987. Mathematical Society of Japan, Cambridge, MA: MIT Press.

Farrell, J. and Saloner, G. 1985. "Standardization, Compatibility, and Innovation," *Rand Journal of Economics*, 16: 70–83.

Franz, W. 1990 "Hysteresis: An Overview," *Empirical Economics*, 15(2): 109–125.
Gould, S. J. 1991. "The Panda Thumb of Technology," in Gould, S. J., *Bully for Brontosaurus*, New York: W. W. Norton.
Henderson, J. V. 1977. *Economic Theory and The Cities*, New York: Academic Press.
Katz, M. and Shapiro, C. 1986. "Technology Adoption in the Presence of Network Externalities," *Journal of Political Economy*, 94: 822–841.
Katzner, D. 1993. "Some Notes on the Role of History and the Definition of Hysteresis and Related Concepts in Economic Analysis," *Journal of Post Keynesian Economics*, 15(3): 323–345
Kitch, E. W. "The Nature and Function of the Patent System," *Journal of Law and Economics*, 20: 265–290.
Klopfenstein, B. 1989. "The Diffusion of the VCR in the United States," in Levy, M. *The VCR Age*. Newberry Park, CA: Sage Publications.
Lardner, J. 1987. *Fast Forward*, New York: W. W. Norton.
Levinson, R. J. and Coleman, M. T. 1992. "Economic Analysis of Compatibility Standards: How Useful is It?," *FTC Working Paper*.
Liebowitz, S. J. and Margolis, S. E. 1990. "The Fable of the Keys," *Journal of Law and Economics*, 33: 1–25; reprinted as Chapter 2 in this volume.
——— 1994a. "Market Processes and the Selection of Standards," *UTD Working Paper*.
——— 1994b. "Network Externality: An Uncommon Tragedy," *Journal of Economic Perspectives*, 8: 133–150; reprinted as Chapter 3 this volume.
——— 1995. "Are Network Externalities a New Source of Market Failure?," *Research in Law and Economics*, 17: 1–22; reprinted as Chapter 4 this volume.
Mills, E. 1967. "An Aggregative Model of Resource Allocation in a Metropolitan Area," *American Economic Review*, 57: 197–210.
Mokyr, J. 1991. "Evolutionary Biology, Technological Change and Economic History," *Bulletin of Economic Research*, 43: 127–147.
Rasmussen, E. 1989. *Games and Information*, Oxford: Basil Blackwell.
Roland, G. 1991. "Gorbachev and the Common European Home: The Convergence Debate Revived?," *Kyklos*, 43: 385–409.
Schelling, T. C. 1978. *Micromotives and Macro Behavior*, New York: W. W. Norton.
Williamson, O. E. 1993a. "Contested Exchange Versus the Governance of Contractual Relations," *Journal of Economic Perspectives*, 7: 103–108.
——— 1993b. "Transaction Cost Economics and Organization Theory," *Industrial and Corporate Change*, 2: 107–156.
——— 1994. "The Politics and Economics of Redistribution and Inefficiency," Working paper, University of California at Berkeley.
Zerbe, R. 1992. "Antitrust Policy in the Presence of Network Externalities," *Working Paper*, August, University of Washington.

6
Should Technology Choice be a Concern of Antitrust Policy? (1990)* **

Introduction

One basic justification for antitrust is that monopoly practices are socially harmful because they decrease total surplus (see, for example, Lande 1982, 65; Bork, 1978, [1997] 90–91). There is disagreement over whether economic efficiency is now or ever was the goal of antitrust (see, for example, Lande 1982, 65, Page 1989, 1221, 1243–244; DiLorenzo 1985, 73) and there are scores of disagreements about exactly what practices result in monopoly inefficiencies (see, for example, Marvel and McCafferty 1985, 363; McGee 1980, 289). But where the *economic* rationale for antitrust is considered, that rationale invariably has to do with welfare losses that follow from behavior that is somehow related to restricted outputs and elevated prices.

But a new concern has recently arisen. It was raised in the White Paper that became a part of the antitrust action against Microsoft (see generally Reback *et al.* 1995, 52); it seems to be an active issue in the Justice Department (see Pearlstein 1995, A1); and it has become a significant theme in the economic literature of industrial organization (see, for example, Tirole 1988, 404–409). The issue can be stated as follows: Are there systematic tendencies for inefficient technologies to become established and resist replacement by superior alternatives? For example, do we drive cars with the wrong type of engines? Do we use the wrong type of nuclear reactors, improperly designed typewriter keyboards, an inferior videocassette recorder ("VCR") format, and a backwards computer operating system? If so, should these potential problems be the focus of antitrust? In particular, are there forms of

* *Harvard Journal of Law and Technology*, 9 (1996): 283–318.

business conduct that facilitate either premature commitment to inferior technologies or the maintenance of their incumbency?

Some analysts have argued in the literature that the answer to these questions is yes (for example, Katz and Shapiro 1985, 424; Arthur 1989, 116). The theoretical support comes from economic models of "path dependence" and "network externality." If this view is accepted as an appropriate concern for antitrust, it would have far-reaching implications. The problem shifts from monopoly versus competition to the choice of one monopoly over another. The problem for antitrust shifts from avoiding monopoly price elevation to choosing among alternative technologies.

The theories of path dependence and network externality are increasingly popular and have migrated from the realm of economic theory to policy. Microsoft's conduct in establishing standards has been the source of alarm in some circles, prompting hyperbole to the point that Microsoft's influence has been alleged to pose a threat to our very freedoms and way of life (see Reback *et al.* 1995).[1] These sorts of concerns have made standards a new concern for antitrust policy.[2] Yet the fundamental premises of these theories have received little in the way of critical examination, and empirical verification of these theories is sorely lacking (see Liebowitz and Margolis 1995a, also Liebowitz and Margolis 1990 [Chapters 5 and 2 in this volume]). In this paper we will put forward a model that illustrates how standards and products are established in the market. With this model we can illustrate the rather stringent conditions that are necessary in order for an inappropriate technology to become established as a standard. Our model shows that it is highly unlikely that antitrust policy could be used to improve upon even an imperfect result.

We begin, however, by discussing several aspects of this literature that have received considerable attention but which we believe are not well understood. The following three sections summarize arguments that we have presented elsewhere which address some of the fundamental claims of this literature.

Network externalities[3]

In making a choice between the Windows and Macintosh operating systems, most of us gave some thought as to what the people around us were choosing or were likely to choose. In deciding whether to switch to Windows 95 or stay with current operating systems, many of us consider what various software companies will do with their products that may provide a motivation to switch to the newer operating system. The software companies' decisions, in turn, depend on their expectations about the number of users who will switch to the newer operating system. Many choices are like this, with one consumer's choice depending on how other consumers are expected to behave. The term "network externality" has been used to denote these network elements (Katz and Shapiro 1985, 424). In light of the discussion that follows, however, we prefer the term *network effect,* however, reserving *network externality* to apply only to those situations in which market failure causes inefficient exploitation of a network effect (Liebowitz and Margolis 1994a, 135).[4] This distinction is important because, while network effects may be found in abundance throughout the economy, network externalities – and the policy implications stemming from the attendant market failures – may be rare or nonexistent.

Michael Katz and Carl Shapiro's 1985 paper on network externality in the *American Economic Review* defines their subject matter as follows: "There are many products for which the utility that a user derives from consumption of the good increases with the number of other agents consuming the good" (1985, 424). They add, "[T]he utility that a given user derives from the good depends upon the number of other users who are in the same 'network' ..." (1985, 424). This idea of a network embraces not only the physically connected examples of computer networks and telecommunications systems but also, according to Katz and Shapiro, goods such as computer software, automobile repair, and video games. It is easy to come up with many more examples of goods that exhibit these so called "positive consumption externalities." When gourmet cooks more easily find preferred ingredients because more people are taking up their avocation, this would be a gourmet-network externality. When fans of live entertainment prefer big cities because the large market for entertainment assures a full variety of acts, this would be an audience-network externality. There is virtually no limit to these examples.

Although positive network effects have been the main focus in this literature, there is no reason that a network externality should necessarily be limited to positive effects. If, for example, a telephone or computer network becomes overloaded, the effect on an individual subscriber will be negative. When we admit the possibility of a negative network externality, the set of goods that exhibit network externalities expands strikingly. As members of a network of highway users, we suffer from a negative network externality because freeways are subject to crowding. And although a larger installed base of computer users might lower the price of computer software, there are many goods, such as housing and filet mignon, where larger networks of users appear to increase the price of the good.

The problem with all of this is that it leads to the conclusion that almost every good exhibits network externalities, which in turn suggests that the concept has not been well specified. In a previous article on this subject (1995b [Chapter 4 in this volume]), we demonstrated that many of the kinds of things that have been called network externalities actually fall into a category that economists have called "pecuniary externalities." The important thing about pecuniary externalities is that while they are an effect that one person has on another, they do not involve any inefficiency. It is important to distinguish, therefore, between network externalities that involve some direct interaction among the network participants, and those that are mediated through the market.

Among the remaining class of network externalities, those that are "real" or nonpecuniary, the interaction occurs through increasing returns in production of some network related good, or some direct interaction among consumers. For either case, a standard result is that as any network gets larger, it becomes increasingly advantaged relative to any smaller competitor networks that might exist. This leads, ineluctably, to a conclusion that only one network can survive in any market. This is equivalent to the phenomenon that economists have long called "natural monopoly" (see Shepard 1990). The problem here becomes the competition among the potential natural monopolists, a special case in the economics of increasing returns, which we take up now.

Increasing returns and path dependence[5]

Path dependence has been offered as an alternative analytical perspective for economics (see also Arthur 1990, 92, 99). This theory takes increasing returns – economic jargon for the condition that bigger is better – as its starting point, and argues that markets and economies often get stuck with inferior products and standards (Arthur 1989). Traditional economic analysis, it is claimed, largely ignores increasing returns, but the "new" "positive feedback economics" embraces the possibility (Arthur 1990). The claim that is made for path dependence is that a minor or fleeting advantage or a seemingly inconsequential lead for some technology, product, or standard can have important and irreversible influences on the ultimate market allocation of resources, even in a world characterized by voluntary decisions and individually maximizing behavior (Liebowitz and Margolis 1995a, 205–206, also Arthur 1989). In short, we get started, perhaps for no good reason, down some path and we are unable to change to an alternative.

In our research, we define three distinct forms of the path dependence claim. The normative implications of these three forms differ sharply, but unfortunately the literature has previously treated all forms of path dependence as interchangeable. Two of these forms – defined as first- and second-degree path dependence – are commonplace. They do not materially differ from the "old" economics that they are said to replace, and they have no normative implications. Only the strongest form of path dependence, which we call third-degree path dependence, significantly challenges the old economics, claiming that not only that market solutions are flawed, but also that there are identifiable and feasible improvements. However, the theoretical arguments for the occurrence of this form of path dependence require either foresight or improbable restrictions on prices and institutions.[6] Moreover, this third form of path dependence is yet to have any empirical verification.

First-degree path dependence is simple durability without error. Initial actions, perhaps insignificant ones, do put us on a path that cannot be left without some cost, but that path happens to be optimal (although not necessarily uniquely optimal). For example, a capricious decision to part one's hair on the left may lead to a lifetime of left-side parting, but the initial urge to part on the left might capture all there is to be taken into account. More seriously, a decision to use a particular electric system for powering the machinery in a plant may be a controlling influence for decades, but the long-term effects of the decision may be fully appreciated by the initial decisionmaker and fully taken into account.

Second-degree path dependence is durability in the presence of imperfect information. Information is never perfect. It is likely therefore that decisions will not always appear to be efficient in retrospect. If we claim that we committed to a good choice in light of available information, but that some other path now looks to be preferable, we are making a second-degree claim of path dependence. In such a case, initial conditions lead to outcomes that are regrettable and costly to change. But, if the current costs of changing are less than the benefits, the change is not made. Such a situation is not inefficient in any meaningful sense, however, given the assumed limitations on knowledge when the decision was first made.

Third-degree path dependence involves error. It occurs where there exists, or existed, some feasible arrangement for recognizing and achieving an outcome that is preferred to the one chosen, but that preferred outcome is not obtained. In this case a bad outcome is remediable, but not remedied. The occurrence of an error that is remediable but not remedied has significant normative policy implications. Such an error would constitute economic inefficiency.

The three types of path dependence make progressively stronger claims. First-degree path dependence is a simple assertion of an intertemporal relationship, with no implied claim of inefficiency. Second-degree path dependence stipulates that intertemporal effects propagate error. Third-degree path dependence requires not only that the intertemporal effects propagate error, but that the error was, or now is, avoidable.

The failure to distinguish among these three discrete forms of path dependence has led to some unfortunate mistakes. The error here involves transferring the plausibility of the empirical and logical support for the two weaker forms of path dependence (first- and second-degree) to the strongest implications of third-degree path dependence. Although it is fairly easy to identify allocations, technologies, or institutions that are path-dependent in some form, it is very difficult to establish the theoretical case or empirical grounding for path-dependent inefficiency.

The importance of path dependence would appear to reside in the third-degree form. The overwhelming share of first- and second-degree dependencies will be garden variety durabilities that have long been well-incorporated into economics. But if third-degree path dependence offers a "new economics," the question arises: Does such a phenomenon exist, and if so, what conditions bring it about?[7]

Brian Arthur and others have suggested that the phenomenon does exist (Arthur 1990). Their work is based on a rather simple story that can be summarized briefly. If there is a value in being compatible with others, then when consumers choose a standard, such as videorecorder format, if they forecast compatibility on the basis of the number of people already committed to each standard, they will tend to choose only the one that is best established, even if that standard is inferior to less well established alternatives. In our critical writing on this [for example, Chapters 4 and 5 in this volume], we have shown that this model, or story, relies on extraordinary restrictions that are not likely to be satisfied for real-world choices. In the following, we present a richer story to consider the possibility of getting stuck with the wrong technology.

Standards contests as a metaphor for technology choices

Rivalries between competing technologies can be thought of as rivalries between standards. Standards are the conventions or commonalities that allow us to interact. Recent examples of battles over standards are numerous: video recording formats, audio taping, audio compact discs, video disks, computer operating systems, spreadsheets, word processors, telecommunications protocols, and HDTV. Standards, networks, and technologies are similar in that the benefits to an adopter of any of these may depend upon the number of adopters. For example, the benefits of a technology may depend on widespread availability of expertise, a body of problem solving experience, and compatibility. Similarly, it is inherent in the nature of a standard that the benefits that accrue to an adopter will depend on the number of other adopters.

The application of path dependence and network externality theories has offered a pessimistic prognosis for firms that would attempt to displace an incumbent standard. It suggests great difficulty, for example, in replacing one generation of software with another. This would seem to promise great rewards for the firm that did manage to control a standard, suggesting that an entrenched standard might fall behind the capabilities of the best available technology without inviting a viable threat from a rival. This was the kind of concern that was raised in the Microsoft case (Sporkin 1995, 1448).

There are, however, important shortcomings with this "entrenched incumbent's" view (Levinson and Coleman 1992). First, it leaves us without an explanation of the successful replacement of one technology with another. How did VHS displace Beta, or graphical user interfaces displace character-based commands, or compact discs replace records, or automobiles replace horses and carriages? Obviously, displacement is quite common. Second, the empirical support for such entrenchment is notably lacking. The continued use of the ever-popular QWERTY versus Dvorak keyboard story, or Beta versus VHS story are sad commentaries on the lack of respect for historical accuracy that has affected this literature.

The following model has implications that contradict the entrenched incumbents' view. It does so by incorporating different characterizations of the production and purchase of goods that embody standards. It allows separate consideration of the coordination advantage of standards (called synchronization effects) and the production technology of these goods. Further, it allows consideration of differences in tastes among consumers. With these departures in modeling come some important results, including these:

- The expected effect of a "standards externality" is on the amount of the standard-using activity, not on choice of standard or the mix of standards.
- Where there are differences in preferences regarding alternative standards, coexistence of standards is a likely outcome. Further, a single-standard equilibrium, if it is achieved, is more readily displaced by an alternative if preferences differ. This suggests that product strategies leading to strong allegiances of some group of customers are likely to be effective in the face of an incumbent standard.
- Entrenched incumbents are less entrenched when consumers react to new sales, and not just the accumulated stocks of goods that embody standards. In particular, a challenging standard that achieves a significant flow of adoptions is shown to be viable. This contrasts with previous models in which a significant installed base gives the incumbent standard an insurmountable advantage.

A model of standards rivalry

The model is based on a fundamental purpose of standards: Standards facilitate interaction among individuals. The term "synchronization" is used to refer to this effect.[8] Synchronization is the benefit received by users of a standard when they interact with other individuals using the same standard. In general, synchronization effects will increase with the number of people using the same standard, although it will often be the case that users' benefits will be less closely tied to the total number of other users of a standard and more closely tied to the number of users with whom they actually interact.

These synchronization benefits are distinguished from the ordinary scale effects on production costs. Synchronization effects in our model may coexist with increasing, decreasing or constant returns to scale. We will demonstrate that neither scale economies in production nor synchronization effects are by themselves necessary or sufficient conditions for an outcome where only one standard survives.

Although it is almost taken for granted among many commentators that average production costs fall with increases in output for most high technology, standardized goods,[9] we are not so sure that this is correct. There are, we would agree, many examples where standardization is associated, rightly or wrongly, with lower prices. The past two decades have witnessed decreases in the costs of computing power, telecommunications, and video-recording, accompanied by increases in the use of computer software, new methods of communications, and video recorders. Consequently, theories that invoke economies of scale have had an easy time capturing our attention.

But there is no reason to believe that the goods referred to as "high-tech" are necessarily subject to increasing returns to scale. The technical advances associated with new technologies may easily disguise actual diseconomies of scale in production. This is the difference between a movement of an entire cost schedule or curve, and a movement along a single schedule, a point made in almost all elementary economic texts, and one that is well understood by economists (see Stigler 1941, 68–76; for a more complete discussion of how this relates to technology choices, see generally Liebowitz and Margolis 1995a [Chapter 5 in this volume]).

Being able to distinguish between these possibilities *on an empirical level,* however, is another matter. Some of the most eminent economists, such as Alfred Marshall,[10] have confused a shift in an average cost curves over time with movements down a single average cost curve. Advances in technology are likely to lead to increases in output and lower prices, but this should not be confused with economies of scale in production.

These new high-technology goods are also likely to be associated with unsettled format choices. The eventual adoption of a standard, which may take several years or even decades, often occurs simultaneously with improvements in technology, making an examination of correlations between time series of standardization efforts and production costs misleading. Certainly, an empirical association exists between the adoption of standards and decreases in costs: IBM's personal computer became the dominant format, and computer and software prices fell while the number of computers and programs rose; prices of fax machines and modems fell dramatically after settlement on a standard compression routine. However, the drop in costs associated with the standardization of many new technologies can not be taken as evidence in favor of increasing returns in the production of standardized goods, since the new technologies often lead to rapid decreases in (quality adjusted) costs over time, with or without standardization. For example, although VCR prices fell after VHS won its standardization battle with Beta, VCR prices had also fallen while both formats possessed significant market shares.[11]

The model that follows provides independent consideration of the impacts of synchronization effects and production cost economies and diseconomies. While the synchronization effect, like the effect of any ordinary fixed cost of production, favors the domination of an industry by a single format, it does not guarantee such a result.[12]

A model of standard selection

Consider a setting in which two formats compete. Current consumer choices are affected by the market share of each format during a recent time period. A consumer commits to a format, for at least a while, by purchasing a product with that particular format. For concreteness and familiarity, the discussion will be presented as a choice between Beta and VHS, in which commitment to a format occurs with the purchase of a VCR.

For several reasons, we assume consumers make purchase decisions on the basis of shares (percentage of market controlled by a standard) rather than scales (total output of a standard). First, there is the issue of synchronization costs: if most of the world uses VHS, the fact that the *number* of Beta users is increasing may be largely irrelevant. Second, for any given scale of a good with standard activity, relative share will determine relative scale. Finally, consumer choices will often be for one format versus another, so that it is the relative, not absolute, benefit of the standard that will affect consumer decisions.

The consumer

Assumptions about consumer values that are the basic building blocks of our model are shown in Figure 6.1. The horizontal axis shows, for the most recent time period, the market share of one format.[13] In our example, the horizontal axis is the share of VHS VCRs as a percentage of all VCRs sold during this period.

We define the autarky value of an individual's investment in a VHS video recorder to be its value assuming no interaction among VHS users (i.e. no other VHS users). A VCR presumably has value even if tapes are never rented or exchanged. But a positive autarky value is not required for the model. In some activities, such as communication with fax machines or modems, it is reasonable to assume an autarky value of zero.

The synchronization value is the additional value that results from the adoption of the format by other consumers.[14] By assumption, the synchronization value assigned by a potential consumer is directly correlated with increases in the consumer's estimate of that format's future market share. Further, we hold that consumers use the format's

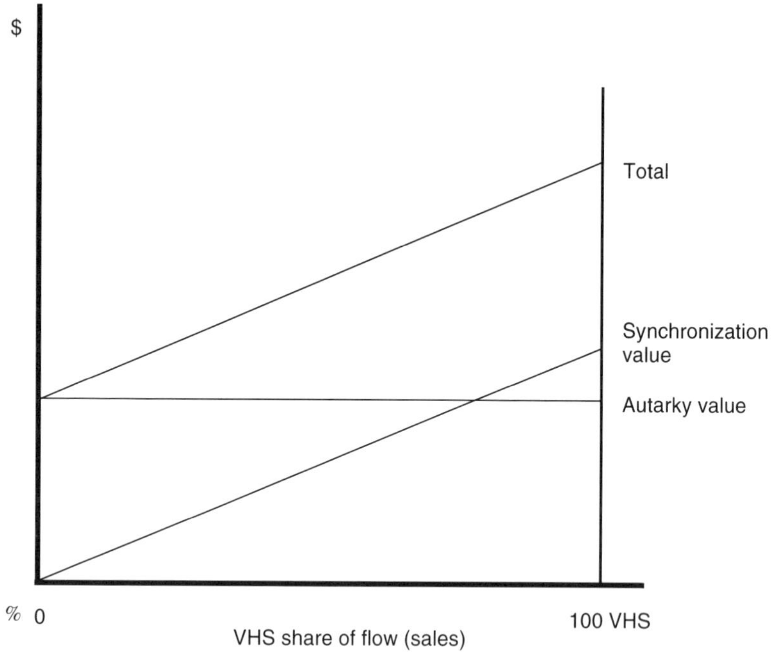

Figure 6.1 A consumer's valuation

current market share to estimate the future share of the stock. Thus, the synchronization value of VHS increases with its share of the market.

Total value, defined as the autarky value plus the synchronization value, will increase as the format's market share increases.

Figure 6.1 shows the value of a format to an average consumer based on its share of the current period's sales (flow).

Production

For many standards, an individual's adoption of the standard occurs with the purchase of a single standard-embodying good, such as a computer, a camera, a typewriter, or a videocassette recorder. For these standards, the conditions of production will influence outcomes in social choices regarding standards.

Production of VCRs could be subject to increasing, decreasing or constant cost. For now, we will assume price-taking behavior by producers. For a given total quantity of VCRs sold, the flow of a particular format will, of course, increase directly with the share. Figure 6.2 shows

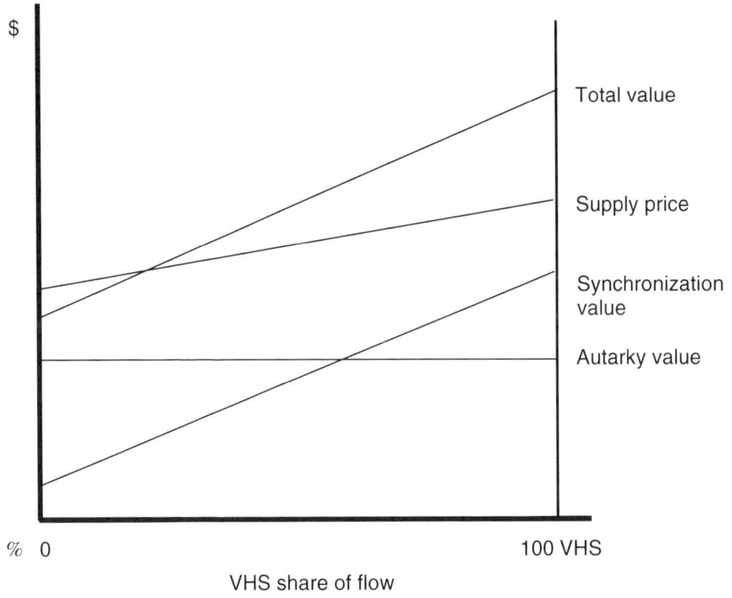

Figure 6.2 Consumer valuation and supply price

the supply price function under the assumption that VCR production involves increasing cost. (Other specifications of cost are allowed and discussed below. Here, the figure illustrates a single possible configuration.)

From these relationships, a net value function for videorecorder formats can be derived. The net value function is equal to the total value (the autarky value plus the synchronization value) less supply price. Since the total value increases more rapidly than supply price in Figure 6.2, the net value increases as VHS's share of the market grows.

The net value functions for machines with the Beta format can be constructed in the same fashion. Net value functions will be upward-sloping if the supply price function is less steeply upward-sloping than the synchronization value function. In other words, if decreasing returns in production overwhelm synchronization benefits, the net value line falls with market share. On the other hand, if synchronization benefits are greater than decreasing returns in production, or if production exhibits increasing returns, then the net value curve is upward-sloping, as in Figure 6.3.

It is only when the net value function is upward-sloping that choices between standards are fundamentally different in character from

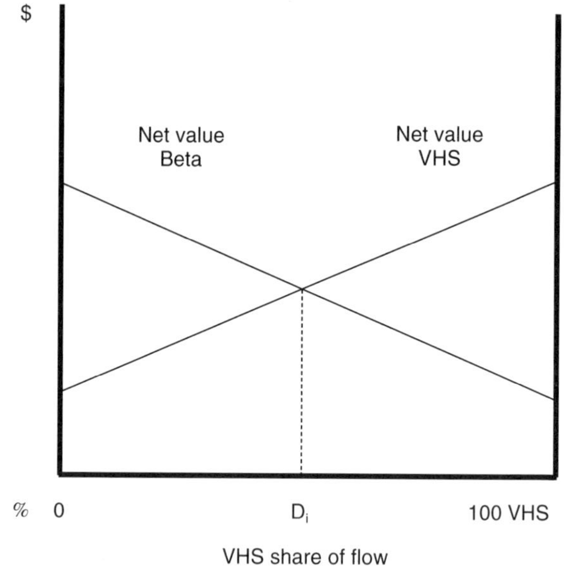

Figure 6.3 Net value for Beta and VHS

choices of other goods (i.e. exhibit increasing returns instead of decreasing returns). We assume throughout the analysis that the slope of the net value function for a given format has the same sign for all consumers.[15]

The net value functions for Beta and VHS are put in a single diagram in Figure 6.3. As VHS share varies from 0 percent to 100 percent, Beta share varies from 100 percent to 0 percent. If the two formats have identical costs and benefits, the Beta net value curve will be the mirror image of the VHS net value curve.

The intersection of the two curves (if they intersect), labeled D_i, represents the market share equilibrium where the consumer is indifferent between the two formats. This value plays a crucial role in our analysis. On either side of D_i, the consumer will have a preference depending on the slopes of these curves. For example, if each net value curve is upward-sloping with respect to its own market share, as in Figure 6.3, the consumer will prefer VHS when its market share increases beyond D_i (VHS has higher value, relative to Beta, as the VHS share increases beyond D_i). If the two net value curves are downward-sloping with respect to their own market shares, however, the consumer will prefer Beta as VHS share increases beyond D_i.

Note that this analysis assumes that the consumer does not take into account the impact of his decisions on other consumers (i.e. he does not consider how his purchase of a video recorder will alter the valuation to other potential purchasers of video recorders). Therefore, the door is still left open for some sort of (network) *externality*.

The market

Each customer has an individual D_i, an equilibrium point at which the two formats are equally valuable. Accordingly, a population of customers will have a distribution of D_i's. Let $G(x_j)$ be the fraction of VCR purchasers with $D_i < x_j$, that is, $G(x)$ is the cumulative distribution function for D_i. This distribution is a key to the selection of a standard.

Perhaps the most basic distribution would be one in which all consumers had the same tastes, so that D_i is the same for all consumers. Call this common value D_i*. This resulting cumulative distribution is shown in Figure 6.4. The cumulative function is actually the share of the population that will buy VHS next period based on different current market shares of VHS.

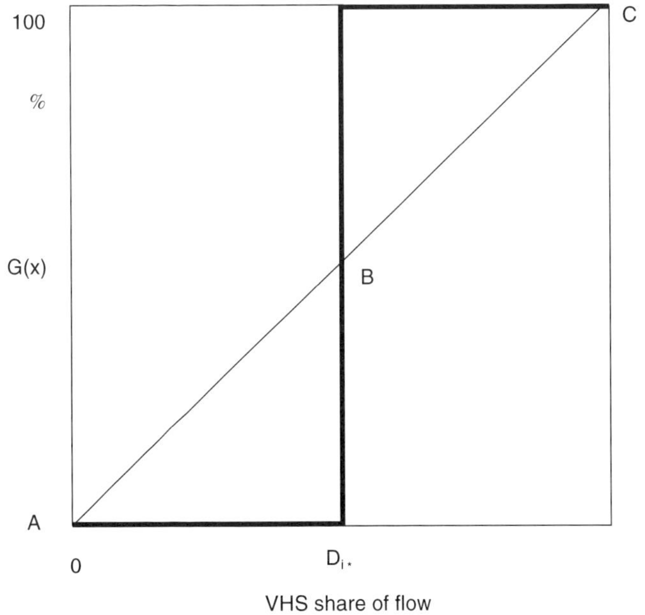

Figure 6.4 Market distribution of D_i

Returning to Figure 6.4, we can now see that the candidates for equilibrium are A, B, and C. Points A and C are single format equilibria which are stable: For flows near 0 percent VHS, all consumers will choose Beta, for flows near 100 percent VHS all consumers will choose VHS. In contrast, B is an unstable equilibrium. At flows near but to the left of D_i* all consumers would choose Beta, at flows near but to the right of D_i*, all consumers choose VHS. So, for the case of upward-sloping net value curves, we obtain an either/or choice that is often argued to be the expected outcome for standards. An upward-sloping net value curve, however, is nothing more than the traditional "natural monopoly."

Consider the outcome for downward-sloping net value curves. In this case, all consumers with D_i less than the prevailing flow choose Beta. The function G(x) thus reveals the fraction choosing Beta. The function 1 – G(x), which is the fraction choosing VHS, is shown in Figure 6.5. The only possible equilibrium is B, a stable equilibrium. At points near, but to the left of D_i*, VHS machines are more advantageous than Beta machines (through effects on supply price) and more consumers would choose VHS. Similarly, displacements of equilibrium to the right of D_i* would increase the relative advantage of Beta machines, moving the outcome back to the left.

Consumers split their purchases so that a VHS purchase and a Beta purchase have identical net value. This describes a circumstance in which the formats will coexist. This result is significant because it demonstrates that even without differences in taste (which favors coexistence), it is still possible for a mixed-format equilibrium to exist.

The mere existence of synchronization effects can now be seen as insufficient to establish the either-or choice with respect to standards. That is because synchronization effects cannot, by themselves, ensure upward-sloping net value curves.

This model of standardization provides some interesting insights. The nature of the equilibrium, either as a mixed format or as an either-or equilibrium, depends on the slopes of the net value curves, and synchronization effects are only part of the story. For example, upward-sloping net value curves can occur when supply price falls, even when there is no synchronization effect. The existence of synchronization effects, the *raison d'être* of standardization, also does not rule out the possibility of downward-sloping net value curves, and the resulting efficient coexistence of formats. *Synchronization effects, therefore, are neither necessary nor sufficient conditions for an either-or equilibrium.*

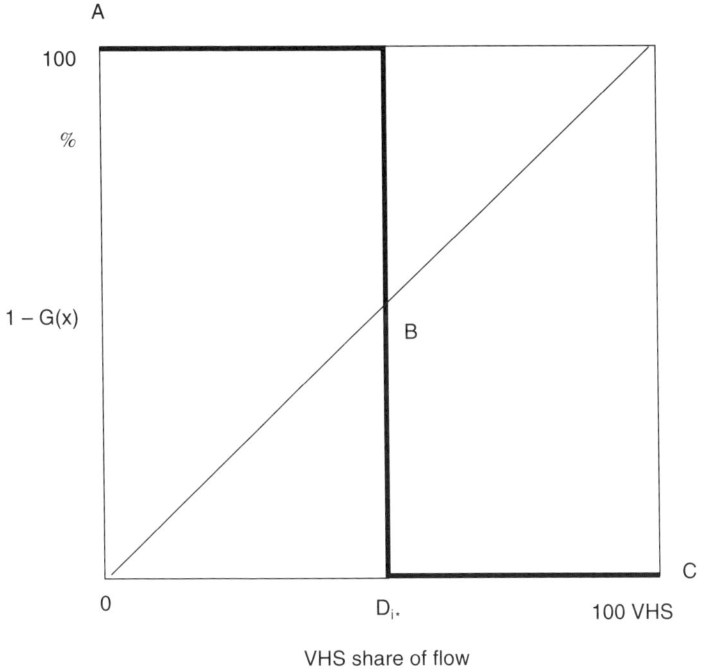

Figure 6.5 Market fraction choosing VHS

In fact, it is possible that the either-or equilibrium is mostly driven by production costs and not network effects. For example, if software categories were to be dominated by single entries, it would likely be due to the large fixed cost element in the *production* of software titles as opposed to synchronization effects.[16] But arguments that network effects might lead to software monopolies (as claimed of Microsoft) miss the point. Software creation may be just a newer version of a natural monopoly in terms of old fashioned, prosaic production costs, which are quite independent of any network effects. Large fixed costs leading to (natural) monopoly can just as well be used to characterize the publishing or movie business.

Yet what would be the implications for antitrust? If the market is a natural monopoly, whether due to synchronization or production costs, there would be no benefit in trying to force the market into a competitive structure with many overly small firms having excessively high production cost structures and low synchronization values for consumers. The government might wish to award natural monopoly franchises, as it does for most public utilities, but the history of publicly regulated utilities does not inspire confidence that technological advancement would be promoted, or that costs would be kept down. Since high technology changes so frequently, a firm that achieved monopoly with one technology will not be able to hold on to its lead unless it is extremely resourceful. This further argues against the value of government intervention in technology markets.

Internalizing synchronization costs

Thus far, the model addresses only private valuations and their effects on outcomes. Since the literature has been preoccupied with how one consumer's format choice affects the values enjoyed by others, we should also examine how internalizing this externality would affect standard choice. We must note, however, that a single owner of a technology or standard is capable of internalizing the impact of consumers' behavior through prices. The following discussion therefore applies to the case in which a technology is not owned by a single entity.

To this point the net value curves have represented private net benefits. Since the synchronization effect is always assumed to have a positive effect on other users of the same format, the social net value function, which includes the synchronization value to others, will always lie above the private net value function, regardless of the slope of the private net value function.[17] The difference in height depends on the relative strength of the synchronization effects and the format's market shares. For example, at zero share of VHS, the VHS private net value curve will be the same as the VHS social net value curve. That is because, where there is no user of VHS to benefit from this individual's purchase, the private and social values must coincide. Where VHS has a positive market share, the social net value curve is everywhere above the private net value curve. This case is shown in Figure 6.6. As the share of VHS increases, and the number of potential beneficiaries of this individual's VHS purchase increases, the difference between the social and private net value curves increases. The same would be true for Beta net value curves.[18]

Depending on the relative sizes of the synchronization effects on users of the two formats the intersection of social net value curves can be to the right or left of the intersections of the private net value curves. In the particular case where the two formats attract users with the same levels of potential interaction and where the private net value curves are the same, internalizing the synchronization externality will

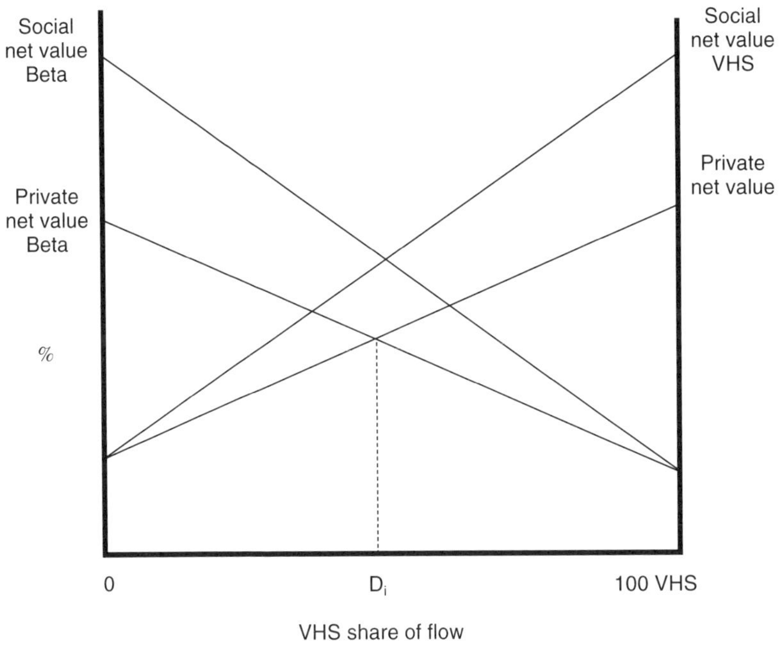

Figure 6.6 Social and private net values

have no effect on any individual's D_i, and thus no effects on the potential equilibria.

If, in the more likely case where the D_is move to the left or right, the cumulative distribution function would also move in the same direction. In that case, internalizing the synchronization externality may lead to a different equilibrium.

But even if the D_i* in Figure 6.4 moves left or right somewhat, when the market starts near point A, that will remain the equilibrium, and if it starts near point B, that will remain the equilibrium. Thus even if internalization of the externality changes D_is, the final market equilibrium need not change. Internalizing the synchronization effect thus might have no impact on the choice of format.

There is one dimension where the internalization of the synchronization effect always has an impact, however. The private net value functions consistently undervalue videorecorders. Therefore, it is not the *relative* market shares, but rather, the size of the overall market that will be affected by this difference between private and social net value functions. *Too few videorecorders of either type will be produced if the synchronization effect is not internalized by the market participants.* Internalizing the externality enhances both VHS and Beta, causing consumption of VCRs to increase even if market shares remain constant (Berg 1989, 361, 362). This is completely compatible with the conventional literature on ordinary externalities (see, for example, Fischer, Dornbusch and Schmalensee 1988, 238). All this is really saying is that too little of a product will be produced if there is a positive externality (e.g. too few golf courses, or too few copies of Microsoft Excel) and too much will be produced if there is a negative externality (e.g. pollution). This is a far more likely consequence of "network externalities" than the more exotic case of winding up with the wrong standard.

Extending the model

There are several natural extensions of this model. The assumption that all consumers have the same D_i can easily be relaxed. Allowing consumers to differ in their D_is acknowledges differences in tastes. These differences may reflect different assessments of the formats, different synchronization values, or both.

Assume that the D_is for consumers range between 20 percent and 80 percent (VHS), and that within this range the distribution of D_is are uniform, as illustrated in Figure 6.7. The height of the distribution of D_is indicates the slope of the cumulative distribution function. The cumulative distribution function, therefore, has a straight line segment between (20,0) and (80,100) as shown in Figure 6.8, and intersects the 45 degree diagonal at points A, B, and C. If the net value functions are upward-sloping with respect to own market share, A and C would be stable equilibria and B would not. Thus, this type of uniform distribution of D_is gives the same general result as the assumption that all consumers have identical D_is. Thus, under these assumptions, we tend to get an either/or equilibrium.

If the net value function were falling with respect to own market share, the corresponding figure would be the vertical mirror image of Figure 6.8. Point B would be the only stable equilibrium in flows. Consumers would buy the format that they most valued, unless it suffered a cost disadvantage due to its popularity. With decreasing returns, we expect many formats (brands, producers) in the market. Because this result is so standard, we focus our attention on the less standard case where net value rises with market share, i.e. where natural monopoly in production is a possible outcome.

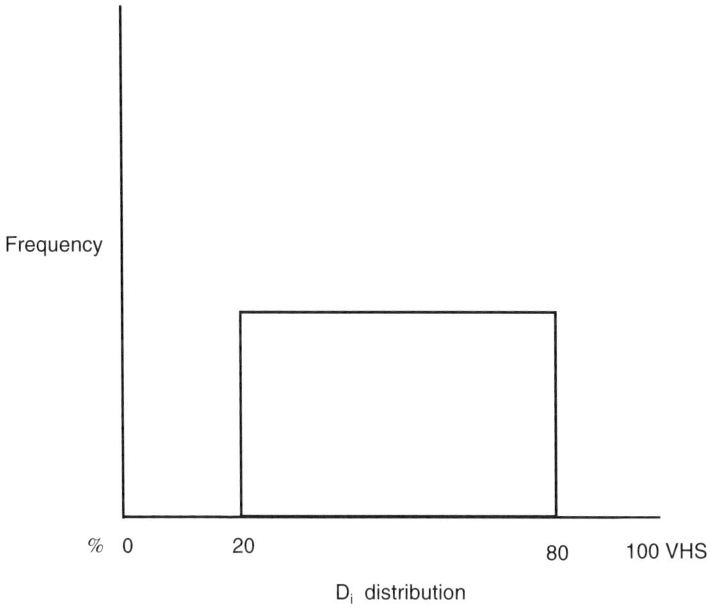

Figure 6.7 Differences in tastes

Strong differences in tastes

Up to this point, the results of the model indicate that when net value curves are upward-sloping, the equilibrium will be of the either/or type. This need not be the case. Figure 6.9 shows a distribution of D_is representing the very reasonable case where each format has a fairly large number of adherents, with the rest of the population of D_is thinly (and uniformly) distributed between 20 percent and 80 percent VHS.

The distribution of D_is in Figure 6.9 results in the cumulative distribution function shown in Figure 6.10. The only stable equilibrium in this case is point B. The differences in tastes allow two standards to coexist in a stable equilibrium, even where net value curves are upward-sloping. This is an important result. In those instances in which each format offers some advantages to different groups of customers, we should expect to find that different formats appeal to different people. When this is so, formats can coexist in a market equilibrium, and individual consumers are not deprived of one of the choices.

It is important to point out that this is the likely path that markets are expected to follow when there are strong natural monopoly

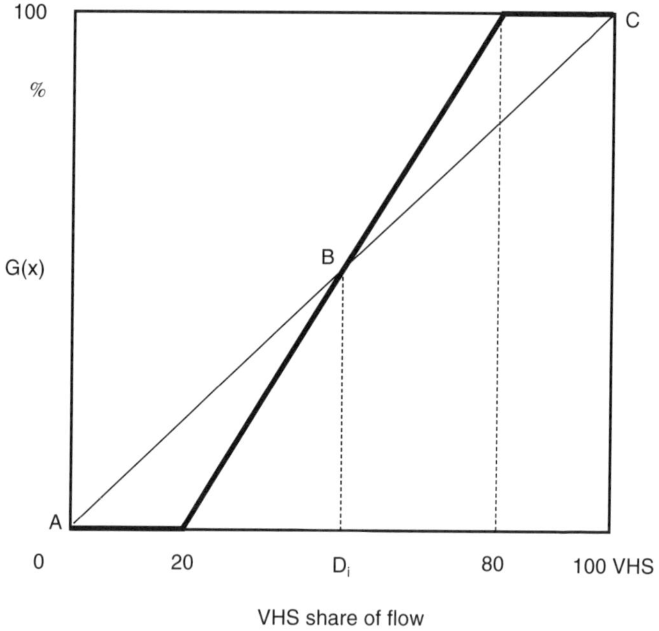

Figure 6.8 Market distribution with difference in tastes

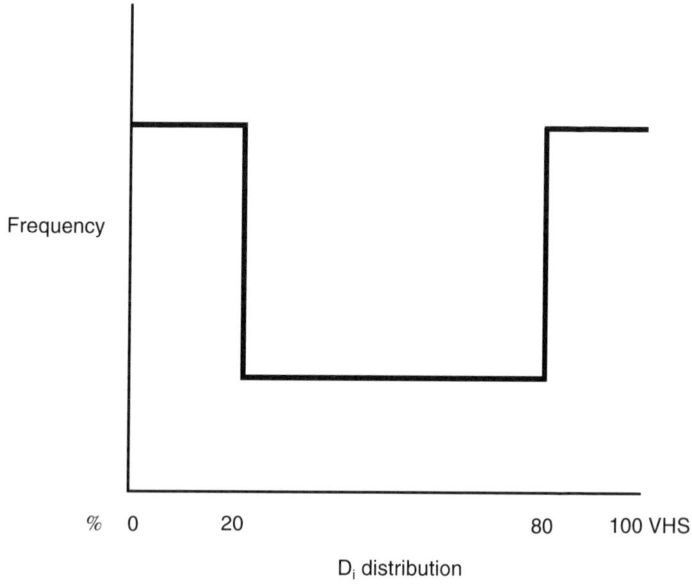

Figure 6.9 Bimodal tastes

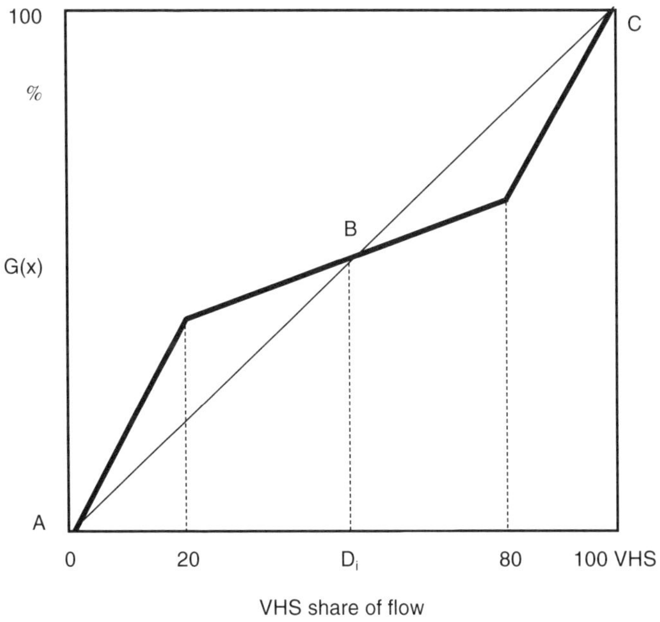

Figure 6.10 Two standards coexist

elements. Although a Hotelling model might predict that two firms will produce nearly identical products, we would expect (entrant) firms to try to specialize their products to appeal to particular groups of users. This is, after all, one simple way for firms to overcome any natural monopoly advantage that might exist in production costs of an incumbent. The incumbent firm, on the other hand, might do well creating products that appeal to the widest possible audience in an attempt to foreclose this possibility.

There are some straightforward implications here. First, even when there are economies of scale and/or network effects, the market can allow more than one format to survive. The key to success is to find a market niche and to produce a product that is as close to the preferences of that market segment as possible. Unless the established firms are much larger and have much lower costs, the superior characteristics for the entrant's product, as viewed by the consumer niche, will provide sufficient advantage for the entrant to survive. If each producer can produce a product that appeals to a segment of the population, then the situation represented by Figure 6.10 will occur. That this result is so grounded in common sense does not, to us, diminish its value.

Results when one product is superior to another

It is more complicated to define a superior standard than might be thought. In the rather lopsided case of one format having higher net values than another by all consumers in all market shares, that format clearly would be superior. It is also not difficult to see that in this case, no D_i would occur in the interior of 0–100 percent, and that the only equilibrium is at a share of 100 percent for the superior format. But it is not common to find such lopsided circumstances. Strongly held, but divergent, preferences lead to different results. If some individuals prefer format A, regardless of share, and others prefer format B, regardless of share, then it is not clear that either can be said to be superior.

For our purposes, however, we shall define standard A to be superior if, for all consumers and any market share X, the net value of A is higher than the net value of B with the same market share (e.g. if all consumers prefer A with 100 percent share to B with 100 percent share; similarly, all prefer A when both A and B share 50 percent of the market).

Assume that VHS is the superior standard. The D_is will then all be less than 50 percent since individuals would only choose Beta when it had the dominant market share. Assume that the D_is are uniformly distributed between 0 percent and 20 percent. Then the cumulative density function lies above the 45 degree line everywhere, as shown in Figure 6.11. Figure 6.11 is the same as Figure 6.8 except that the upward-sloping segment is displaced to the left. A and C are the only two equilibrium points, but only C is a stable equilibrium. *This analysis implies that if society starts at 100 percent Beta, it could get stuck at A, but only if no one ever purchases a single VHS machine. The trap at A, being an unstable equilibrium, is incredibly fragile.*

In this case it is almost certain that the superior format dominates the market. If VHS is superior and both formats originate at the same time, VHS will win unless Beta, although inferior, can somehow capture *and keep* a market share of 100 percent. This would seem an almost impossible task for the Beta producers. It is unlikely, however, that both formats would come to market at the same time. If VHS arrives first, Beta need not bother showing up. If Beta arrives first, as it in reality did, then it has a market share of 100 percent prior to the arrival of VHS. If the entrenched stock is large and if it also has an influence on expected future market shares, then the distribution of D_is would be shifted to the right. This implies the possibility of an

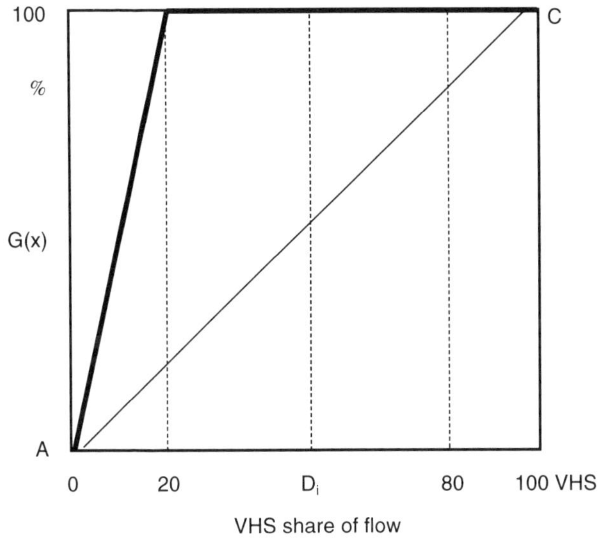

Figure 6.11 VHS dominant

equilibrium that is different from C. This is the instance of being "stuck" in an inferior format.

An example of getting stuck

It is not difficult to alter the previous example so that A becomes a stable equilibrium, even though VHS is preferred by all consumers. One simple alteration is merely to assume some minor changes from those conditions represented in Figure 6.11. For example, as noted above, Beta might have an advantage in the existing stock and consumers might take into account the established base of previous sales in addition to sales this period. Under that assumption we let the D_is range between 10 percent and 30 percent, instead of the former 0 percent and 20 percent. The market now can be represented by Figure 6.12. Because all consumers prefer Beta when the share of Beta is greater than 90 percent, the cumulative distribution function is no longer always above the diagonal, and point A becomes a stable equilibrium in addition to point C. Point B, at 12.5 percent VHS, now is an unstable equilibrium.

Notice that the possibility of getting stuck does not require the existence of any synchronization (network) effect. Upward-sloping net value curves are all that are necessary, and this can be achieved merely with old-fashioned scale economies in production.

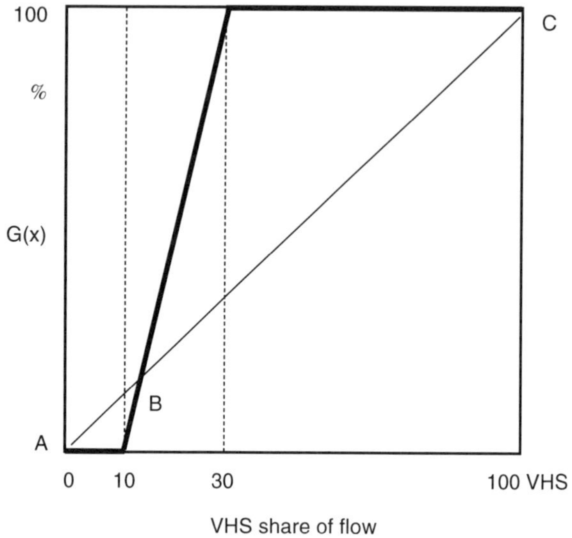

Figure 6.12 Multiple equilibria

Getting unstuck

Under the conditions discussed above, where the market settles at A, owners of the VHS format have an incentive to alter conditions to attempt to dislodge the market from A. One method might be to dump a large number of VHS machines on the market, perhaps by lowering the price, in order to generate an immediate 12.6 percent market share, driving the equilibrium to C.[19]

Producers of VHS can also try to prime the pump on sales by providing deals to the largest users, or distributors, or retailers (perhaps offering side payments) to convince them to switch to VHS.[20] If this action can provide a market share of 12.5 percent, VHS can dislodge Beta (as of course it did). Of course, if the VHS format were not owned, there would have been a potential free rider problem for the VHS producers to solve before these strategies could have been adopted.

There are other alternatives as well, including advertising, publicity, and services to allow partial or total compatibility. (VHS, with RCA's expertise, did put on a large publicity blitz in the US). Interestingly, VHS, through a combination of lower prices, clever advertising, and most of all, a product considered superior by most consumers, overtook Beta within six months of introduction in the US.

It is important to note that the larger the difference between the two formats, the easier it is for the superior format to overcome any initial lead of an inferior standard. For truly large differentials, we should expect diagrams like Figure 6.11, not Figure 6.12. Thus, the greater the potential error in the choice of a standard, the less likely it is that an error would be made.

Additionally, the greater the difference in the format, the greater the difference in potential profits between formats and the more likely the superior format can get financing to engage in the pump-priming type of activities that we alluded to above. In a circumstance like the ones presented above, all other things equal, the technology that creates more wealth will have an advantage over a technology that creates less. While the owner of a technology may not be able to appropriate its value perfectly, owners of a superior format can be less perfect at overcoming their appropriation problems and still win the competition.

The role of antitrust should be, basically, to get out of the way here. The various pump-priming measures discussed above may well look predatory, but the superior format must be allowed to engage in actions that can help ensure it survives and prospers, particularly if it is not the first format offered to users. If the superior technology is offered first, we are unlikely to see a sustained attempt to dislodge the leader by the owners of inferior technologies, unless they expect that they can achieve their ends through political means, since their expenditures in the market are likely to be futile. If government is to do anything useful, it should help to ensure that the capital market is functioning properly so that new technologies have access to sufficient financing. The recent episode with Netscape and its enormous market capitalization[21] seems to indicate that such financing is more than abundant.

It may not always be apparent how or if a technology is owned. Ownership of a technology can take various forms including ownership of critical inputs, patent, copyright, and industrial design. Literal networks such as telephones, pipelines, and computer systems are most often owed by private parties. Sony licensed the Beta system, JVC–Matsushita the VHS system. Standards are often protected by patent or copyright. Resolution of these startup problems may be an important and as yet not fully recognized function of the patent system (see Kitch 1977, 265) and other legal institutions.

Other methods for getting unstuck

Transactions are one method for avoiding an inefficient standard or moving from one standard to another. In some circumstances, the numbers of people who interact through a standard is small enough that transactions are a feasible method of resolving any externalities regarding the standard. A small group of engineers working together can certainly get together and decide to use a different CAD package. Or an extended family can coordinate the choice of Camcorder format so that tapes of grandchildren can be exchanged.

Another tactic for dislodging an inferior standard is convertibility. Suppliers of new-generation computers occasionally offer a service to convert files to new formats. Cable-television companies have offered hardware and services to adapt old televisions to new antenna systems for an interim period. For a time before and after the Second World War typewriter manufacturers offered to convert QWERTY typewriters to Dvorak for a very small fee (see Liebowitz and Margolis 1990 [Chapter 2 in this volume]).[22]

All of these tactics tend to unravel the apparent trap of an inefficient standard. But there are additional conditions that can contribute to the ascendancy of the efficient standard. An important one is the growth of the activity that uses the standard. If a market is growing rapidly the number of users who have made commitments to any standard is small relative to the number of future users. Sales of audiocassette players were barely hindered by their incompatibility with the reel-to-reel or eight-track players that preceded them. Sales of sixteen-bit computers were scarcely hampered by their incompatibility with the disks or operating systems of eight-bit computers [see chapter 2 in this volume]. In each of these cases, rapid market growth was sufficient to overcome operating such incompatibility.

We thus conclude that instances of getting stuck with the wrong standards, when the standards are chosen in the market, should be few and far between. In the next section, we present a summary of our prior work that critically examines two popular case studies used to support the notion of an inferior standard "trap." We conclude by applying the lessons of this work to the recent computer operating system debate.

Empirical examples of standard choice

"The fable of the keys" ... [see Chapter 2 in this volume]

...

A tale of the tape: Beta vs. VHS

After the typewriter story, the second most popular illustration of harmful lock-in is the contest between the Beta and VHS videotaping format ... [see Chapter 5 in this volume].

Computer operating systems – Mac vs. IBM

It is often claimed that the Macintosh operating system is better than either the DOS system or the DOS-based Windows system that followed. However, these standards are not fixed, but instead can and do evolve. The IBM operating system evolved into one that is very similar to the Macintosh. It is possible, in fact, that the Macintosh was introduced too early, for its operating system was more than the hardware of the time could handle with reasonable performance and cost.

DOS had advantages when processors were slow and memory was scarce, since text based displays were much more rapidly displayed and required far less memory. Printers also were not generally up to the task of printing graphical images of pages, except for PostScript printers which required gobs of memory, a very expensive license to use the PostScript page description language, and a fast processor to interpret the language and convert the textual commands into graphical images. For ordinary businesses and ordinary users, these advantages of the Macintosh were largely extravagances that could easily be forgone. Even Windows did not really take off until the power of computers was able to overcome its sluggish performance relative to DOS.

As processors, hard drives, and memory increased in speed and power, graphical interfaces increased in attractiveness. Printers also increased commensurately in power. If the MS-DOS world were still using DOS, there is little doubt that Macintosh would have dramatically increased its market share and might now be the dominant brand. But Microsoft apparently understood this. Windows, and now Windows 95, have migrated toward the Macintosh path (which in fact was the path originated by the Xerox Palo Alto Research Center), so the original Macintosh backers were correct in their view that many of the features that confronted the user in the Macintosh system were theoretically and aesthetically better than DOS. The fact that a particular *brand* did not dominate should not be confused with the inability of a *technology* to dominate. Again, individual choices led to a solution that appears to be efficient.

Conclusions

High-technology goods, and computer software in particular, pose interesting problems for economic analysis. It may be that some types of software products should be produced by only a single supplier. But, this is not the usual venue for antitrust. There might be reason to intervene in the market if there were evidence that rivalry in the marketplace was moribund. But, the evidence seems to be overwhelmingly to the contrary. Or, there might be reason to intervene if there were evidence that these industries were seriously deficient in technological progress. But, there is no such evidence. There might be reason to overturn the market's selection of a standard if it could be shown that markets are systematically deficient at such choices. But, as we have shown, this is an unlikely event, and there is as yet no evidence to support such a view.

We have presented a different view of how markets generally function. In our model individuals have foresight, entrepreneurs have ambition, and knowledge is a prized asset. In the alternative world view consumers are myopic and entrepreneurs are either timid or impotent. In this latter world it is not surprising that accidents have considerable permanence and that mistakes are not corrected. In such a world there are no agents who might profit by devising some means of capturing a part of the aggregate benefits of correction.

If we follow the advice given by many proponents of concepts such as path dependence and network externalities we will likely be handicapping a sector of the economy that has been one of, if not the most, powerful sources of growth, innovation and vitality in domestic and international markets. This government interference with high-technology markets would not be based on well supported theories of monopoly behavior, but rather would be based on theories that are highly speculative and generally without any empirical support. Further, attempts to convert these theories into an antitrust agenda as proposed by the Reback White paper (Reback 1994) have carried these economic theories to extremes.

The misuse of economic theory for public policy purposes cannot be in the country's long run interest. Even if one does not like Microsoft, its CEO, or its products, it is still a mistake to use antitrust as an instrument with which to bludgeon Microsoft, since there is no telling where the misuse of antitrust will next appear. The high-technology marketplace appears to be quite capable of disciplining any firm that does not address the needs of its consumers, as is demonstrated by the extraordinary rate of turnover of product leaders in these markets. Above all else, the theory that is alleged to underpin such antitrust action is a theory that, at best, is of limited applicability and, at worst, is simply wrong. Consumers, manufacturers, regulators, and economists will all be better off when our discourse is based on theories that have empirical confirmation in the real world.

Notes

** Textual format has been altered to conform to the style in the rest of this volume.

1. The authors argue that Microsoft's ownership of operating system standards will be leveraged into eventual domination of the entire information mechanism of society.

   > It is difficult to imagine that in an open society such as this one with multiple information sources, a single company could seize sufficient control of information transmission so as to constitute a threat to the underpinnings of a free society. But such a scenario is a realistic (and perhaps probable) outcome. (Reback *et al.* 1995, 65)

2. Arguments of this type were apparently important in the federal district court's decision to reject a settlement between Microsoft and the United States Department of Justice (Sporkin 1995).

   > Microsoft is a company that has a monopolistic position in a field that is central to this country's well being, not only for the balance of this century, but also for the 21st Century ... In this technological age, this nation's cutting edge companies must guard against being captured by their own technology and becoming robotized. (Sporkin 1995, 337–338)

   The Justice Department's recent examination of the Microsoft Network and Windows 95 seems to be based on similar reasoning, particularly since it is hard to imagine any reasonable context using standard antitrust criteria for such an investigation at the embryonic stages of a product. Even the roadblocks thrown up by the Justice Department during Microsoft's proposed acquisition of Intuit (the leader in personal finance software) seem likely to have been influenced by such thinking.
3. The material in this section draws from the authors' previous publications on the subject of network externalities. See generally Liebowitz and. Margolis (1994a, 1995b) [Chapters 3 and 4 in this volume].
4. Other researchers seem to have adopted this distinction between network effect and network externality. See Katz and Shapiro (1994, 93, 95).
5. The material in this section draws on a previous publication. See generally Liebowitz and Margolis (1995a) [Chapter 5 in this volume].
6. For an illustration of the role that this idea of path dependence has played in challenging the neoclassical economic paradigm, see the recent exchange between Samuel Bowles and Herbert Gintis (1993, 83) and Williamson (1993a, 103). See also Williamson (1993b) (discussing influence of institutional characteristics and state of knowledge on scope for improving on market outcomes).
7. See David (1992), "The accretion of technological innovations inherited from the past therefore cannot legitimately be presumed to constitute socially optimal solutions provided for us – either by heroic entrepreneurs, or by herds of rational managers operating in efficient markets."
8. We have defined *synchronization* to have a meaning similar to that which the literature has given to the term *compatibility*. Katz and Shapiro (1985, 424–425).

9. Arthur (1990, 93), "the parts of the economy that are knowledge based, on the other hand, are largely subject to increasing returns. Products such as computers, pharmaceuticals, missiles, aircraft, automobiles, software, telecommunications equipments or fiber optics."
10. Marshall thought that increasing returns was the norm for production of all goods except agricultural and extraction goods. However, as Stigler pointed out, Marshall's discussion of increasing returns indicates that he confused movements along the cost curves with movement of the cost curves, Stigler (1941, n.32; see also Ellis and Fellner 1943, 493). Some modern authors have made the same claim, almost precisely echoing Marshall, for example, Arthur (1989, n.116).
11. It is possible, and perhaps likely, that the competition between VHS and Beta enhanced the speed of innovation, as the formats fought for market leadership. Increased recording time, hi-fi sound, wireless remote controls, increased picture resolution, etc. all came about very quickly, with each format striving to keep ahead of the other. We are somewhat surprised that there are only few, if any, suggestions that competition between formats might be beneficial in the same way as competition between producers. Carlton and Klamer (1983, 446) illustrates the traditional view of a tradeoff between competition and efficiency.
12. If there were production economies at the firm level, we should see many natural and entrenched monopolies. Many early leaders of new technology industries are not those who now dominate their industries – e.g. Sony's video recorder Betamax, Digital Research's operating system (CPM) VisiCalc's spreadsheet standard, Lotus 1–2–3 (which appears to be losing to Excel) and so forth.
13. Although it may appear that we are modeling consumer behavior only with respect to the purchase flow, the impact of stocks will be added into the model later. A somewhat more general mathematical model based on both stocks and flows gives the same basic results. See Liebowitz and Margolis (1994b).
14. We assume that all members in the network are equally likely to interact with another user. If some members of the network were more important than others (i.e. greater likelihood of interaction), the overall share would be less essential than shares weighted by the importance of members in the network.
15. Of course, for any consumer, the two net value curves need not have the same sign. Moreover, different consumers need not have the same signs on their net value curves. In the latter case, there would be a group of customers with density functions like Figure 6.4, and another group with density function like Figure 6.5. The overall density function would be a mixture of these two. In the former case, if one format had a positive-sloping (with respect to market share) net value curve, and the other a downward-sloping net value curve, the relative size of the slopes in absolute terms would decide whether the result was a mixed-share, or a either-or equilibrium. If the upward-sloping curve were steeper than the downward-sloping curve, the result is identical to the case in which both curves are upward-sloping, and the either-or result prevails. If the upward-sloping curve is less steep, the results are the same as when both are downward-sloping, and a mixed-share equilibrium would prevail.

16. Even here we shouldn't let ourselves be seduced by the natural monopoly story. Yes, the (large) fixed costs imply an element of natural monopoly, but after millions of copies have been sold, how steep is the slope of the average fixed cost curve? We suspect that for many software products, the fixed costs are overwhelmed by variable costs.
17. This discussion invokes the usual assumption that the supply function does not reflect a real or technological externality
18. One possible consequence of internalizing the synchronization effect occurs when the sign of the slope of the social net value function is different from the sign of the slope of the private net value function. Since the social net value function must have a larger slope than the private net value function, this change in sign can only occur when the private net value function is downward-sloping, and the social net value function upward-sloping. In this case, the private net value function implies a mixed-share equilibrium, but the social net value function with an either-or equilibrium would result if the externality were internalized
19. In fact, when VHS came to the US market, largely under the RCA brand, it significantly undercut the price of Beta although Beta almost immediately matched the price cut. See Liebowitz and Margolis (1995a).
20. In fact, both VHS and Beta, aware of the need to generate market share, allowed other firms to put their brands on video recorders. This was the first time that Sony was willing to allow another firm to put its name on a Sony produced product (Liebowitz and Margolis 1995a [Chapter 5 in this volume]).
21. Netscape became worth nearly 6 billion dollars although the company had virtually no profits and very small sales. See *IAC Newsletter* (1995 §204).
22. Present day keyboard machines may be converted to the simplified Dvorak keyboard in local typewriter shops. "It is now available on any typewriter. And it costs as little as $5 to convert a Standard to a simplified keyboard" (Foulke 1961 160).

References

Arthur, W. B. 1989. "Competing Technologies, Increasing Returns, and Lock-in by Historical Events," *Economic Journal*, 99: 116–131.

——— 1990. "Positive Feedbacks in the Economy," *Scientific American*, 262: 92–99.

Berg, S. V. 1989. "The Production of Compatibility: Technical Standards as Collective Goods," *Kyklos*, 42.

Bork, R. H. 1978 [1997]. *The Antitrust Paradox*, New York: Free Press.

Bowles, S. and Gintis, H. 1993. "The Revenge of Homo Economicus: Contested Exchange and the Revival of Political Economy," *Journal of Economic Perspectives*, 7: 83–102.

Carlton, D. W. and Klamer, J. M. 1983. The Need for Coordination Among Firms with Special Reference to Network Industries," *University of Chicago Law Review* 50: 446–456.

David, P. A. 1992. "Heroes, Herds and Hysteresis in Technology History: Thomas Edison and 'The Battle of the Systems' Reconsidered," *Industrial and Corporate Change*, 1: 129–180.

DiLorenzo, T. J. 1985. "The Origins of Antitrust: An Interest Group Perspective," *International Review of Law and Economics*, 73.

Ellis H. S. and Fellner, W. 1943. "External Economies and Diseconomies," *American Economic Review*, 33: 493–511.

Fischer, S., Dornbusch, R. and Schmalensee, R. 1988. *Economics*, (New York: McGraw-Hill, 2nd edn.

Foulke, A. 1961. *Mr. Typewriter: A Biography of Christopher Latham Sholes*, Boston: Christopher Publishing.

IAC Newsletter 1995. "Datacoms in Brief: Netscape Communications Corp. Dec. 22," available in LEXIS.

Katz, M and Shapiro, C. 1985. "Network Externalities, Competition, and Compatibility," *American Economic Review*, 75(3): 425–440.

———— 1994. Systems Competition and Network Effects," *Journal of Economic Perspectives*, 8: 93–115.

Kitsch, E. W. K. 1997. "The Nature and Function of the Patent System," *Journal of Law and Economics*, 265: 275–280.

———— 1988. "The Nature and Function of the Patent System," *Journal of Law and Economics*, 20: 265–290.

Lande, R. H. 1982. "Wealth Transfers as the Original and Primary Concern of Antitrust: The Efficiency Interpretation Challenged," *Hastings Law Journal*, 34.

Levinson, R. J. and Coleman, M. T. 1992. "How Useful is It?," unpublished paper presented at the Western Economic Association Meetings, San Francisco, CA (July); *FTC Working Paper*.

Liebowitz, S. J. and Margolis, S. E. 1990. "The Fable of the Keys," *Journal of Law and Economics*, 33, 1–25; reprinted as Chapter 2 in this volume.

———— 1994a "Network Externality: An Uncommon Tragedy," *Journal of Economic Perspectives*, 8: 133–150; reprinted as Chapter 3 in this volume.

———— 1994b "Market Processes and the Selection of Standards," *UTD Working Paper*

———— 1995a. "Path Dependence, Lock-in, and History," *Journal of Law, Economics and Organization*, 11: 205–226; reprinted as Chapter 5 in this volume.

———— 1995b "Are Network Externalities a New Source of Market Failure?," *Research in Law and Economics*, 17: 1–22; reprinted as Chapter 4 in this volume.

Marvel, H. P. and McCafferty, S. 1985. "The Welfare Effects of Resale Price Maintenance," *Journal of Law and Economics*, 28.

McGee, J. 1980. "Predatory Pricing Revisited," *Journal of Law and Economics*, 23.

Page, W. H. 1989. "The Chicago School and the Evolution of Antitrust: Characterization, Antitrust Inquiry , and Evidentiary Sufficiency," *Virginia Law Review*, 75: 1221–1244.

Pearlstein, S. 1995. "Big Retailers Rewrite Rules of Competition Series: Winner Takes All; Microsoft, Starbucks and More," *Washington Post* (November).

Reback, G. L. 1994. Memorandum of *Amici Curiae* in Opposition to Proposed Final Judgment, *US* v. *Microsoft Corp.*, No. 94-1564 (DDC).

———— *et al.* 1995. "Why Microsoft Must be Stopped," *Upside* (February): 52–67.

Shepard, W. G. 1990. *The Economics of Industrial Organization* (Prospect Heights: Waveland Press).

Sporkin, J. 1995. "*US* v. *Microsoft Corp.*" 159 F.R.D. 318, 333–38 (DDC 1995) Rev'd, 56 F. 3d 1448 (DC circuit).

Stigler, G. J. 1941. *Production and Distribution Theories*, New York: Macmillan.

Tirole J. 1988. *The Theory of Industrial Organization*, Cambridge, MA: MIT Press.

Williamson, O. E. 1993a. "Contested Exchange Versus the Governance of Contractual Relations," *Journal of Economic Perspectives*, 7: 103–108.

——— 1993b. "Transaction Cost Economics and Organization Theory," *Industrial and Corporate Change*, 2, 107–156.

7
Path Dependence (1998)*

Path dependence is a term that has come into common use in both economics and law. In all instances that path dependence is asserted, the assertion amounts to some version of "history matters." Path dependence can mean just that: Where we are today is a result of what has happened in the past. For example, the statement "we saved and invested last year and therefore we have assets today" might be more fashionably expressed as, "the capital stock is path dependent."

Path dependence is an idea that spilled over to economics from intellectual movements that arose elsewhere. In physics and mathematics the related ideas come from chaos theory. One potential of the nonlinear models of chaos theory is sensitive dependence on initial conditions: Determination, and perhaps lock-in, by small, insignificant events. In biology, the related idea is called contingency – the irreversible character of natural selection. Scientific popularizations (Gleick 1987, Gould 1991) have moved these ideas into the public view.

We must caution, however, that the analogies are incomplete. If turtles become extinct, they will not reappear suddenly when circumstance change to make it advantageous to have a shell. But if people stop using large gas guzzling engines because gasoline has become expensive, or extend patent protection to the "look and feel" of software, they can always revert to their old ways if they came to regret the switch.

Similarly, path dependence and chaos have an apparent unity that may be misleading. In chaos theory, small events or perturbations tend to cause a system to evolve in very different ways but the system never

* *The New Palgrave Dictionary of Economics and Law*, ed. P. Newman, London: Macmillan, 1998: 17–23.

settles down in any repeatable path or fixed equilibrium. The essence of "chaos theory" is that this seemingly endless pattern, which never finds an equilibrium, is not random but rather has a determinate structure. Path dependence in economics has imported the view that minor initial perturbations are important, but has grafted this on to a theory where there are a finite number of perfectly stable alternative states, one of which will arise based on the particular initial conditions. The never ending "disequilibrium" that seems the essence of chaos theory is thus missing from the economic analysis of path dependence.

In mathematics, path independence is a condition for the existence of exact solutions for differential equations. In probability theory, a stochastic process is path dependent if the probability distribution for period t + 1 is conditioned on more than the value of the system in period t. In both cases, path independence means that it doesn't matter how you got to a particular point, only that you got there. What is interesting is that in both of these mathematical uses of path independence, history does matter in the ordinary sense. History matters in that it is what gets us to the present state. In a game of coin tossing, for example, the history of coin tosses does determine the winnings of each player. But the particular sequence of winnings does not influence the probabilities on the next toss. In contrast, if a process is path dependent, the sequence does influence the next step. So in mathematics, path dependence is a stronger claim than simply that history matters. Unfortunately, as path dependence has been borrowed into the social sciences, it has taken on several different and often conflicting meanings. Sometimes it means only that history matters in the very narrowest sense, and other times it means something more.

The issue

Economics has always recognized that history matters. The wealth of nations has much to do with the accumulation of capital of every sort; our saving, investing, studying and inventing. All this is history.

Some writers have lately raised concerns that current economic circumstances may depend in important ways on the quirks and accidents of history. Further, they raise a concern that our circumstances may depend on these quirks and accidents in particularly perverse ways. The present that we inherit or the future that we build may come about not as a result of endowments and preferences – the important givens or the inevitable forces of economic history – but rather from little things that we might easily change if we only realized how they affected us. A shelter is built at a particular clearing for no very important reason, which leads to the development of a village. In turn, the village may develop into a city. Similarly, a chance experiment with one technology leads to additional experimentation with that technology, which increases its advantages over untried alternatives. In each instance, we build on what we have, making the best of it. In this context, individuals may have limited incentives to examine whether what we have is what we ought to have and limited opportunity to effect a change. Are we optimizing in some global sense, or are we just finding some minor, local and insignificant optimum? This is the concern raised by path dependence as it has been applied to economic allocations.

A taxonomy of path dependence

Several very different types of claims appear in the literature as path dependence. Unfortunately, although these different claims may have vastly different implications, discussions of path dependence have not always distinguished among them. An earlier paper (Liebowitz and Margolis 1995 [Chapter 5 in this volume]) elaborates on these different sorts of claims and explains the potential for error in treating these claims as if they were equivalent. A summary of that taxonomy follows.

A minimal form of path dependence is present whenever there is an element of persistence or durability in a decision. For example, an individual does not alter his consumption of housing services every day in response to changes income or relative prices. Since one's exact consumption of housing is largely determined by a rental or purchase decision made some time in the past, an observer could not expect to determine the values of a consumer's housing consumption today even with full knowledge of the current values that enter that consumer's optimization problem. So here we have something that could be called path dependence. What we have today depends critically on conditions that prevailed and decisions taken at some time in the past. The observation that the consumer's bundle is narrowly wrong, given today's income and prices, would not, however, prompt anyone to claim that the consumer is irrational, nor would it prompt us to discard consumer rationality as a basis for analysis. In any practical approach to modeling the consumer's choice problem, we would recognize the presence of some fixed or quasi-fixed factors and the presence of transaction costs, and examine the consumer's action as a rational pursuit of his interests. Here we have persistence and perhaps nothing else. The consumer may well have properly predicted all future prices, incomes, family size developments, and so on. If so, there is no error or inefficiency. This is what we have termed "first-degree" path dependence. Path dependence here does no harm, it is simply the fact of durability.

Since information is always imperfect, a second circumstance is always possible. When individuals fail to predict the future perfectly, it is likely that *ex ante* efficient decisions may not turn out to be efficient in retrospect. You may build a house without knowing that five years hence a sewage treatment plant will be built nearby, lowering property values and the neighborhood amenities available. Here the inferiority of a chosen path is unknowable at the time a choice is made, but we later recognize that some alternative path would have yielded greater wealth. In such a situation, which we have termed second-degree path dependence, there is a dependence on past conditions that leads to outcomes that are regrettable and costly to change. We would not have built the house had we known what was going to transpire. This dependence is not, however, inefficient in any meaningful sense, given the assumed limitations on knowledge.

The strongest form of path dependence claim, which we have termed third-degree path dependence, is a claim that alleges the existence of remediable inefficiencies. You know a sewage plant is going to be built but build a house nearby anyway since all of your friends are buying houses there and you value being part of that neighborhood. You would rather buy a house away from the sewage plant, and so would your friends, but you and your friends are somehow unable to coordinate your actions.

The three types of path dependence make progressively stronger claims. First-degree path dependence is a simple assertion of an intertemporal relationship, with no implied error of prediction or claim of inefficiency. Second-degree path dependence stipulates that intertemporal effects together with imperfect prediction result in actions that are regrettable, though not inefficient. Third-degree path dependence requires not only that the intertemporal effects propagate error, but also that the error was avoidable.

Williamson (1993b, 140) introduces the term "remediability" to refer to the circumstance in which known feasible and preferable alternatives exist. He argues that it is necessary to establish remediability in this sense in making any claim that an allocation is inefficient. Demsetz (1973), Coase (1964), Calabresi (1968), and Dahlman (1979) have made similar points.

Clearly, the phenomena that we are calling first- and second-degree path dependence are extremely common. They are a reflection of ordinary durability and they have always been a part of economic thought. Ordinary theories of capital and decision making under uncertainty acknowledge the considerations that give us the first- and second-degree forms of path dependence.

All this is not to claim that there is nothing new to be said with regard to first- and second-degree forms. It can be both novel and important to observe persistence in circumstances where it might not be immediately apparent. For example, people will adapt their behavior and make fixed investments in response to laws and other economic institutions. These adaptations can make it costly to change these laws and institutions later on. Nevertheless the main focus and novelty of the current economic literature of path dependence is on the third-degree form, and prominent examples in this literature feature specific claims of inefficiency. For example, listen to Paul David: "The accretion of technological innovations inherited from the past therefore cannot legitimately be presumed to constitute socially optimal solutions provided for us – either by heroic enterprises or herds of rational managers operating in efficient markets" (1992, 137).

It is the third-degree path dependence claim that constitutes a new challenge to invisible-hand theorems that private optimization leads individuals to wealth maximizing allocations. Consider this example. It *could* happen that we each prefer the Beta format for video tape recording, but if we each think everyone else is buying VHS recorders, and we care about compatibility, we might all buy VHS. We each maximize privately given this expectation, and it turns out that our forecasts are correct, yet we each end up worse off that we might have. Of course, that such a thing *could* happen does not mean that it *does*. Because there is wealth loss in third-degree path dependence, various agents will have interests in avoiding this loss. It is an empirical issue, therefore, whether we do get the wrong video recorder, or more generally whether we enter or remain on inefficient paths where known, feasible, and superior alternatives exist.

While some writers do use path dependence simply to mean that history matters, many are explicitly concerned with efficiency claims. A prominent example is Mark Roe (1996), who offers a taxonomy of path dependence that upon first reading appears very similar to that offered in Liebowitz and Margolis (1995). Roe seeks to establish a contrast between the economists' alleged presumption of evolution towards efficiency and what he refers to as a "richer understanding."

In his "weak path dependence" two alternatives are equally efficient, but one is chosen and it survives. Although these alternatives may differ from one another in important ways, the choice has no efficiency consequences. Roe's "weak path dependence" is not noticeably different from his "false path dependence" which appears to be his terminology for first-degree path dependence. The only difference between Roe's "false" and "weak" path dependencies appears to be that the former are efficient and the latter are not inefficient. This appears to be a distinction without a difference.

Roe's "semi-strong form" path dependence is a choice that "has become inefficient but is not worth changing." Roe tells us on p. 648 that this form arises from errors in forecasting the future. At that point, Roe's semi-strong form appears to be parallel in most respects to our second-degree path dependence, though we have emphasized that is it misleading to call this circumstance "inefficient." An additional problem is that while the definition (1996, 648) seems clear enough, Roe's discussion of the durability of certain US financial institutions (1996, 650) demonstrates the pitfalls of his taxonomy. Roe ponders whether this durability constitutes path dependence of the weak form or the semi-strong form. In so pondering, he ignores entirely the possibility that the persistence of American financial arrangements might just be efficient, that is, an instance of his "false path dependence." Since it would only be by remarkable serendipity that the alternative arrangements would be exactly as efficient as the ones that now exist (his "weak-form" path dependence), Roe argues that current American financial institutions seem overwhelmingly likely to exhibit the semi-strong form of path dependence, at best. All this with no actual evidence that these American institutions are locked in to any inefficiencies at all.

Finally, Roe offers strong-form path dependence as "highly inefficient structures that society cannot eliminate." If we understand that "cannot eliminate" means that the costs of eliminating these structures are prohibitive, an immediate problem with this definition is that the circumstance in which something is inefficient but not worth changing is not distinct from to the circumstance that Roe calls the semi-strong form.

The distinction Roe would like to sustain here is that the costs that prevent change in the strong form are "information and public choice costs." But these costs are not fundamentally different from other sorts of cost. Roe does acknowledge this, but not its full import. He writes: "We can reinterpret [the strong form] as a variant of the second [semi-strong] form: public choice and information are real costs of action" (1996, 651). Again we have a distinction that doesn't seem to make a difference. Nevertheless, in observing this possibility, Roe does join most other observers in his observation that with rational agents, inefficiencies from path dependence can only occur where there is some coordination problem among agents. His definitional novelty would seem to be in his focus on path-created coordination (information) costs, although how and why path-created costs differ from other coordination costs is unclear.

For all his emphasis on efficiency, however, Roe's framework does not allow us to consider the possibility of *remediable* losses. In both the strong and semi-strong forms that Roe defines, there is no possibility of improvement and therefore no socially relevant inefficiency or remediable loss to be considered.

The theory of path dependence

Brian Arthur's writings on path dependence, as well as many other writings in this field (most prominently by Katz and Shapiro 1986; Farrell and Saloner 1986) share certain elements. First, most of them incorporate some version of increasing returns, which in this context may result from the usual economies of scale in the firm or from network effects. These increasing-returns economies often give rise to a second common element in this literature, models of multiple equilibria.

The role of increasing returns may be readily understood using Arthur's own numerical example (1989). In this example, society is faced with an opportunity to develop one of two technologies. For each technology, the greater the number of adopters of the technology, the greater the payoffs to those adopters.

Individuals make decisions based on their private interests and receive payoffs as shown in Table 7.1. A first adopter of any technology would expect a payoff of 10 if he adopts technology A or 4 if he adopts technology B. Under these circumstances, Arthur notes, the adopter would certainly choose A. A second adopter would reach the same conclusion, and so on, as the advantage of technology A over technology

Table 7.1 Payoffs to adopters of two technologies

Number of adoptions	0	10	20	30	40	50	60	70	80	90	100
Technology A	10	11	12	13	14	15	16	17	18	19	20
Technology B	4	7	10	13	16	19	22	25	28	31	34

B would only increase with additional adoptions of A. But notice that if the number of adopters does eventually become large, technology B offers greater payoffs. Thus for Arthur, the table tells us a story of lock-in, and lock-in to an undesirable outcome.

But there are problems with this table and the lessons that are drawn from it. First, note that the increasing payoffs in the table must be stronger for B than for A if this story is to unfold as presented (see the entry on network externalities [chapter 8 in this volume] for an explanation of why this is unlikely where increasing returns are due to network effects).

Also, the table does not allow adopters to anticipate or influence the outcome. But people clearly do both. If the first person who was faced with the opportunity to purchase a fax machine had assumed that he was going to be the only user, we might still be waiting for this technology to catch on. If a technology is owned, the owner of the technology may assure adopters that they will receive highest available payoffs by leasing applications with a cancellation option and can publicize current and planned adoptions. Additionally, technology owners could simply bribe early adopters through low prices or other compensation. Of course, the owners of both of these technologies can do this, but the owner of the technology that creates more wealth can profitably invest more to win such a contest. Concluding that lock-in is inevitable here requires that we assume a very passive role for both consumers and entrepreneurs. It requires that we assume away consumer and trade magazines, trade associations, guarantees, advertising, brand names, and so on.

If agents in the economy have the kind of information that is revealed to us in the table, they will have the motive, and some of them may have the means, of bringing about the preferred outcome. Of course, if no one has this kind of information, any alleged inefficiencies are entirely hypothetical. The alternative technology does not really present us with a known feasible alternative that is an improvement, but rather just an alternative roll of the dice. (See Liebowitz and Margolis 1995 [Chapter 5 above in this volume] for further discussion of this table.)

Models of multiple equilibria generally begin by assuming increasing returns in some form, and then adding either differences among consumers or a stochastic choice process. Figure 7.1 illustrates a typical modeling (see Liebowitz and Margolis 1996). Assume, for example, that consumers must chose between two technologies, A and B. This could be the choice between Beta and VHS or between DOS and Macintosh.

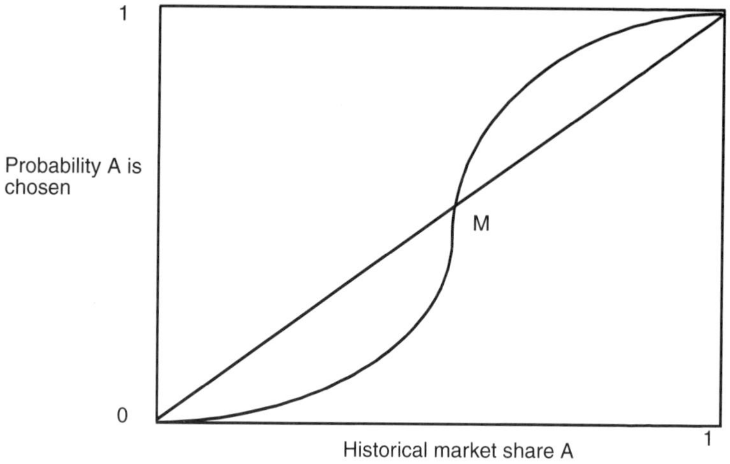

Figure 7.1 Competing technologies

An equilibrium condition is shown on the upward-sloping forty-five degree line. For an equilibrium, the fraction choosing a particular alternative must equal the fraction that has chosen that alternative. (For example, if 75 percent are using VHS, new purchases must be at 75 percent VHS for that share to persist.)

The S-shaped curve reflects consumer behavior and is consistent with increasing returns. The curve is upward-sloping because as more consumers are A users, option A is more attractive, so the probability that a consumer will chose A is larger. The S shape reflects a kind of critical mass influence. There are three equilibria. The one at M is unstable. At small displacements to the left of this intersection, the fraction choosing A is less than the fraction that have chosen A. This will lead to a smaller share for A, which leads fewer consumers to chose A, and so on. The share of A will decline to zero. To the right of M, A's share will increase until all consumers are choosing A.

These models are often invoked to illustrate that the outcome depends crucially, though perhaps perversely, on history. If we get started just slightly to the left of M, technology A will fail, regardless of the intrinsic merits of A. If we get started slightly to the right of M, A succeeds, again regardless of its merits. If A were inherently better than the alternative, a differently shaped S-shaped curve would have point M somewhere to the left of center, but the possibility of a non-A equilibrium would not be removed. History, perhaps some whimsical or coincidental start to things, will dictate the outcome.

All this comes to us dressed in the full rigor of mathematical proofs, supported by theorems on stochastic processes. The weak link, however, is in the phrase, "if we get started." That phrase buries a world of assumptions. In particular, it again abstracts from all of the things that companies do to win technological races and all of the things that consumers do to purchase well. Where we get started is a choice, not an entirely random process. The reasoning that leads to the conclusion of sensitive dependence on initial conditions – the accidents of history – is that some initial decision-maker just happens to choose A, or B, and that decision has enormous influence. But a single agent with only minimal interest in the process, who might be expected to have chosen whimsically or idiosyncratically, is not likely to have the powerful influence that is assumed for this process.

This model is often used to analyze markets in which consumers benefit from their compatibility with other consumers. In such cases, some researchers have suggested that consumers respond to the installed base of a particular technology, that is, the entire stock of commitments to a technology. Liebowitz and Margolis (1996) notes that if consumers are assumed to base their decisions on the entire stock of old commitments, the resulting models will show great deal of inertia. But if consumers are assumed to respond to concurrent sales, the resulting models will suggest that markets are much more agile. Further, Liebowitz and Margolis (1996) argue that consumers ought to be interested in predicting future compatibility, and therefore should be interested in recent and current activity rather that the entire history of consumers' commitments. Markets are more agile under these circumstances because it is much easier to change the flow of new commitments that it is to change all of history. That is to say, it is a fairly manageable matter for the owner of a technology to choose, or change, the position from which we start out on Figure 7.1. The owner of a viable technology might invoke any of the strategies we discussed above, or might just simply give some product away in order to move the market from the left of M to the right of M.

None of which proves that the best technology necessarily prevails. It only goes to demonstrate that these models are merely models. They demonstrate particular results in the context of particular assumptions. Whether we are considering the increasing returns story of Table 7.1, or the multiple equilibrium model that is illustrated with Figure 7.1, we are left with an empirical question: Have the modeling choices that give us these models captured something important about the way that markets work?

Evidence for third-degree path dependence

The literature of path dependence, both theoretical and empirical, contains a number of claims that path dependent processes lead us to inefficiencies, even for products sold in open markets. Brian Arthur cites as examples of this inefficiency the QWERTY typewriter keyboard and the internal combustion engine (Arthur 1989), and the VHS videorecorder (Arthur 1990). Paul David (1985) tells the story of the QWERTY keyboard as a clear example of market failure. Paul Krugman's *Peddling Prosperity* (1994) contains an entire chapter called "The Economics of QWERTY," where he concludes, "In QWERTY worlds, markets cannot be trusted."

Empirical support for the third-degree claim for path dependence rests almost entirely on a handful of cases. Of these, the typewriter keyboard history is the case that is most often invoked both to illustrate and to support third-degree path dependence paradigm. (Liebowitz and Margolis (1990 [Chapter 2 in this volume] is a detailed account of this.)

There are other cases that have been presented at one time or another as path dependent inefficiency. For example, Van Vleck (1997) reconsiders the case of Britain's small coal cars, long considered an example of "technical backwardness." She finds that the small coal car was in fact well suited to Britain's geography and coal distribution systems. Ribstein and Kobayashi (1996) examine the possibility that the adoption of state laws concerning limited liability companies exhibits path dependence and find little persistence of initial statutory forms.

Our reading of the evidence is that there are as yet no proven examples of third-degree path dependence in markets. In nonmarket arenas, where there may be less opportunity for entrepreneurs to profit from removing inefficiencies, third-degree path dependence is more likely to occur. Of course, these nonmarket arenas may exist largely because political bodies have chosen to pursue objectives other than economic efficiency.

References

Arthur, W. B. 1989. "Competing Technologies, Increasing Returns, and Lock-in by Historical Events," *Economic Journal*, 99: 116–131.

———— 1990. "Positive Feedbacks In the Economy," *Scientific American*, 262: 92–99.

———— 1994. *Increasing Returns And Path Dependence in the Economy*, Ann Arbor: University of Michigan Press.

Calabresi, V. 1968. "Transactions Costs, Resource Allocation and Liability Rules: A Comment," *Journal of Law And Economics*, 11: 67–74.

Coase, R. H. 1964. "The Regulated Industries: Discussion," *American Economic Review*, 54: 194–197.
Dahlman, C. 1979. "The Problem Of Externality," *Journal of Law And Economics*, 22: 141–163.
David, P. A. 1985. "Clio and the Economics Of QWERTY," *American Economic Review*, 75: 332–337.
———— 1992. "Heroes, Herds and Hysteresis In Technological History: Thomas Edison and 'The Battle Of the Systems' Reconsidered," *Industrial and Corporate Change*, 1: 129–180.
Demsetz, H. 1973. "Information and Efficiency: Another Viewpoint," *Journal of Law And Economics*, 10: 1–22.
Gleick, J. 1987. *Chaos: Making A New Science*, New York: Penguin.
Gould, S. J. 1991. "The Panda Thumb Of Technology," In Gould, S. J. *Bully For Brontosaurus*, New York: W. W. Norton.
Katz, M. and Shapiro, C. 1986. "Technology Adoption in the Presence of Network Externalities," *Journal of Political Economy*, 94: 822–841.
Katzner, D. 1993. "Some Notes On the Role of History and the Definition of Hysteresis and Related Concepts in Economic Analysis," *Journal of Post Keynesian Economics*, 15(3): 323–345.
Kobayashi, B. and Ribstein, L. 1996. "Evolutions of Spontaneous Uniformity: Evidence From the Evolution of the Limited Liability Company," *Economic Inquiry*, 34: 464–483.
Krugman, P. 1994. *Peddling Prosperity*, New York: W. W. Norton.
Lardner, J. 1987. *Fast Forward*, New York: W. W. Norton,.
Liébowitz, S. J. and Margolis, S. E. 1990. "The Fable of the Keys," *Journal of Law and Economics*, 33: 1–25; reprinted as Chapter 2 in this volume.
———— 1995. "Path Dependence, Lock-in, and History," *Journal of Law, Economics and Organization*, 11: 205–226; reprinted as Chapter 5 in this volume.
———— 1996. "Should Technology Choice be a Concern of Antitrust Policy?," *Harvard Journal of Law and Technology*, 9: 283–318; reprinted as Chapter 6 in this volume.
Lopatka, J. E. and Page, W. 1995. "Microsoft, Monopolization, and Network Externalities: Some Uses and Abuses of Economic Theory in Antitrust Decision Making," *The Antitrust Bulletin*, 40: 317–369.
Mokyr, J. 1991. "Evolutionary Biology, Technological Change and Economic History," *Bulletin of Economic Research*, 43: 127–147.
Ribstein, L. and Kobayashi, B. 1996. "An Economic Analysis of Uniform State Laws," *Journal of Legal Studies*, 34: 131–199.
Roe, M. J. 1996. "Chaos and Evolution in Law and Economics," *Harvard Law Review*, 109: 641–668.
Van Vleck, V. N. 1997. "Delivering Coal by Road and by Rail in Great Britain: The Efficiency of the 'Silly Little Bobtailed Coal Wagons'," *Journal of Economic History*, 57: 139–160.
Williamson, O. E. 1993a. "Contested Exchange Versus the Governance of Contractual Relations," *Journal of Economic Perspectives*, 7: 103–108.
———— 1993b. "Transaction Cost Economics and Organization Theory," *Industrial and Corporate Change*, 2: 107–156.

8
Network Externalities (Effects) (1998)*

Network externality has been defined as a change in the benefit, or surplus, that an agent derives from a good when the number of other agents consuming the same kind of good changes (Katz and Shapiro 1985). As fax machines increase in popularity, for example, your fax machine becomes increasingly valuable since you will have greater use for it. This allows, in principle, the value received by consumers to be separated into two distinct parts. One component, which elsewhere we have labeled the autarky value, is the value generated by the product even if there are no other users. The second component, which we have called synchronization value, is the additional value derived from being able to interact with other users of the product, and it is this latter value that is the essence of network effects.

An illustration: As this essay is being written, commentators are speculating whether Apple computer will survive, since some analysts think that its network (base of users) is shrinking below a minimum acceptable level. Because the actual quantity of Apple computers being sold is still amongst the very largest of all personal computer manufacturers, allowing Apple to take advantage of any economies of scale in production, and its computers are not thought to be deficient in terms of quality, any lack of viability must be due to the fact that the network of Apple computer users is too small. In other words, the synchronization value of Apple computers is thought to be too low.

First a definitional concern: Network effects should not properly be called network externalities unless the participants in the market fail to internalize these effects. After all, it would not be useful to have the

* *The New Palgrave Dictionary of Economics and Law*, ed P. Newman, London: Macmillan, 1998: 671–675.

term "externality" mean something different in this literature than it does in the rest of economics. Unfortunately, however, the term externality has indeed been used somewhat carelessly. Although the individual consumers of a product are not likely to internalize the effect of their joining a network on the network's other members, the owner of the network may very well internalize such effects. When the owner of a network (or technology) is able to internalize such network effects, they are no longer externalities. This distinction, first discussed in Liebowitz and Margolis (1994 [Chapter 3 in this volume]) now seems to be adopted by some authors (e.g. Katz and Shapiro 1994) but has not been universally adopted.

Putting aside definitional concerns, the import of network effects comes largely from the belief that they are endemic to new, high-tech industries, and that accordingly such industries experience problems that are different in character from the problems that have, for more ordinary commodities, been solved by markets (Farrell and Saloner 1985; Katz and Shapiro 1985; Arthur 1996). The purported problems due to network effects are several, but the most arresting is a claim that markets may adopt an inferior product or network in the place of some superior alternative. Thus if network effects are a typical characteristic of modern technologies, the theory suggests that markets may be inadequate for managing the fruits of such technologies.

The concept of network externality has been applied in the economics of standards, where a primary concern is the choice of a correct standard (Farrell and Saloner 1985; Katz and Shapiro 1985; Besen and Farrell 1994; Liebowitz and Margolis 1996 [Chapter 6 in this volume]). The concept has also played a role in discussions of path dependence (Arthur 1989, 1990; David 1985; Liebowitz and Margolis 1990, 1995a [Chapters 2 and 5 in this volume]).

Two types of network effects have been identified. *Direct* network effects have been defined as those generated through a direct physical effect of the number of purchasers on the value of a product (e.g. fax machines). *Indirect* network effects are "market mediated effects" such as cases where complementary goods (e.g. toner cartridges) are more readily available or lower in price as the number of users of a good (laser printers) increases. In early contributions, however, this distinction was not carried into models of network effects. Once network effects were embodied in payoff functions, any distinction between direct and indirect effects was ignored in developing models and drawing conclusions. However, our 1994 paper demonstrates that the two types of effects will typically have different economic implications.

It is now generally agreed (Katz and Shapiro, 1994) that the consequences of internalizing direct and indirect network effects are quite different. Generally, indirect network effects are pecuniary in nature and therefore should not be internalized. Pecuniary externalities do not impose deadweight losses if left uninternalized, whereas they do impose (monopoly or monopsony) losses if internalized. An interesting aspect of the literature on network externalities is that it has seemed to ignore, and thus repeat, earlier mistakes regarding pecuniary externalities (for the resolution of pecuniary externalities see Young 1913; Knight 1924; Ellis and Fellner 1943).

Concern about marginal adjustment of the level of network activity has not been the primary focus of network externality modeling; it has focused, instead, primarily on selection among competing networks. The discussion below follows this relative emphasis. It briefly considers the issue of levels of network activities in the next section, and then turns to the choice of networks.

Levels of network related activities

Harvey Leibenstein's work on bandwagon and snob effects (1950) anticipated much of the current discussion of network effects. His main result was that demand curves are more elastic when consumers derive positive value from increases in the size of the market.

One branch of the more recent network literature would fit easily into the Leibenstein framework. Such research has reexamined various economic models with network effects introduced. For example, an analysis of the impacts of unauthorized software copying will change when network effects are introduced. Since unauthorized users increase the size of a network just as do authorized users, and larger network sizes increase the value derived by authorized (paying) users, any harm from unauthorized copying might be mitigated, or perhaps reversed.

The difference between a network effect and a network externality lies in whether the impact of an additional user on other users is somehow internalized. Since the synchronization effect is almost always assumed to be positive in this literature, the social value from another network user will always be greater than the private value. If network effects are not internalized, the equilibrium network size may be smaller than is efficient. For example, if the network of telephone users were not owned, it would likely be smaller than optimal since no agent would capture the benefits that an additional member of the network would confer on other members. (Alternatively, if the network effects were negative a congestion externality might imply that networks tend to be larger than optimal.) Where networks are owned, this effect is internalized and under certain conditions the profit maximizing network size will also be socially optimal. (see Liebowitz and Margolis 1995b [Chapter 4 in this volume]).

Perhaps surprisingly, the problem of internalizing the network externality is largely unrelated to the problem of choice between competing networks that is taken up in the next section. In the case of positive network effects, all networks are too small. Therefore, it is not the *relative* market shares of two competing formats but rather the overall level of network activity that will be affected by this difference between private and social values. This is completely compatible with standard results on conventional externalities. For reasons that we will expand on below, this is a far more likely consequence of uninternalized network effects than the more exotic cases of incorrect choices of networks, standards or technologies.

Network size is a real and significant issue that is raised by network effects. Nevertheless, this issue has received fairly little attention in contemporary discussions of network externality, perhaps because it is well handled by more conventional economic models.

Choice among competing networks under increasing returns

Recent work on network externalities challenges economists' traditional use of decreasing returns and grants primacy to economies to scale. Positive network effects, which raise the value received by consumers as markets get larger, have impacts that are very similar to conventional firm-level economies of scale. If we start an analysis with the assumption that firms produce similar but incompatible products (networks), and that the network effects operate only within the class of compatible products, then competitors (networks) with larger market shares will have an advantage over smaller competitors, *ceteris paribus*. If larger competitors have a forever widening advantage over smaller firms, we have entered the realm of natural monopoly, which is exactly where most models that address network and standards choices find themselves.

It is critical to note, however, that network effects are not in general *sufficient* for natural-monopoly-type results. In cases where average production costs are falling, constant, or nonexistent, network effects would be sufficient for a result of natural monopoly. Many, if not most, models in this area ignore production costs and thus with any assumption of positive network effects are unavoidably constructed as instances of natural monopoly. But notice that if production costs exhibit decreasing returns, and if these decreasing returns overwhelm the network effects, then natural monopoly is not implied, and competing incompatible networks (standards) will be possible.

Though economists have long accepted the possibility of increasing returns, they have generally judged that, except in fairly rare instances, the economy operates in a range of decreasing returns. Some proponents of network externalities models predict that as newer technologies take over a larger share of the economy, the share of the economy described by increasing returns will increase. Brian Arthur has emphasized these points to a general audience: "[R]oughly speaking, diminishing returns hold sway in the traditional part of the economy – the processing industries. Increasing returns reign in the newer part – the knowledge-based industries ... They call for different management techniques, strategies, and codes of government regulation. They call for different understandings" (Arthur 1996, 101).

If the choice of a standard or network is dominated by natural monopoly elements, then only one standard will survive in the market. It is thus of great importance that the standard that comes to dominate the market also be the best of the alternative standards available. Traditionally it has been assumed that the natural monopolist who comes to dominate a market will be at least as efficient as any other producer. This assumption is challenged in the network literature although specifics differ across the many models populating it. The issue that occurs time and again is that we lose the usual assurances that the products that prevail in markets are those that yield the greatest surpluses.

The mere existence of network effects and increasing returns is not sufficient to lead to the choice of an inferior technology. For that, some additional assumptions are needed. One common assumption that can generate a prediction of inefficient network choice is that the network effect differs across the alternative networks. In particular, it is sometimes assumed that the network offering the greatest surplus when network participation is large also offers the smallest surplus when participation is small. This condition, however, is not likely to be satisfied, since synchronization effects are likely to be uniform. For example, if there is value in a cellular telephone network becoming larger, this should be equally true whether the network is digital or analog. Similarly, the network value of an additional user of a particular videorecorder format is purported to be the benefits accrued by having more opportunities to exchange video tapes. But this extra value does not depend on the particular format of videorecorder chosen. If network effects are the same for all versions of a given product, it is very unlikely that the wrong format would be chosen if both are available at the same time [see Chapter 7 in this volume].

Common restrictions in network effects models

As we have noted, network externality models often feature particular outcomes: Survival of only one network or standard, unreliability of market selection, and the entrenchment of incumbents. In formal models, these results follow inevitably from assumptions that are common simplifications in economic theory and that appear to be relatively unrestrictive. As applied in these network models, however, these assumptions are both critically responsible for the results and unappealingly restrictive.

Two important limitations of many network externalities models are the assumptions of constant marginal production cost and network value functions that rise without limit (see, for example, Chou and Shy 1990, 260; Church and Gandal 1993, 246; Katz and Shapiro 1986, 829; and Farrell and Saloner 1992, 16). Matutes and Regibeau (1992) consider issues of duopoly and compatibility under a similar structure. Such assumptions impose an inexhaustible economy of large-scale operation. If network size could reach a point where additional participation did not provide additional value to participants, then increases in scale would no longer be advantageous and it would be possible for multiple networks to compete at an efficient output.

Without investigation, it seems unreasonable that in all or most new-technology industries the law of diminishing marginal product is somehow suspended. While the scale properties of a technology pertain to the simultaneous expansion of all inputs, it seems evident that resource limitations do ultimately constrain firm size. Economists have long supposed that limitations of management play a role in this, a relationship formalized in Radner (1992). The resource constraints faced by America Online in early 1997 is an example of this type of effect, even if it was only a short run phenomenon at that time.

Another limitation is the common assumption that consumers are identical in their valuations of competing networks. Once heterogeneous tastes are allowed it becomes feasible for competing networks to coexist with one another even though each exhibits natural monopoly characteristics (e.g. If some computer owners much prefer Macintoshes and others much prefer the PC, they could both coexist).

A further restriction in the modeling is the undifferentiated value received by consumers when another consumer joins a network, regardless of who the new consumer is. If economists, for example, much prefer to have other economists join their network as opposed to, say, sociologists, then a sociologist has a smaller network effect than another economist. Such differential network impacts make it possible for economists to form a coalition that switches to a new standard even if the new standard failed to attract many sociologists. This latter point will prove to be of great importance when examining empirical examples of choosing the wrong standard, where large entities such as multinational firms and governments play an important role.

The empirical relevance of network effects and increasing returns

Although many technologies have tended to evolve into single formats (e.g. home-use VCRs are almost all of the VHS variety) some portion of these may actually have evolved for reasons having little to do with either network effects *or* increasing returns. We should not be surprised to find that where there are differences in the performance of various standards, one may prevail over the others simply because it is better suited to the market.

First of all, the extent (and homogeneity) of network effects may be much more limited than is commonly assumed. For example, in the case of word-processors, it may be quite important for a small group of collaborators to use identical software so as to be perfectly compatible with each other. Similarly, compatibility may be important for employees within a firm. But compatibility with the rest of the world may be relatively unimportant, unimportant enough to be overwhelmed by differences in preferences, so that multiple networks could survive. Networks that serve niche markets well (such as word-processors specializing in mathematical notation), might not be significantly disadvantaged by network effects.

As an illustration, consider the empirical examples of tax software and financial software. By far the dominant firm in North America is Intuit, with its Turbo-Tax products and Quicken financial software. This market seems to have tilted strongly toward a single producer. Yet network effects should be virtually nonexistent for these products. Consumers do *not* exchange this type of information with one another. A better explanation that is consistent with the product reviews in computer magazines is that these products are just *better* than the alternatives.

Similarly, for large firms, compatibility within the firm should be of great importance, but compatibility outside the firm might be of little consequence. For many products where the majority of customers are large firms, producers will not encounter natural monopoly elements since there may be little or no network advantage in selling to multiple firms. Firms using spreadsheets, for example, will likely benefit from compatibility within the firm and there will be strong network effects *within* a firm. Across firms, however, network effects might be non-existent. If the only natural monopoly element in spreadsheet production was the network effect (e.g. constant or increasing spreadsheet-production costs), we might find multiple producers of spreadsheets, each with a natural monopoly over the firms that had adopted that particular spreadsheet, but with no producer being a natural monopolist for the market as a whole.

Regarding increasing returns in production leading to a single product or standard (independent of network effects), it is true that the past decades have evidenced a number of technologies that have experienced enormous declines in prices and tremendous growth in sales. Nevertheless, it is not clear that this is the result of increasing returns to (network) scale *per se*. Since bigger has been cheaper, it has often been assumed that bigger causes cheaper. But an available alternative explanation is that as technologies have advanced with time, the average cost curves (derived under *ceteris paribus* assumptions) have themselves been shifting down over time. If that is the case, the implied causality may be reversed: Cheaper causes bigger. Consider for example the history of old technologies, such as refrigerators and automobiles (or a modern product such as the personal computer). These industries, currently thought to exhibit conventional decreasing returns in production (beyond a minimum efficient scale), experienced tremendous cost decreases, along with tremendous increases in utilization, early in their histories. Changes in technology may have been more important than changes in scale. (For a related discussion of increasing returns and monopolization, see Stigler 1941 68–76.)

Policy implications

The theory of network externality is currently playing a role in several antitrust actions, the most prominent of which are the investigations of Microsoft by the Justice Department over various aspects of Microsoft's behavior including its attempted purchase of Intuit, the inclusion of the Microsoft Network as an icon in Windows 95, Microsoft's attempt to wrest control of the web browser market from Netscape and so forth. The claim seems to be that since markets cannot be relied upon to choose the best standards or bring about the right networks, governments might wish to investigate and control firms' efforts to make standards or establish networks. These theories played a central role in the *Amicus Curiae* brief against the Microsoft consent decree presented by four anonymous parties (Sporkin 1995, *Microsoft Corp.*).

Clearly the potential to misuse such as yet unsubstantiated theories in antitrust actions by competitors unable to win in the marketplace is very great, not unlike that of various theories of predation. With so little empirical support for these theories, it appears at best premature and at worst simply wrong to use them as the basis for antitrust decisions.

It is also possible that network effects may cast in a new light the role of copyright and patent laws. First, networks are likely to be too small if network effects are not internalized. Intellectual property laws are one means by which such network effects can be internalized, since ownership is an ideal method of internalization.

The possibility that networks can compete with each other suggests a further consideration regarding intellectual property law. Where one standard is owned and another is not, we can have less confidence that an unowned but superior standard will be able to prevail against an owned standard, since the owner of a standard can appropriate the benefits of internalizing any network effects. Although we do not have any evidence that inferior standards have prevailed against superior standards (in free markets), this may be in large part because most standards are supported by companies that have some form of ownership such as patent, copyright, or business positioning. The greatest chance for some form of third-degree path dependence [see Chapter 7 in this volume] to arise would be if an unowned standard with dispersed adherents were to engage in competition with a standard that had well defined ownership. Further research in this area is needed before any firm conclusions can be drawn, however.

Conclusions

Network effects are undoubtedly real and important phenomena. The popular and very compelling example is the telephone network. Who would deny that the value of phone service depends heavily on the number of other people who have phone service? Contemporary technologies expand that example enormously.

The enthusiasm for recognizing and understanding these phenomena should not, however, lead us to inappropriate or premature conclusions. As we have noted above, there are distinctions and reservations that ought to be maintained. The first and broadest is that between network effects and network externalities. A further distinction is between pecuniary externalities and real ones. Even for the set of real externalities, it is important to note the distinction between the problem of network size and that of network choice, the boundedness of the network effect, the likely symmetry of network effects for alternative products, the ability of large consumers to self-internalize network effects, and the influence of differences in tastes.

Finally, we would urge some reservation about the empirical validity of economies of production scale for many high-tech products. If these products have diseconomies of scale at some production level, these production costs may overturn other natural monopoly elements. Improvements in production costs, as with many other economic results, may have more to do with being smarter than with being bigger.

References

Arthur, W. B. 1989. "Competing Technologies, Increasing Returns, and Lock-in by Historical Events," *Economic Journal*, 99: 116–131.

——— 1990. "Positive Feedbacks in the Economy," *Scientific American*, 262: 92–99.

——— 1996. "Increasing Returns and the New World of Business," *Harvard Business Review*, 72: 100–109.

Besen, S. M. and Farrell, J. 1994. "Choosing How to Compete: Strategies and Tactics in Standardization," *Journal of Economic Perspectives*, 8: 117–131.

Chou, D. and Shy, O. 1990. "Network Effects Without Network Externalities," *International Journal of Industrial Organization*, 8: 259–270.

Church, J. and Gandal, N. 1993. "Complementary Network Externalities and Technological Adoption," *International Journal of Industrial Organization*, 11: 239–260.

David, P. A. 1985. "Clio and the Economics of QWERTY," *American Economic Review*, 75: 332–337.

Ellis, H. S. and Fellner, W. 1943. "External Economies and Diseconomies," *American Economic Review*, 33: 493–511.

Farrell, J. and Saloner, G. "Standardization, Compatibility, and Control," *American Economic Review*, 75: 424–440.

——— 1985. "Standardization, Compatibility, and Innovation," *Rand Journal of Economics*, 16: 70–83.

——— 1992. "Converters, Compatibility, and Control of Interfaces," *The Journal of Industrial Economics*, 40: 9–36.

Katz, M. L. and Shapiro, C. 1985. "Network Externalities, Competition, and Compatibility," *American Economic Review*, 75: 424–440.

——— 1986. "Technology Adoption in the Presence of Network Externalities," *Journal of Political Economy*, 94(4): 822–841.

——— 1994. "Systems Competition and Network Effects," *Journal of Economic Perspectives*, 8: 93–115.

Knight, F. H. 1924. "Some Fallacies in the Interpretation of Social Cost," *Quarterly Journal of Economics*, 38: 582–606.

Leibenstein, H. 1950. "Bandwagon, Snob, and Veblen Effects in the Theory of Consumer's Demand," *Quarterly Journal of Economics*, 64: 183–207.

Liebowitz, S. J. and Margolis, S. E. 1990. "The Fable of the Keys," *Journal of Law and Economics*, 33: 1–25; reprinted as Chapter 2 in this volume.

——— 1994. "Network Externality: An Uncommon Tragedy," *Journal of Economic Perspectives*, 8: 133–150; reprinted as Chapter 3 in this volume.

——— 1995a. "Path Dependence, Lock-in, and History," *Journal of Law, Economics and Organization*, 11: 205–226; reprinted as Chapter 5 in this volume.

——— 1995b. "Are Network Externalities a New Source of Market Failure?," *Research in Law and Economics*, 17: 1–22; reprinted as Chapter 5 in this volume.

——— 1996. "Should Technology Choice be a Concern of Antitrust Policy?," *Harvard Journal of Law and Technology*, 9: 283–318; reprinted as Chapter 6 in this volume.

Matutes, C. and Regibeau, P. 1992. "Compatibility and Bundling of Complementary Goods in a Duopoly," *The Journal of Industrial Economics*, 40: 37–54.

Radner, R. 1992. "Hierarchy: the Economics of Managing," *Journal of Economic Literature*, 30: 1382–1415.

Sporkin, J. 1995. "*United States of America* v. *Microsoft Corporation*," Civil Action No. 94-1564 (United States District Court for the District of Columbia), 159 F.R.D. 318; 1995 U.S. Dist. LEXIS 1654; 1995–1 Trade Cas. (CCH) P70,897.

Stigler, G. J. 1941. *Production and Distribution Theories*, New York: Macmillan.

Young, A. A. 1913. "Pigou's Wealth and Welfare," *Quarterly Journal of Economics*, 27: 672–686.

9

Dismal Science Fictions: Network Effects, Microsoft, and Antitrust Speculation (1998)*

Introduction

Revolutions in science and technology, while bringing benefits to large numbers of people, also bring stresses of various sorts. New technologies can alter the scale of business activities, the geographic distribution of these activities, the types of firms that are involved in production and distribution, and the distribution of wealth. The benefits are many: consumers may enjoy cheaper goods and new products; firms that implement the new technology may make very substantial profits; workers may enjoy higher wages, new types of careers, and generally expanded opportunities. At the same time, some businesses and workers will lose as new skills and methods of commerce supplant old ones.

In these circumstances, interested parties have often enlisted legislation or regulation to preserve old interests or defend new ones. The historical motivations for U S antitrust law have been at least in part an attempt by various parties to defend their stakes in the economy. The antitrust debates over new computer technologies in general, and Microsoft in particular, are consistent with this pattern. In particular, today, as in the past, there are calls for restrictions on the leading firms in new technology industries. While the focus for scrutiny is Microsoft, the effects are likely to reach much further. As with past generations of antitrust law, the precedent and enforcement practice reached in the current debate are likely to have a wide and long-lasting influence.

In the policy debates surrounding the antitrust campaign against Microsoft, both the Justice Department and various parties that have

* *Cato Policy Analysis*, Washington, DC: Cato Insitute, 1998.

aligned against Microsoft have invoked novel and incomplete economic theories to justify action against a firm with a large market share. In markets for high-technology products, it is alleged, a company with a head start or the largest market share will have what may prove to be an insurmountable advantage over its rivals. These new theories are associated with terminology such as increasing returns, network effects, path dependence, or lock-in.

According to these theories, where industries exhibit increasing returns, certain old-fashioned beliefs about market outcomes and market processes should be cast aside in favor of the following: First, the success of products in the marketplace comes from size, good timing, aggressive strategies, or luck, rather than their inherent values. Second, we should have no confidence that new products, technologies, or standards should be able to displace their established counterparts, even if they offer important advantages. Finally, and perhaps most directly of interest to the antitrust enforcers, any action taken by a market leader that might increase market share, such as lowering price, should receive heightened scrutiny, since such actions have the likely consequence of locking-out superior products.

Widespread acceptance of such theories would necessitate a radical rethinking of antitrust policy. Further, it appears that such theories are holding considerable sway in today's antitrust debates. For example, *Business Week* reported:

> Instead of basing his attack against Microsoft on outdated economic theories that demonize bigness, Assistant Attorney General Joel I. Klein is relying on a developing body of antitrust thinking that warns that the threat of anticompetitive behavior could be even greater in high technology than in traditional industries. This research on "network externalities" deserves to be taken seriously ... The Microsoft case is one of the first ever in which Justice has made use of network theory. (Garland 1997)

Even the pundits at the *Wall Street Journal*, a publication not known for embracing radical expansions of antitrust law, have fallen for lock-in theory. Alan Murray recently opined, on the paper's front page, that: "[H]igh-tech industries might be more susceptible to antitrust problems than their low-tech brethren. That's because consumers often feel a need to buy the product that everyone else is using, even if it isn't the best, so their equipment is compatible. Economists call this 'network externalities'."

> It's why most people use a keyboard that begins clumsily with the letters QWERTY; why most videos are now available only in VHS format; and why Windows has become the dominant operating system. (Murray 1997)

These new theories provide a convenient solution for those who would bring antitrust claims to bear against market leaders such as Microsoft. Those "outdated economic theories," so cavalierly dismissed in the above quote, might fail to support antitrust enforcement against the current generation of market leaders in high-tech industries. Standard theories of monopoly, which have long provided what economic foundation there was for antitrust, hold that monopoly restricts output in order to elevate prices. Monopoly was bad only for these reasons. In contrast to this concern, what we seem to see in high-technology markets are falling prices and increased quantities, even as market shares of the market leaders become extremely large.[1] Absent an allegation of high prices, antitrust authorities have looked to these new lock-in theories in order to provide some economic support for their actions against such high-technology firms.

The problem with all this is that these new economic theories are fundamentally flawed. Our writings, appearing in academic journals since 1990 [and reprinted in this volume], show that the case for lock-in is an extraordinarily weak one.

While our work has criticized lock-in theories as being based on overly restricted assumptions, the more telling criticism has to do with the lack of empirical support for these theories. Alleged examples of lock-in seem, when held up to critical scrutiny, to be more the products of wishful thinking than the fruits of serious study. This essay reviews the case against the economic theory of lock-in and analyzes the lock-in claims levied against Microsoft in recent months. With regard to Microsoft, as elsewhere, neither theory nor fact supports the call for antitrust enforcement measures.

The economics of increasing returns, network effects, and path dependence

There is a closely related group of ideas that come together under the theory of lock-in. *Increasing returns* are said to occur wherever the net benefits of an activity increase with the scale of the activity. Within a firm, increasing returns are present if the average cost of producing goods decreases as the output of the firm increases. All firms are thought to have increasing returns at outputs that are small. Economists have also long considered cases in which increasing returns are more persistent, such that even if a single firm were supplying the entire industry demand, it would still experience decreases in average costs as output increased. In such a case, known as *natural monopoly*, monopoly is the likely evolution of a free market. Further, in this instance, monopoly offers society the opportunity for the lowest possible production cost because it takes full advantage of decreasing costs: *In this instance monopoly is socially desirable.* The problem, however, is that even though such a monopoly would minimize costs, it would be expected to restrict output and elevate price.

Many industries regarded as experiencing these persistent economies to scale are those treated as public utilities: Electricity, telephone, natural gas, cable TV, and others. The policy response to this circumstance has been price (or rate of return) regulation. It is interesting, particularly in the context of the antitrust debate over operating systems, that the industries that we have traditionally regarded as natural monopolies are now being widely deregulated.

Network effects, also sometimes called *network externalities*, may be understood as a special case of increasing returns. With a network effect, the benefit that someone gets from purchasing a product depends upon the number of other users of the product. For example, people who buy fax machines will find them to be more valuable as other people buy compatible fax machines. The relationship to increasing returns is straightforward. As a product becomes more popular, it will become more valuable to consumers, giving it an ever-increasing advantage over its smaller rivals. As a result, smaller rivals are likely to disappear. We may settle on a single format for videocassette recorders or a single communication protocol for fax machines. This need not constitute a monopoly in the usual sense of a single firm, depending on ownership of the standard, but in many cases it will.

As is the case for natural monopoly, a monopoly outcome may be socially desirable. This observation is critical for consideration of antitrust policies. Of course, the potential for monopoly price elevation still applies, and if it occurred, such price elevation might result in social losses. But this has not been the concern of the network externality literature that apparently has influenced the Justice Department.

The problem of path dependence, or lock-in, begins with the observation that monopoly is a likely outcome of network effects. But the concern here shifts to whether the best technology or product is chosen. The allegation of this literature is that we are likely to get the wrong monopolist, producing the wrong product, not that the monopolist charges the wrong price or produces the wrong quantity.

Theories of lock-in

A useful starting point in understanding the theory of lock-in is an example [examined also in earlier chapters in this volume] presented by Brian Arthur, one of the leading figures in the literature of lock-in.

Table 9.1 presents his example (see Arthur 1989). In Arthur's table, society faces an opportunity to develop one of two technologies. For each technology, the greater the number of adopters of the technology, the greater the payoffs to those adopters. Network effects, for example, could cause this relationship.

Individuals make decisions based on their private interests and receive payoffs as shown in the table. The first adopter of technology A would expect a payoff of 10. Similarly, the first adopter of technology B would expect a payoff of 4. Under these circumstances, Arthur notes, the very first adopter of any technology would certainly choose A, thus receiving 10 instead of 4. A second adopter would reach the same conclusion, and so on, since the advantage of technology A over technology B would only increase with additional adoptions of A. But notice that if the number of adopters does eventually become large, technology B offers greater payoffs. Thus for Arthur, the table tells a story of lock-in to an undesirable outcome.

There are problems with this table and the lessons that are drawn from it. First, note that the increasing payoffs in the table must be stronger for B than for A if this story is to unfold as presented. Yet there is no reason to think that among competing technologies the one with the greatest payoffs with many users does not also have greater payoffs with smaller numbers of users. At a minimum, this restriction narrows the set of possible lock-ins.

Also, the table does not allow adopters to anticipate or influence the outcome. But people clearly do both. If the first person faced with the opportunity to purchase a fax machine had assumed that he was going to be the only user, we would still be waiting for this technology to

Table 9.1 Payoffs to adopters of two technologies

Number of adoptions	0	10	20	30	40	50	60	70	80	90	100
Technology A	10	11	12	13	14	15	16	17	18	19	20
Technology B	4	7	10	13	16	19	22	25	28	31	34

catch on. If a technology is owned, the owner of the technology may assure adopters that they will receive highest available payoffs by leasing applications with a cancellation option, publicizing current and planned adoptions, or simply bribing adopters through low prices or other compensation. Of course, the owners of both of these technologies can do this, but the owner of the technology that creates more wealth can profitably invest more to win such a contest (For a more complete discussion of this table see Liebowitz and Margolis 1995 [Chapters in this volume].)

Lock-in theory is often argued in the context of formal models with multiple equilibria. In these models, several different outcomes are equally likely, even though they may not be equally desirable, and the choice among them is largely a matter of coincidence. Better products, it is shown, may not win. All of this comes to us dressed in the full rigor of mathematical proofs, supported by theorems on stochastic processes. These models, although seemingly more complex than the simple table in Arthur (1989), again abstract from most of the things that companies do to win technological races and most of the things that consumers do to purchase well (see Liebowitz and Margolis 1996 [Chapter 6 in this volume] for an example of a multiple equilibria model). Inclusion of these factors is difficult, and can not prove that markets always choose correctly. Therefore, whether we are considering the increasing returns story of Table 9.1, or multiple equilibrium models, we are left with an empirical question: Have these models captured something important about the way that markets work? The next section addresses that empirical question.

Evidence for lock-in in the economy: do we get the wrong monopolist?

Facts, or empirical evidence, must be the final arbiters of these theories, as they are with all theories. Given the extensive publicity received by these theories, one might conclude that they are supported by a large body of evidence. Nothing, however, could be further from the truth. The little support that has been offered consists of a few key examples where markets have supposedly settled on the wrong system or standard and failed to change to a purportedly better system or standard. The key examples are presented in the following subsections.

The QWERTY keyboard

The most commonly cited example in the network-externality, path dependence literature is the prosaic typewriter keyboard [Chapter 2 in this volume]. The importance of this example can be gleaned from Paul Krugman's book *Peddling Prosperity* (1994). In that book Krugman speaks glowingly of this entire literature in a chapter entitled "The Economics of QWERTY." He does, however, appear to have altered his views when made aware of the facts [we have] presented (see Gomes 1998) ...

The acceptance of this story, wrong as it is in almost every detail, illustrates both the desire by path dependence theorists for empirical support and their reluctance to check the facts. The economic historian who wrote an influential paper on the keyboard story and who cites a Navy study to provide support for path dependence theories never actually examined the Navy study.[2]

We published a very detailed account of all this in the spring of 1990 [Chapter 2 in this volume]. Yet in spite of our paper, which has not been factually disputed, Garth Saloner, who is certainly aware of our paper, used the keyboard example as recently as last fall at the Ralph Nader's anti-Microsoft conference.[3] One could hardly find better evidence of this theory's lack of empirical support then the continued use of a result that is known to be incorrect.

Beta–VHS

The second most popular example of how markets allegedly get locked-in to poor standards is the Beta–VHS videorecorder format struggle. It is sometimes claimed that Beta was a better format and that VHS won the competition between formats only because it fortuitously got a large market share early on in the competition with Beta. But this story turns out to be just as inaccurate as the keyboard story [as discussed in previous chapters in this volume] ...

[As we have shown] the story [Arthur 1990] is little more than an inaccurate anecdote. The elevation of poorly researched anecdotes to the category of "proof" for narrowly constructed theories reappears in the current discussions surrounding Microsoft, as shown below.

Other purported examples, including the Macintosh

Path dependence advocates have sometimes claimed that the continued use of FORTRAN by academics and scientists is an example of getting stuck on a wrong standard. But one doesn't have to peruse too many computer magazines to realize that FORTRAN has long ago been superseded by languages such as Pascal, C, C++, and now, perhaps, Java. Individuals continue to use FORTRAN not because they want to be like everyone else, but because their cost of switching is too high. Network effects, as normally modeled, should have induced them to switch years ago. This is a story of ordinary sunk costs, not of network "externality" or other market failure.

Path dependence proponents have also sometimes claimed that the gasoline-powered engine might have been a mistake, and that steam or electricity might have been a superior choice for vehicle propulsion. This is in spite of the fact that in the century since automobiles became common, with all of the applications of motors and batteries in other endeavors, and with all the advantages of digital electronic power-management systems, today's most advanced electric automobiles do not yet equal state of the art internal-combustion automobiles of the late nineteen-twenties.

The most captivating of these other stories, however, is the success of the PC over the Macintosh. Mac users naturally favor the claim that they chose operating systems wisely whereas the rest of the world ignorantly opted for Microsoft's products. The presence of this large and somewhat embittered audience probably explains why the idea of getting stuck with an inferior product resonates so strongly in the Microsoft case, playing as it does in the arena of personal computer aficionados.[4]

Yet even here the facts do not support the lock-in thesis. Yes, Macintosh owners were forward-looking when they made their purchases in the early and mid-1980s. At that time, the advantages of a graphical interface were clearly understood, if not fully implemented. The lack of implementation, however, had to do with the high price, in terms of speed and cost, that owners of graphical computers had to pay at a time when processors were slow and memory was expensive.

A graphical user interface requires considerably more power to get the job done, significantly increasing costs when that power was hard to come by. Macintosh owners had to wait for their screen displays to change, whereas PCs owners had almost instantaneous updates.[5] True, Macintosh owners could see italics and bold onscreen, but to print the screen as they saw it required a PostScript printer, and such printers cost in the vicinity of a thousand dollars more than ordinary laser printers. The graphical user interface allowed users to learn programs much more easily, but in many business settings, a computer tended to be used for only a single application. In that environment, the operator had very little interaction with the operating system interface, and once the operator had learned the application, the advantages of the graphical user interface were diminished.

The case for DOS therefore, was stronger than appears from the vantage of the 1990s with our multimegabyte memories and multigigabyte hard drives. Now that we routinely use computers that, compared to those old DOS machines, can run thirty times as fast, with fifty times the memory and one hundred times the hard drive capacity, the requirements of a graphical operating system seem rather puny. But they were enormous back in the days of DOS.

As processors became faster, memory cheaper, and hard drives larger, the advantages of a graphical user interface should have overcome any command (text) based system such as DOS. If we were still using DOS, that would certainly be an example of being stuck with an inferior product. But we are not using DOS.

Instead we are using a Mac-like graphical user interface. If someone went to sleep in 1983 and awoke in 1995 to see a modern PC, they most likely would think that the Macintosh graphical user interface had been colorized and updated, with a second button added to the mouse.[6] Our modern Rip van Winkle might be surprised to learn, however, that the owner of the graphical user interface was not Apple, but Microsoft.

The movement from DOS to Windows was costly, yet it occurred quite rapidly. As in the other examples, what the evidence shows is quite the opposite of what the path dependence pundits predicts: not markets getting stuck in ruts, but instead markets that make changes when there is a clear advantage in doing so.

Microsoft's dispute with the justice department

Historically, new antitrust doctrines have developed in connection with the big cases of the times. These big cases most often involved the biggest and most successful companies. That pattern is being repeated today. Various antitrust actions against Microsoft have been the main venue for discussions and actions that propose and explore new economic foundations for antitrust and new interpretations of old antitrust doctrines.

Microsoft's antitrust problems began with a government investigation of Microsoft's pricing of software sold to original equipment manufacturers (OEMs). Microsoft agreed to end these practices in a highly publicized 1994 Consent Decree with the Department of Justice (DOJ). Whether these practices were anticompetitive or not, there can be little doubt that these practices had little to do with Microsoft's successes in the market.[7]

The Consent Decree did little, however, to end Microsoft's legal problems with the DOJ. When Microsoft attempted to purchase Intuit, a maker of financial software, the DOJ opposed the deal. In a highly publicized decision, the Consent Decree itself was temporarily overturned by Judge Stanley Sporkin's (later overturned) decision, which appears to be the first time that path dependence theory had reached the point of having a serious influence on policy.

There were other skirmishes as well. The DOJ examined Microsoft's inclusion of the Microsoft Network icon on the Windows 95 desktop. It was claimed that consumers would be unwittingly forced into acceptance of this product to the detriment of competition in the online service industry.

The most recent twist in the DOJ's continuing investigation is its interest in Microsoft's channel partners on its "active desktop" (Wilke and Band 1998). The antitrust theory behind this investigation is still unclear, but appears to be related to the exclusionary claims being made against Microsoft with regard to Internet Explorer.

The DOJ's primary focus appears to be an investigation of the competition between Netscape and Microsoft that was initiated in 1996. This investigation erupted into activity recently when the DOJ accused Microsoft of violating the 1994 Consent Decree. The current issue revolves around Microsoft's inclusion of its web browser in the Windows operating system, and Microsoft's insistence that its browser not be removed by OEMs. The next section will discuss that.

Newspaper accounts and public statements by DOJ officials and other participants indicate that the economics behind these investigations are either partly or completely based on the theories of path dependence. The most famous, and perhaps most influential, attempt to connect these theories to antitrust is a series of briefs prepared by Gary Reback, a lawyer working for several of Microsoft's competitors, along with two economists who have played prominent roles in this literature: Brian Arthur and Garth Saloner.

These briefs actually go much farther than the economics literature has gone. Reback does not stop with the traditional path dependence claim that a market-based economy is likely to choose all sorts of wrong products. Nor does he stop with the claim that innovation might be eliminated in the computing industry. Instead, Reback portrays Microsoft as an evil empire intent on nothing less than world domination. To hear him tell it, the American Way of Life will be imperiled if Microsoft is not reined in by the government: "It is difficult to imagine that in an open society such as this one with multiple information sources, a single company could seize sufficient control of information transmission so as to constitute a threat to the underpinnings of a free society. But such a scenario is a realistic (and perhaps probable) outcome."[8]

These are fantastic claims indeed. They were repeated at the conference on Microsoft recently held by Ralph Nader.[9] Brian Arthur, Gary Reback, and Garth Saloner all made presentations.

Antitrust doctrines and network technologies

Both the DOJ and some of Microsoft's private competitors have used theories of lock-in to support a call for heightened antitrust scrutiny of Microsoft. By itself, lock-in would seem not to constitute an antitrust offense. There is nothing in the law that makes it a crime to have technologies that are less than the best available or less than the best imaginable.[10] Instead, lock-in theories offer an alternative way to claim harm in the absence of the usual monopoly problem of elevated prices and restricted outputs. Also lock-in stories offer new life and a contemporary spin on old antitrust doctrines. The following two subsections considers some of the antitrust issues that have been raised in the software industry. The first subsection describes why monopoly leverage requires special conditions that make it nearly impossible. The second describes why no smart monopolist would try predatory bundling.

Monopoly leverage, tie-ins, and bundling

In theory, monopoly leverage occurs when a firm uses its monopoly in one industry to win a monopoly in another industry. Tie-in sales and bundling are contractual practices that are sometimes alleged to facilitate monopoly leverage, but tie-ins and bundling do not have to create new monopoly to be profitable. Nor do tie-ins necessarily harm consumers.[11] In fact, as this subsection explains, the theory of monopoly leverage requires so many special conditions that it seems certain to remain just that: A theoretical problem.

Economists have long been skeptical that monopoly leverage is either feasible or profitable. In most circumstances, forcing consumers to purchase some other product so as to create a second monopoly will not add to a firm's profits. A monopolist can instead simply extract the value of its monopoly through the pricing of the good in the market where it has its first monopoly.

Suppose, for example, that a firm held a monopoly on oil furnaces. Such a monopoly might be quite profitable; oil furnaces are useful things that offer some advantages over other kinds of furnaces. The monopolist's ability to maximize profits would face some limits, of course, such as the availability of substitutes like propane and electric heating.[12] Still, the monopolist could devise a pricing system that captures the extra value of using an oil furnace rather than a competing source of heat. The lower the price of heating oil relative to the price of propane or electricity, the greater that value would be. If the furnace monopolist were to become the oil monopolist too, he might raise the price of heating oil, but that would only reduce what he could extract through the furnace price.

Consider this analogy: Regardless of whether or not it worried you that someone had a key to the front door of your house, it would not worry you more if that person also had a key to your back door. Nevertheless, the idea that the second monopoly could be used for something has intuitive appeal. Even if the monopoly in furnaces could be used to extract everything that can be extracted from the furnace users, could not a monopoly in heating oil be used to extract something from people who use heating oil for another purpose? It turns out that, yes, there is a circumstance in which a second monopoly is worth something. That circumstance is a very limited one, however. If the furnace monopolist could also monopolize the heating oil industry, he could extract additional monopoly rents from heating-oil users who were not also his furnace customers.

The question then arises whether one monopoly could ever be extended to capture customers of solely another market. The answer again is yes, it is possible – but, again, only under very special circumstances. *If* there were economies of scale in the heating oil industry and *if* too few customers bought heating oil for non-furnace uses to support a separate supply of heating oil, then the furnace seller could lever his monopoly in furnaces into a monopoly in heating oil by preventing furnace customers from buying heating oil from other sources. By assumption, the nonfurnace customers would not offer a large enough market to support any independent oil supplier and the furnace monopolist could then extract new monopoly rents in this other market. This explanation of leverage is sometimes referred to as market foreclosure.[13] Ironically, *the larger the furnace monopolist relative to the heating oil industry, the less likely it will benefit from monopolizing heating oil* since it will already have virtually all the potential customers.[14]

This explanation is a theoretical possibility of harmful monopoly leverage – but it requires very special conditions. The levered market must be big enough to matter, but not so big as to allow competitive independent suppliers to survive. There must be some economies of scale in the levered market, but not enough to have caused prior monopolization of the market. The levered market must have many of the same customers as the initial monopoly, so as to provide control of the new market, but not too many, or there will be no new rents to extract by establishing the second monopoly. In short, leveraging can be viewed as the Goldilocks theory of monopoly extension – everything has to be *just the right size*.

Do the facts of the Microsoft case fit within the leverage story at all? If Microsoft requires each customer to buy one copy of some other Microsoft product, this would, in and of itself, add nothing to its profits. That sort of tie-in sale with fixed proportions has long been understood to offer no particular advantage to the monopolist.[15] So the issue becomes whether Microsoft could crowd out any rivals that sell to customers who do not use Microsoft's own operating system.

Here the application to Microsoft of the market foreclosure theory runs into trouble. If the products allegedly crowded out by Microsoft's bundling are products that run only under the Windows operating system, then monopoly leverage offers Microsoft no advantage.

To illustrate this point, consider a hypothetical example of successful tying-foreclosure using personal software products, such as Quicken and Microsoft Money. Both are sold in the Macintosh market and the Windows market. *If* Microsoft were to build Microsoft Money into the Windows operating system, *and if* this eliminated Quicken in the Windows market, *and if* the Macintosh market were too small to allow a product like Quicken to be produced at reasonable average cost in that market alone, *and if* Microsoft continued to sell the product separately in the Macintosh market (now at a monopoly price), *and if* there were few additional costs for Microsoft in creating a Macintosh version, then, and *only then*, would Microsoft benefit from leveraging monopoly.

Has this been done? Does Microsoft sell in the Macintosh market disk compression, backup, fax software, or any other program that is included in the Windows operating system? Although we have not performed an exhaustive search, the only product that comes to mind is a Macintosh version of Internet Explorer. But Microsoft *gives away* this product in the Macintosh market, and promises a permanent price of zero. If Microsoft sticks to its promise, it cannot profit from including the browser in the operating system. Even then, the other required conditions for market foreclosure (the Macintosh market being too small to support Navigator and the costs of Microsoft creating a Macintosh version not being too large) may very well fail to obtain.

A simple rule that would prevent this type of foreclosure would prevent Microsoft from including in its operating system any program that it sells separately in another market. But although such a rule might remove the risk of this sort of market leverage, it also would penalize customers in other markets who would be excluded from the benefits of these programs in cases where no market leverage was contemplated. Given all the special conditions required for successful leveraging, it would be unwise to implement such a rule without further investigation of the potential harm of denying Microsoft products to consumers in tied markets.

Predatory bundling

The most recent allegations against Microsoft concern predatory use of its ownership of the Windows operating system. The specific allegation is that Microsoft's integration of its browser into the operating system is largely predatory in intent, aimed at forcing other firms out of the browser market. The implications of this issue, however, extend well beyond the browser market, and extend to the very issues of what an operating system can be and the nature of progress in the software industry.

Antitrust law defines as predatory those actions that are inconsistent with profit maximizing behavior except when they succeed in driving a competitor out of business. In predatory pricing, for example, a would-be monopolist allegedly charges a price that is so low that other firms cannot sell their outputs at prices that will cover even their variable costs. These other firms are then forced either into bankruptcy or to exit the industry because they have become unprofitable. Upon completing the predatory episode, the predator then gets to enjoy the benefits of monopoly pricing. It should be noted that during the predatory episode, consumers benefit greatly from the low prices, so it is only the later monopoly pricing that causes harm to consumers.

Economists are generally skeptical of claims that price cuts or other actions have predatory intent because they have determined, both in theory and practice, that predatory campaigns are unlikely to have profitable endings. First, the predatory action is likely to be more expensive for the predator than for the prey. The predator cannot just cut price; it must also meet market demand at the lower price. Otherwise, customers will be forced to patronize the prey, even if at higher prices. If the predator is a large firm, it stands to lose money at a faster rate than the prey. Second, even if the predation succeeds in bankrupting the prey, there is no guarantee that a reestablished firm will not just re-enter the industry once the predator has established monopoly pricing. If there are fixed investments in the industry, such as durable specialized equipment, the predator cannot establish monopoly prices as long as these durable assets can return to the market. If there are no durable assets, then the prey can cheaply exit the industry and re-enter when monopoly prices return. Either way, the predatory episode drains the predator while imposing uncertain burdens on the prey.

Another problem with predation is that almost any action that a firm takes to become more attractive to consumers can be alleged to be predatory. If customers like something a firm is doing, its competitors will not. In the most elementary case, a price cut or product improvement will damage the prospects for some competitor. It bears noting that most of the alleged cases of predation have been demonstrated to be false.[16]

Predatory bundling, like predatory pricing, is a simple idea that ultimately has the same failings as pure predation. If a firm with a controlling share of one product bundles in some other product, competitors who sell the bundled-in product will have to compete with a product that, to the consumer, has a zero cost. If Microsoft includes in its operating system a piece of software that competes with other vendors in what had been a separate market, Microsoft ensures that virtually all purchasers of computers then have a copy of the new software.

Suppose Microsoft bundles a fax program into Windows 98. If Microsoft's fax program, relative to its cost, is better than other fax products, then the bundling can not really be predatory. The Microsoft product would win in the marketplace anyway and adding it to the operating system costs less than its value to consumers. If the product is worth more to consumers than the costs of creating it, then bundling will also be profitable without any exclusionary consequences. In contrast, if Microsoft's fax program, again considering its cost, is inferior to alternatives or provides less value than its cost, then Microsoft would profit only if bundling caused other firms to exit the market and Microsoft were able to raise the price of the operating system by the now higher implicit monopoly price for its fax product.

As a strategy, however, predatory bundling has the same liabilities as predatory pricing. As in predatory pricing, Microsoft stands to lose money (relative to not including the fax software) faster than its rivals if its fax program costs more to produce than its value to consumers. Moreover, a rival with a superior fax program could keep the product on the market for a price that reflects the advantages that it offers over the bundled product. The rival could not charge more than that because the Windows consumer would already have the inferior fax program. The rival could still capture the extra value that its own intellectual property contributes, however. While it may lose profits or market share, the rival will *retire* its fax program only if it is inferior to Microsoft's.

From a social or consumer welfare perspective, then, Microsoft's bundling action would do no harm. The rival software is a fixed asset in the industry; it does not wear out. In the extreme case, a bankrupt producer might put its fax program on the web, making it freely available to all. This would limit what consumers would be willing to pay for the program bundled into Windows 98 to its extra value, which is zero. Thus Microsoft would be unable to charge a higher price for the bundled software despite having incurred the costs of creating the fax program. Microsoft would lose money and fail to monopolize the market. Furthermore, the creative talents used to make the rival fax program still exist, ready for some other firm to hire should Microsoft ever achieve a monopoly price on the fax program.

Of course, an antitrust enforcer might reply that the OS producer has distribution or coordination advantages that an independent rival lacks. But if these are real advantages that outweigh any quality advantages of the rival, then it is efficient for the OS producer to bundle its fax program.

All this suggests that bundling, as a predatory action, is unlikely to succeed. Furthermore, the software industry has very important nonpredatory reasons to bundle functions into operating systems and other software products. As we explain below, new sales of software will *require* continual additions to functionality.

In the Netscape case, antitrust enforcers might allege that Microsoft is not interested in defeating the Netscape *browser* so much as destroying Netscape as a *company*. Industry pundits have often theorized that web browsers might constitute a means of establishing a new operating system. Netscape, they allege, constitutes a threat to Microsoft's position in the operating system market. Regardless of the technical reasonableness of this claim, however, it runs into the same problems as other allegations of predation.

Here, as elsewhere, predation would not destroy the durable assets of the prey. Netscape's software will hardly disappear if Microsoft bundles a browser into Windows. Indeed, Netscape has already made the source code for its Navigator program publicly available. Even if Microsoft still tried to destroy Netscape in order to protect Windows' market share, it would ultimately fail. Any of Microsoft's several large and vigorous competitors, such as IBM or Sun, would happily purchase Netscape, or hire its engineers, if they thought that by so doing they could share some of Microsoft's enviable profits.

The rate of innovation

Putative dangers

One concern that has been raised by the DOJ, in the Judiciary committee hearings, by some journalists, and by several path-dependence theorists, is that Microsoft's dominant position in the market will somehow inhibit innovation. The suggestion is that Microsoft will be able to so dominate the software market that no small firms will dare compete with it. Firms will be unwilling to create new products in any market that is likely to attract Microsoft's attention, especially in products that are possible additions to the operating system. It is not clear that current antitrust law addresses such concerns. If valid, however, and if not addressed by antitrust law, they might encourage new legislation. Of course, the impact of such legislation would probably reach beyond the computer industry.

Concerns about lock-in drive the accusations against Microsoft. Consumers are viewed as being so locked-in to Microsoft's products that even if the Wintel platform fell far behind the cutting edge of computer technology, no other combination of an operating system, applications, and support could displace it. Obviously, no one can empirically disprove the claim that products that might have been created would have been better than currently existing products. Instead, the analysis here focuses whether lock-in theory correctly concludes that Microsoft will stifle innovation in the computer industry.

Certainly there are instances where Microsoft has incorporated programs into the operating system where the former providers of such programs have gone on to other things. Disk compression and memory management programs are two examples. Fax programs, backup programs, and disk-defragmenting programs are counter-examples where the inclusion of such programs in the operating system has not eliminated the separate market. The difference appears to be in whether the programs Microsoft includes in its operating system are as good as the separate programs or not. When Microsoft produces a product as good or better than the competition, the separate market usually does disappear. It is difficult, however to conceive of consumer harm in this case.

The general claim that innovation will suffer if Microsoft is allowed to grow and add programs to the operating system has several shortcomings. It does not just assume that creative ideas are more likely to come from small startup companies than from Microsoft. That assumption is likely to be true, since the number of outside programmers developing products for Windows is more than fifteen times as large as the number of programmers working for Microsoft. Instead, it assumes that Microsoft could not, or would not, use these programmers to produce as much creative activity as they would produce if they continued to work independently.

It is, of course, conceivable that large firms produce less innovation than small firms do (adjusting for size). But this has been investigated at length in the economics literature with no clear consensus.[17] If there were a reason to believe that the software industry would be different from most other industries in this regard, it would tend to support a view that large software firms will continue to innovate.

Firms benefit from good new ideas. Profits will increase when these new products are brought to market. Monopolists benefit just as much from an extra dollar of profit as do competitive firms. The argument that large firms might innovate less than small firms do usually relies on some variation of the view that large firms are fat and lazy. That is, that they do not innovate because they do not have to. Still, a dollar is a dollar. Most investors are just as eager for their large-firm stocks to perform well as they are for their small-firm stocks to perform well. For the fat-and-lazy condition to hold, it must be that large firms with dispersed ownership of their stock do not have the same incentives to maximize shareholder value and profits as do small firms which are usually closely held. This real possibility is known as the problem of separation of ownership and control.

With regard to Microsoft and many other successful high-technology firms, however, this argument would seem to have little force. The ownership of Microsoft and most other high-tech firms is not widely disbursed. For example, Bill Gates owns almost 25 percent of Microsoft and several other early Microsoft investors own very substantial stakes. This may in fact explain why Microsoft is still considered such an intense competitor.

Alternatively, it is vaguely suggested that Microsoft stifles innovation because it copies software ideas from others, leaving these other firms no reward for their efforts. If there were any truth to this claim, the problem would appear to lie in intellectual property law, not in any potential monopoly power on the part of Microsoft. After all, if

Microsoft could copy the ideas of its rivals, so could a host of other large (or small) firms in the industry, in each instance lowering the profits of the innovator, large or small.[18]

It would be a serious problem if innovators in software were not being properly rewarded for their efforts. The purpose of intellectual property laws is to allow innovators to collect economic rewards for their efforts. Without such laws, imitators could free ride off the efforts of innovators and produce similar products at lower cost, driving true innovators out of business. So, while deserving of investigation, these problems do not seem fundamental in any way to Microsoft, or its ownership of the operating system. Perhaps a reevaluation of intellectual property laws would be in order. But this claim seems to have little to do with antitrust.

There are some factual matters that do not seem consistent with the claim that Microsoft reduces innovation. Microsoft's behavior toward its developers, for example, does not seem to square with the claim that it is intent on driving out independent software producers:

> Microsoft doesn't court only the powers from other industries. It's also spending $85 million this year ministering to the needs of 300 000 computer software developers. It subsidizes trade-show space for hundreds of partners. And it's not above lavishing attention on small companies when it needs their support ... "The platforms that succeed are the ones that appeal to developers," admits Alan Baratz, president of Sun Microsystem Inc.'s JavaSoft division. He calls Microsoft's hold on the developer community its "crown jewel" (Hamm 1998).

More broadly, there seems to be a paucity of evidence to support the concern that the pace of innovation is insufficiently rapid. The pace of innovation in the computer industry is generally regarded with some awe. Certainly, the Windows market does not appear to have suffered from stifled development of applications.[19]

Finally, there seem to be tremendous rewards to those who do innovate in this industry. Even in the instance of Netscape, a supposed victim of Microsoft's power, the founders walked away with hundreds of millions of dollars. Does this discourage others from taking the same path? Unless and until careful research answers these sorts of questions, any antitrust action would be premature and potentially dangerous to the software industry and the economy as a whole.

A real danger to innovation

The nature of software markets requires that software producers continually add functionality to their products. Unlike most other products, software never wears out. If Big Macs never change, Mcdonald's can keep selling them because consumers still want to purchase Big Macs that are just like the ones that they ate the day before. This is true for most goods, which eventually need replacement. But because software lasts forever, with no diminution in quality, there is no reason for consumers to purchase more than once a word processor or operating system unless new improved versions come to market. Undoubtedly, improvement will mean additional functionality.

To aid in understanding this, consider what it means to improve software. Software could be made faster and perhaps more intuitive, with no additional functionality. But this is not likely to win over many new customers. First, consumers will discover that real speed improvements are likely to come from the inevitable speed increases that occur when they replace their old computers with faster ones. Further, although intuitive interfaces are useful, practice overcomes inherent design imperfections. So the natural inclination of consumers would be to stick with any familiar version of a program (or operating system) unless the newer version could perform some useful tasks not available in the old version. This requires adding functionality not found in previous versions.

Added functionality can be seen in every category of software. Word processors have far more functionality than they used to – spell and grammar checkers, mail merge programs, thesauruses – which were not included with the original generation of word processors. Spreadsheets, database programs, and virtually every other category of program also have far more functionality than before.[20] That is one reason why new software seems to fill our ever-expanding hard drives, which have hundreds or thousands of times the storage capacity of earlier machines.

The consumer benefits in many ways from this added functionality. These large programs almost always cost far less than the sum of the prices that the individual component products used to command. The various components also tend to work together far better then separate components because they are made for each other. If it were not the case, consumers would not purchase new generations of software products.

As this process of adding functionality to programs continues, it is possible that the number of small companies specializing in add-ons will shrink. But is this any reasons to prevent creators of word processors from including grammar checkers and thesauruses? Should the producers of dominant programs be forbidden to add functionality while producers of less successful programs are allowed to add new functions? That hardly seems a recipe for success. Do we really believe that innovation was retarded because add-on companies feared that they might have been put out of business? Do we even know if they have been put out of business? That those programmers are no longer working on new ideas? Again, questionable logic and a dearth of evidence make these claims suspect.

Yet it appears that some Microsoft's critics, including those within the government, have proposed freezing the operating system, putting an end to adding functionality. If this proposal were accepted for the operating system, it would also seem to apply to other categories of software. The results would be disastrous for software producers, who would have no new sales except to new computer users, for computer manufacturers, who would find little demand for more capable hardware, and most importantly for users, who would be forced to use seriously crippled software. The proposal to freeze Windows reflects a view that all the useful things have already been invented. Few proposed antitrust policies are as dangerous as this one.

Who should get to assign desktop icons? The irrelevance of the 'browser wars'

At the Senate hearings, and in the media, considerable attention has been given to the claim that Microsoft's desire to prevent OEMs from removing the Internet Explorer icon from the desktop was somehow inimical to competition. This section explains why Microsoft and OEMs might each want to control the placement of desktop icons and provides an economic framework for deciding who should be allowed to control the desktop icons. Ultimately, though, it turns out that icon placement should probably not matter to even the computer and software industry, much less to antitrust enforcers.

Control of the desktop might be valuable since, as a practical matter, all computer users see the desktop. In principle, desktop placements of "advertisements," whether a program or a message, could be sold to companies interested in such exposure. For example, assume that an icon for America Online appears on the desktop. Consumers interested in an online service might just click on the icon and begin the process of becoming an America Online customer. Knowing this, a company such as America Online might be willing to pay the controller of the desktop for a good placement of its icon.[21]

Assume for the moment, then, that these icon placements are indeed valuable. The next subsection explains why, nonetheless, regulators should not care whether Microsoft or OEMs control icon placement. Following that, the discussion critically re-examines the assumption that control of icons should matter even to the computer industry.

A simple theory of "desktop rights"

If revenues can be generated by placing icons on the desktop, it should not be surprising that both OEMs and the owner of the operating system (Microsoft) each will claim the rights to place the icons. Economic analysis allows us to examine whether it makes any difference who has this right. It also may provide some guidance as to who should get this right.

The Coase theorem can help to explain the tradeoffs involved.[22] If the rights to place desktop icons were well defined, and if there were no transactions costs or wealth effects, the Coase theorem tells use that regardless of who initially has these rights, they would end up where they have the greatest value. Consider the following example. If the rights to sell desktop placement were worth $5 to Microsoft and $10 to OEMs, then OEMs would wind up controlling the desktop icons regardless of who initially had the rights. If Microsoft initially controlled the desktop, OEMs would be willing to pay up to $10 to Microsoft for these rights, and Microsoft would be better off selling the rights to OEMs. It would do this by raising the price of the operating system by more than $5 (but no more than the $10 that OEMs would pay) and granting OEMs the right to place the icons.

If, on the other hand, OEMs initially control desktop placements, Microsoft would be willing to lower the price of the desktop by up to $5 in exchange for the right to control icon placements. OEMs would prefer to keep the rights themselves, however, since they can generate more than $5 in revenues by maintaining this control. In either case, OEMs wind up with the rights, and both parties share the $10 in extra revenue brought about by icon placement sales. Although the two parties might be expected to fight over the rights, it makes no difference to the rest of us who gets the rights. By analogy, as virtually all microeconomics textbooks explain, if the government subsidizes gasoline purchases it makes no difference whether automobile drivers or service stations receive the subsidy, because in either case the subsidy would be shared in exactly the same way.

Sometimes the assumptions of the Coase theorem are not met. For example, if negotiations between OEMs and Microsoft were not feasible, efficiency considerations would require that the property rights be assigned to the party who can generate the highest value for desktop placements.[23] Since Microsoft and OEMs are already negotiating over other aspects of the desktop (e.g. price), however, there is little reason to believe that the market will not work efficiently. Since this is a matter of contract, property rights can be defined and transacted within the contract.

The current anxiety regarding desktop placements is misplaced. So long as the parties freely enter into new contracts, neither party will benefit from a legal stipulation of who initially controls the desktop. It should not matter at all to the government who has the rights.

The reader may naturally ask "if it makes no difference, why is there fighting over who places the icons?" There are two answers. First, there is no evidence that Microsoft and OEMs disagree. It is Microsoft's competitors who are complaining. Second, it is not unusual in such circumstances for there to be contract disputes or strategic behavior. Two parties can negotiate a contract, then subsequently dispute their understanding of the terms of that contract. If, for example, OEMs are receiving a lower price from Microsoft because Microsoft thought it controlled desktop placement, but now OEMs have a chance to sell icon placement while remaining under a fixed contractual price for Windows, it would not be surprising that a dispute would arise.

Is icon placement valuable?

In order for icon placement to be valuable, it must generate *future* revenues. America Online benefits in the previous example because consumers could not use its services without paying a monthly fee. Having its icon on the desktop increased the chances that consumers would sign up for the service.

For a typical software product to be on the desktop, however, it is usually the case that the software is already installed on the computer, and thus already purchased. The icon placement only increases its likelihood of use. The only additional benefits to the software producer from having the consumer *use* the software after purchasing it is that the consumer might purchase upgrades or ancillary products.

For the Netscape and Microsoft browsers there are several reasons why the icon placement might be important. (This analysis ignores any future revenues from upgrades since both companies have agreed not to charge for browsers or upgrades.) It is possible that Netscape and Microsoft might be able to trade off the success of their browsers to sell software specializing in serving up web pages (known as servers) because of their large presence among the base of users and the (presumably) assured compatibility with these browsers.

There is another possible reason for the web browser icon to have value. When a browser is first put into use, it goes to a default starting location on the Internet.[24] If large numbers of web users (surfers) view a particular location, advertising revenues can be generated as some popular locations on the Internet, such as Yahoo!, have discovered. Yahoo! in fact paid Netscape many millions of dollars to provide Netscape users an easy way to reach the Yahoo! page. Netscape and Microsoft, although somewhat late to this game, both are working on new start pages (to which the browsers will be preprogrammed to go) in the hopes of enticing users to stay at their web sites. It is thought that browsers might become a potent revenue generating force by leading consumers to particular pages,.

There are serious reservations to the claim that the browser icons are valuable for the control they provide of the start page, however. First, it is possible, and quite easy, for users to alter the start page. Would it make sense for radio stations to pay automobile dealers to have car radios set at certain stations when the cars leave the new car lot? This is virtually a perfect analogy to the browser icon story. Yet it seems hard to believe that radio stations would benefit, mainly because it is so easy to change stations. Is it really that much more difficult for consumers to change the icons on the desktop? This is an empirical question whose answer may change as consumers become more accustomed to the operating system.

There is, however, a more fundamental impediment to the claim that desktop placement is important for Browsers. *Just having the icon on the desktop is insufficient to gain access to the Internet.* Clicking on that icon will not connect users to the Internet. For that they will have to use one of many Internet service providers. The Internet service provider will almost certainly provide its own browser, independent of what icon is on the desktop.[25] Therefore, it is hard to see how the icon on the desktop at the time of sale provides much value at all.

Finally, the concept of detailed governmental control over desktop placement leads to other seemingly endless and seemingly absurd questions. What about the Start button in Windows? The order of programs tends to be alphabetical. Should the government be concerned about the ordering of these programs, and who gets the rights to order these programs? Has anyone investigated whether the various color schemes found in Windows work to benefit Microsoft's icons over the alternatives? Is the screen saver in Windows that shows the Microsoft Windows icon moving around anticompetitive in its subliminal effects? In conclusion, and in all seriousness, we should ask this: Should the government really be involved in these types of decisions?

Implications

The theories of path dependence and lock-in are relatively new to the economic literature. These theories have not won over the economics profession after years of debate and they have not made their way into many economics textbooks. Nor do these theories draw on first principles in obvious and secure ways. That does not make theories of path dependence and lock-in bad economics, or wrong economics, or inappropriate topics for academic research. On the contrary, it makes the academic debate that much more important. It makes these theories, however, a poor foundation for public policies that could affect the progressiveness of the American economy.

If we were treating a dying industry, even speculative economic medicine might be worth a try. But the computer and software industries continue to astound most people both with the rates at which products improve and at which prices decline. It makes no sense to submit such a robust patient to the risks of economic quackery.

In our academic writings collected above, we have shown that there is a poor connection between theories of path dependence and the real-world behaviors of entrepreneurs and consumers. Our work also demonstrates that there is no connection between the alleged empirical support for these theories and real events. Contrary to the lock-in claim, and contrary to some popular stories of markets gone awry, good products do seem to displace bad ones. Since there is no real support for the supposition that markets fail in increasing returns environments, there is no more basis for antitrust in increasing returns markets than in any others.

There might even be less reason to apply antitrust to such markets. Our most basic theory of increasing returns implies that monopoly or near-monopoly equilibria are likely. Where people do value compatibility, or where increases in firm scale really do lower costs, dominant formats or single producers will probably result at any particular moment.

Furthermore, consumers want it that way. Anything else will frustrate the urge for compatibility, unnecessarily raise costs, or both. So monopoly outcomes need not imply that anything has gone wrong or been done wrong. Monopolies that are undone by the government may lead only to monopolies that are redone in the market. The faces may change, but market structure may not. If we insist that natural monopolies be populated by several firms kept at inefficiently small shares, we are likely to find these markets taken over by foreign companies without such restrictions.

In such markets, firms will compete to be the monopolist. It is in this competition that products that create more value for consumers prevail against those that create less. Notice what that means. The very acts of competition that bring about the market tests of these products – the strategies that save us from inferior keyboards – will look like monopolizing acts. That is because they are. They determine which monopoly prevails until better products prompt new campaigns to capture an increasing returns market.

Many of the other claims that surround the new antitrust debate are disconnected, not only from real-world observations, but also from any real theoretical support. One such claim is that Microsoft would like to crush any would be direct competitor. It probably would. Theory and history, however, do not tell us how predation could ever work in a world in which assets are perfectly durable. Further, Microsoft has been visibly unsuccessful in crushing anything except where their products are better than the opposition. They had to resort to (the attempted) buying of uncrushed Intuit, they have barely dented America On Line with the much ballyhooed Microsoft Network, and they only began to erode Netscape's near monopoly when their own browser came up to snuff. Microsoft's products that dominate in the Windows environment are the very ones that have dominated elsewhere.[26]

There is, finally, the vaguely posed claim that Microsoft stifles innovation – another disconnect. The claim fails to conform with several prominent features of the PC landscape. First, Microsoft courts and supports its many software developers, who now number in the hundreds of thousands. Second, the personal computing industry, by any practical standard of comparison, seem to be astonishingly innovative.

Finally and most importantly, antitrust doctrines brought to bear against Microsoft cannot be constructed to apply to Microsoft alone. If doctrines emerge that the biggest operating system must be kept on a short leash, then why not also a big producer of database software that sets the standards for that activity, or the biggest producer of printers, or scanners, or modems, of microprocessors, and so on? If these new technologies do exhibit increasing returns, or important reliance on standards, or network effects, then we are likely to see high concentration in all of these areas. Unless we are to embark on a relentless attack on whatever it is that succeeds, we need to acknowledge that the constructive competitive actions that firms take in this environment – new products, new capabilities, new deals – will often hurt competitors by the very fact that they make consumers better off.

Notes

1. We are not, however, aware of any formal studies that examine market shares and prices in high tech markets.
2. Gomes (1998) reports that Paul David, the author of the paper bringing this story to economists, never saw the Navy study.
3. "Appraising Microsoft and Its Global Strategy," Washington, DC, November 13–14, 1997. RealAudio files of the conference are available at <http://www.appraising-microsoft.org/day1rm.html>.
4. Pick up *Newsweek* in 1996 and there is Steve Wozniak, the engineering *Wunderkind* largely responsible for Apple's early success, explaining that Apple's recent failures were just another example of a better product losing out to an inferior alternative. "Like the Dvorak keyboard, Apple's superior operating system lost the market-share war" he is quoted as saying. See Steve Wozniak, "We Failed Apple," *Newsweek*, February 19, 1996.
5. The screen display on the PC required only 5 or 10 percent of the computer memory that was required by the Macintosh screen.
6. The original graphical user interface, developed at the Xerox PARC research center, had three buttons. The Microsoft community takes great pride in its use of but a single button and often defends it as optimal.
7. See the declaration of Kenneth J. Arrow (January 17, 1995) as part of the Memorandum of the United States of America in Support of Motion to Enter Final Judgment and in Opposition to the Positions of IDE Corporation and Amici.
8. See Gary L. Reback *et al.*, 1995
9. See RealAudio files of Nader's conference, held in Washington, DC on November 13 and 14, 1997 "Appraising Microsoft and Its Global Strategy," available at <http://www.appraising-microsoft.org/day1rm.html>
10. This is not to say, however, that antitrust laws as written are ideal. If there really were serious problems with lock-ins to inferior technology we might want to rewrite the antitrust laws. For reasons set forth here, however, there is no evidence supporting that supposition.
11. Tie-in sales may allow the monopolist to capture more of the surplus created by the monopolized good, may spread risk, may contribute to quality control or may provide a cheap means for monitoring intellectual property infringement. Such effects of tie-ins do not require monopolization of a second market. Further, where tie-ins are profitable for any of these reasons, they may contribute to economic efficiency. See Liebowitz (1983). Bundling is very common for all kinds of goods. People buy season

tickets, cars with tires and transmissions, and houses with microwaves and furnaces. Bundling can be explained by efficiencies of either production or purchase and commonly occurs in highly competitive markets.

12. This analysis ignores natural gas, which in fact is usually cheaper than oil where it can be had.
13. While this explanation has been around in antitrust economics for some time, it is formalized in Whinston (1990)
14. Furthermore, the existence of economies of scale in heating oil make it likely that someone else has already monopolized the industry, in which case extending the monopoly from furnaces to oil would cause no economic harm; it would merely change the identity of the monopolist. The furnace monopolist is likely to benefit if can avoid dealing with an oil monopolist who can share in the furnace monopolists' profits, or lead to lower joint profits if the two monopolists each try to take larger shares of the profit.
15. This does not hold true if a different firm monopolizes the tied market, as discussed in the previous footnote. However, consumers suffer no harm at all if Microsoft replaces the other monopolist and thus there is no reason that antitrust should care about that outcome.
16. The most famous of these cases is John D. Rockefeller's Standard Oil. John McGee (1958), however, demonstrates that there were virtually no instances of predatory pricing by Rockefeller.
17. See Scherer (1980, 418): "One conclusion relevant to public policy follows immediately. No single firm size is uniquely conducive to technological progress. There is room for firms of all sizes." Similarly, Shughart (1990, 356): "Industrial creativity does seem to depend on something other than pure size."
18. Note that many small start-ups have in fact gained access to enormous amounts of capital in the equities market when they were able to convince investors of the potential value of their ideas. These would include Netscape, Yahoo!, and many other Internet companies.
19. Surely it is difficult to argue that the software market has been insufficiently innovative in recent years. Nonetheless, it remains very difficult to prove that the industry has been optimally innovative.
20. For example, word processors now contain draw packages, paint packages, graphing packages, dictionaries, thesauruses, grammar-checkers, equation editors, outliners, and so forth. Spreadsheets now routinely include spell-checkers, graphics packages, statistics programs, financial programs, programming languages, linear and non-linear programming routines, and so forth. Even fax programs now contain optical character recognition software (to convert faxes to text, draw packages to create cover pages, and so forth).
21. This was supposedly the main ingredient in a well-publicized deal whereby America Online agreed to include Internet Explorer on its installation disks (although users could use Netscape's browser if they so desired). See Wilke and Band (1998).
22. This refers to a paper by Ronald Coase that is the most highly cited paper in the field of economics, and for which he received the Nobel prize.

23. Who is most likely to maximize the value of desktop placement? The ability to generate value in desktop placement depends largely on the costs of searching, marketing, and negotiating desktop placement with both users and placement purchasers. In this case, it might appear that that Microsoft would be able to transact at lower costs with placement purchasers than could OEMs, arguing for giving Microsoft the property rights. First, OEMs are not included in the upgrade market, and thus Microsoft already would be negotiating for these desktop placements. The additional costs for Microsoft controlling OEM placements would seem trivial. Second, each OEM would likely duplicate the marketing, search, and negotiation costs of other OEMs. On the other hand, OEMs often sell other software to customers of which Microsoft has no knowledge. Although the placement of these icons could be pre-ordered in a particular way, this might impose its own inefficiencies. It is conceivable that this would tilt the result toward giving OEMs property rights. The bottom line is that at this time it remains unclear who can maximize desktop value.
24. Early in the history of the Internet, it was possible to have a browser and not know what to do to get started. Start pages cropped up to help consumers learn to maneuver their way around the web.
25. For example, both America Online and AT&T's Worldcom Internet services use a version of Internet Explorer that is specially set up to go to America Online's and AT&T's homepage, respectively. Note that control of the start page is a Coasian problem analogous to the icon placement problem.
26. The market share for Microsoft applications (such as Word and Excel) in the Macintosh market, for example, has historically been far larger than in the Windows market.

References

Arthur, W. B. 1989. "Competing Technologies, Increasing Returns, and Lock-in by Historical Events," *Economic Journal*, 99: 116–131.

———— 1990. "Positive Feedbacks in the Economy," *Scientific American*, 262: 92–99.

Garland S. 1997. "Commentary: Justice Vs. Microsoft – Why it has a Case," *Business Week* (November 17).

Gomes L. 1998. "QWERTY Spells a Saga of Market Economics," *Wall Street Journal* (February 25): B1.

Hamm, S. 1998. "The Secrets to Microsoft's Might," *Business Week* (January 19); available on the web as part of the hardcopy story "Microsoft's Future," by Steve Hamm in Redmond, Washington, with Amy Cortese in New York and Susan B. Garland in Washington, DC.

Krugman, P. 1994. *Peddling Prosperity* (New York: Norton) Coase, R. 1960 "The Problem of Social Cost," *Journal of Law and Economics*, 3: 1–44.

Liebowitz. S. J. 1983. "Tie-in Sales, Risk Reduction and Price Discrimination," *Economic Inquiry*, 21: 387–399.

Liebowitz, S. J. and Margolis, S. E. 1995. "Path Dependence, Lock-in, and History," *Journal of Law, Economics and Organization*, 11: 205–226; reprinted as Chapter 5 in this volume.

———— 1996. "Should Technology Choice be a Concern of Antitrust Policy," *Harvard Journal of Law and Technology*, 9: 283–318; reprinted as Chapter 6 in this volume.
McGee J. 1958. "Predatory Price Cutting: The Standard Oil of NJ Case," *Journal of Law and Economics*, 1: 137–169.
Murray, A. 1997. "The Outlook: Antitrust Isn't Obsolete in an Era of High-Tech," *Wall Street Journal*, (November 10): A1.
Reback G. L. *et al.* 1995. "Why Microsoft Must Be Stopped," *Upside* (February: 52–67).
Scherer, F. M. 1980. *Industrial Market Structure and Economic Performance*, 2nd edn., New York: Rand McNally.
Shughart, W. 1990 *The Organization of Industry*, Toronto: Irwin.
Whinston, M. 1990. "Tying, Foreclosure and Exclusion," *American Economic Review*, 80: 837–859.
Wilke J. R. and Band, D. 1998. "Microsoft Allies in 'Active Desktop' Are Subpoenaed in Antitrust Probe," *Wall Street Journal* (February 5).
———— 1998. "AOL, MCI Are Subpoenaed in Microsoft Antitrust Case," *Wall Street Journal Interactive Edition* (February 20).

10
Network Effects and the Microsoft Case (2001)*

Networks, competition, and Microsoft[1]

Much of our work has examined the logic and empirical support for concepts of lock-in and path dependence. These topics have now entered the realm of public policy in what may be the most important antitrust action, or at least the most famous, since the Standard Oil case almost one hundred years ago.

Network effects occur when the value consumers receive from a product increases as the number of users of that product increases. The archetypal example would be a fax machine, or telephone, where the product has virtually no value to a consumer if only that consumer has one, but whose value begins to increase as additional users adopt the product.

As long as other factors, such as increasing costs, do not overpower network effects, larger firms or networks will have advantages over smaller firms or networks. Following through the logic of the model, this leads, naturally enough, to a single winning firm or network.[2] Network effects share an important characteristic with economies of scale. In particular, both tend to advantage larger firms in an industry, although the former does it by increasing demand and the latter by decreasing costs.

A portion of this literature claims that network effects tend to keep a leading firm's position intact, even if there is a superior product available, a result otherwise known as lock-in.[3] We need to make clear that our definition of "lock-in" does not just imply that costs of switching

---

* *Dynamic Competition and Public Policy: Technology, Innovation, and Antitrust Issues*, ed. J. Ellig, Cambridge: Cambridge University Press 2001, originally adapted with permission from *Winners, Losers & Microsoft: Competition and Antitrust in High Technology*, S. Liebowitz and S. Margolis, Oakland, Calif., The Independent Institute, 2001.

make it uneconomic to switch. If it is uneconomic to switch, we do not want the switch to occur. Instead, our definition of lock-in implies that a superior product is not adopted even when all costs (except coordination costs) are less than the benefits. In case it appears that we are setting up a straw man, the reader should note that it is exactly this form of lock-in that generated so much excitement about the typewriter keyboard fable in the profession.[4] Our previous investigations of supposed real-world cases of lock-in, however, forced us to conclude that were as yet no known real-world instances.[5]

The first use of these concepts against Microsoft, in the mid 1990s, was the claim the network effects in software would lead to lock-in, or the wrong choice of software product.[6] The more recent use of network effects has modified this claim very slightly. For example, Franklin Fisher, in his testimony against Microsoft, claims that network effects enhance Microsoft's monopoly power. Judge Jackson, in his finding of fact, claimed that the "chicken-and-egg" nature of software markets let to an "application barrier to entry" meaning that incumbent operating system producers were protected from competitors by the fact that network effects and coordination costs would be working against the challenger. The implication would seem to be that the challenger might not be superior, but that the barrier to entry prevents the equal or inferior product from ever getting a chance to seriously compete with the incumbent.

This concept of entrenched incumbents is, apparently, a beguiling idea because it has seduced a large portion of the economists who have encountered it. This is so in spite of the fact that the economic theory is itself ambiguous, as demonstrated by the concept of excess momentum (Farrell and Saloner, 1985). Perhaps an even more telling criticism is the fact that it is unclear that there is any empirical support for this claim. Nonetheless, this concept has achieved considerable acceptance, perhaps in part riding on the coattails of the popularity of the concept of network effects, which itself has been the focus of only a very limited and suspect empirical literature, particularly as regards software markets.[7]

Since it has been claimed that software manifests network effects, and since increasing returns in production (decreasing average cost as output increases) are also likely in the software industry, the conditions would seem to be in place for software to be an incubator for lock-in and/or inertia. In the following section we will examine some implications of these theories. The analysis of software markets that follows examines evidence regarding the general predictions of these theories and some specific allegations of Microsoft's "monopolist" behavior in these markets.

Implications of network effects

Network effects are thought to be common in many technology industries. A virtual mountain of papers have been written about these effects in spite of the lack of evidence of their overall strength, such is its theoretical appeal. In the Microsoft case it has just been assumed that network effects were pervasive, which does not seem out of line with many academic articles. Legal standards, however, probably should require more stringent standards than current academic fads since so much is at stake, but the standards, in antitrust at least, have not been historically high. Just because there is so much uncorroborated agreement about network effects, however, does not mean that it is so. It is important that we try to verify these beliefs. Here we suggest some implications of network effects. If these implications are not found in software (or other network) markets, then we believe that the importance of network effects in software or other markets should be reexamined.

Price: the neglected implication

We start with this not because it is easily testable, but because it has been entirely ignored in the literature and because it is about as direct an impact as one can find.

Network effects increase the demand for the product. *Ceteris paribus*, as network effects get stronger, prices should rise. This should be true for individual firms as they increase their market shares and also for the market as a whole as the size of the network increases, at least as network effects are usually modeled. This is in complete contrast with the impact of economies of scale, which by lowering the costs of the firm, should lower the price of the product for any given level of monopoly power exerted in the market.

It is somewhat surprising, then, that this clear implication of network effects has not received much attention in the literature.[8] The higher prices that should be caused by the increase in demand brought about, in turn, by larger networks, the relationship at the very core of this theory, has been neglected.

Because so many factors are involved in setting market prices, it may be difficult to generate a definitive test relating prices to network size, but the general claim of higher prices as networks get larger should be observable in some fashion. The reader should keep this in mind as actual prices in various markets are examined.

Winner-take-all (or most)

The implication of network effects that has received most attention is the winner-take-all (or winner-take-most) result coming from increasing returns. A potential problem in testing this implication is that it applies equally well to old-fashioned economies of scale. For many high-tech products, particularly software, economies of scale seem very likely, thus making it difficult to separately distinguish the impact of network effects.

Another difficulty is that software has a characteristic that we refer to as "instant scalability" meaning that the output can be increased very rapidly without the usual additional costs associated with sudden increases in output. This instant scalability is due to the fact that reproduction equipment is not specialized. Instant scalability will also be found for compact disc music recordings and long-playing records prior to that.

Note that this is not the same as zero or low reproduction costs. Printed books using specialized plates can be reproduced at very low marginal cost, but the scale of output is limited to that one printing location using those plates since it is time consuming to create other plates.

Software has this attribute because disc-reproducing machines are not specialized for any particular software title and thus it is considerably easier to increase output of a software title than to increase output of automobiles or even books. In a world where output can be changed so quickly, market shares can adjust to meet every whim of consumers. The market need not have unfilled orders or higher prices; no Cabbage Patch dolls or Furbys here.[9] This provides yet another potential explanation for winner-take-all outcomes in software. The difference, however, is that market shares can change dramatically here since a product that better strikes a fancy will quickly come to dominate the market. The software markets that we look at appear to change in a manner consistent with this view of the world.

We believe that this concept of instant scalability may have been at work for some time and is worthy of further examination to determine how important its impacts may be. We hope some readers will join us in putting this concept to some empirical testing.

Winner-take-all results, therefore, are consistent with network effects, but also with economies of scale and instant scalability.

Lock in or inertia

The concept of lock-in would seem to apply to software if it applies anywhere. Network effects should be stronger in most software markets than would have been expected in the other suspected havens of lock-in – typewriters or videorecorders, say.

If large firms have advantages over small firms, then we have the possibility of what we have defined elsewhere (1995 [Chapter 5 in this volume]) as third-degree lock-in or inertia. Obviously, this is not to say that an incumbent remains forever entrenched, but instead that when a better product comes along it might not get adopted even if there were economic advantages to its adoption. This is to be distinguished from weaker cases of lock-in where real costs of switching make it uneconomical to switch to another product.

Confirmation of the lock-in hypothesis requires finding better products that are not adopted.[10] Testing for inertia would require that we know the optimal switching speed and compare that to the actual speed with which a switch is made. Testing for inertia obviously requires more detailed knowledge than testing for lock-in, and considerably more detail that we are likely to find. Instead, we ask the reader to compare the speed of changes in software markets to speed of changes elsewhere, admittedly an imperfect measure.

As already mentioned, Judge Jackson in his *Finding of Fact* converted the lock-in concept to a barrier to entry. As we all know, barrier to entry is a slippery concept, meaning anything from a high cost of entry to a cost incurred by the challenger but not the incumbent. The latter definition has always seems correct to us, and in that case it is unclear how network effects, economies of scale, or any of the other factors at work favor the incumbent relative to the challenger. The incumbent had to coordinate consumers to adopt his product, whether it was first in the market or replaced a previous incumbent. In either case, getting consumers to come on board is a cost imposed on all market entrants, late or early and does not necessarily favor early firms.

In contrast to much of the path dependence literature which focuses on excess inertia, we note the possibility that the speed at which market leaders replace one another might be greater in software markets than in many "ordinary" markets due to the *instant scalability* feature of software. In fact, the software markets that we examine below exhibit extremely rapid changes in market leadership. Although we are not aware of any precise benchmarks with which to make comparisons to other industries, it appears on casual inspection that changes in market share occur at a far more rapid rate in software markets than in other markets.

Tipping

Tipping is a term that has been used rather vaguely in the literature and in Microsoft antitrust testimony. A market is considered to have "tipped" when one product or standard has become dominant. A market is tipping when it is sliding toward the eventual domination by a single firm. It is generally claimed that tipping occurs when a product has generated sufficient momentum with regard to network effects that its domination is inevitable. Although there is considerable vagueness in the literature, the general idea seems to be that after a period of struggle, one firm breaks out from the pack and tipping ensues.

We assume that tipping has some meaning other than just market dominance. Since network effects only strengthen as market share increases, there should be a pattern to market share growth. First, when a firm is smaller than it competitors, growth should be slow since network effects should be working against the firm. Later, when consumers anticipate that a firm will become larger than its competitors, market share increases should come more easily, since network effects are self-reinforcing. This tipping point, or critical mass, should mark an acceleration in market share growth. In such instances, increases in market share for leading products would occur even without any advantages in product quality. As we will see, there is no evidence for markets tipping in this manner.

Software markets: background

We will focus on a few key software application markets. We are particularly interested in markets where Microsoft has achieved or failed to achieve a dominant status. We examine spreadsheets and personal finance as two markets where Microsoft has had very different success, and Internet browsers since this market was so crucial to the case.

The consumer's choice

When faced with software choices, whether changing to a completely different product, or just upgrading a current choice,[11] the logic of the choice facing the consumer is straightforward. First, the consumer must evaluate the increased value that would be brought about by using the new software relative to remaining with the current software. This extra value might come from new features, increased speed, better compatibility with other users, and so forth. On the other side of the ledger go the costs of purchasing the software, the costs of the transition (presumably users will be less productive as they learn to use the new software), and the costs of any file incompatibility with previous software (the cost of imperfect access to old data).

Software has several characteristics that will make it appealing for consumers to remain with the same vendor. First and foremost is a concern with backwards-compatibility – a compatibility with the learned skills associated with previous versions of a program, and compatibility with file formats that were created with previous versions of the program. If the adoption of a new spreadsheet or word processor removed any ability to read the consumer's old files, it is very unlikely the consumer would make the change. That is why virtually all software products try to provide some degree of backward-compatibility with older versions. Note that this is a real cost and it is not a form of inefficient lock-in for the consumer to avoid changing if the benefits to changing are less than this cost.

It is also common for software products to provide some ability to read files produced by other products so as to entice the users of other products to switch and to increase the value of the product to users who exchange files. Some software products try to lower the consumer's costs of switching by mimicking aspects of the user interface of other products.

There are, of course, numerous reasons why a user might have an interest in changing their software applications. Even if they are happy with their current product, it might be that the user needs to move to a new operating system that doesn't run the old product (say from PC to Mac). Or, as is more commonly the case, the user might be looking for some additional features missing from his current product.

Another factor that influences consumers' choices and is likely to be related to large changes in market shares are paradigm changes, or market displacements. These are external changes in the markets that provide motivations for large numbers of current users to switch to a new product. These changes might be a design alteration in the nature of the product itself, or a change in the operating environment of the product. Examples would be the removal of copy-protection, allowing the product work in networked environments, the movement from 8 bit to 16 or 16 to 32 bit architectures, the growth of the Internet, the invention of macros, graphical systems, voice recognition, and so forth. If consumers find these changes compelling, they will be willing to switch products if necessary in order to take advantage of the new environment. Two such displacements were the movement from DOS programs to Windows programs and the creation of Office Suites.[12]

Measurement issues

How does one go about measuring the quality of a software product? We have decided to leave the examination of the software quality to experts writing for (mainly) computer magazines. There are, however, still some issues that require judgment calls. First, many magazines do not give numerical scores to competing software products. In many instances, particularly during the 1980s, magazines compared features of various products without making judgments. When judgments were made, magazines often picked a "winner" or "editor's choice" without indicating the quality differential between winners and losers, and without differentiating among the losers.

To overcome some of these limitations, we used more than one method of comparison. The rankings generated with either of these methods are presented as timelines, which can then be compared with market shares.

When magazines numerically rated individual software products, we used these ratings. When numerical scores were given we report these scores, normalized so that the highest rated product always receives a "10." In cases where reviewers rated software by qualitative category such as "excellent," "good," and so forth, we converted these categories into numerical equivalents. In those cases where no overall rating was given, but only ratings for particular characteristics (ease of use, speed, and so forth) we take the average value of the characteristics to get an overall quality ranking for the software application relative to its competitors. In these cases we assigned numerical scores to these ratings (excellent = 10, good = 7.5, fair = 5, poor = 2.5) and summed the ratings across categories to arrive at a score for the package as a whole.[13]

For those reviews that provide clear winners, but no overall evaluation, we count the number of reviewers who state that a particular product is the best. We refer to the number of reviews make such judgments as the number of "wins." This latter measure, even though it provides no information about the remaining products, provides a relatively large number of data points.

To avoid clutter we often remove from the diagrams products that were not important players. Occasionally, therefore, the winner in a particular review may be one of those packages that we have removed, but the reader can easily tell its presence from the fact that the highest score listed will be less than 10. In fact, this occurred quite infrequently.

Although both measures were constructed for each market, only the measure of wins is reported in this paper. Interested readers will need to refer to our book [Liebowitz and Margolis 1999] for complete coverage.

There are also choices regarding the measurement of market share. It can be measured either in units, or in revenues. Most of the time it makes little difference, but we report shares based on revenues unless otherwise specified. Since we usually report prices as well as market shares, the reader can determine unit based market shares for themselves.

Some computers come with a set of software products installed. Although the consumer may not use these preinstalled products, market share statistics treat these preinstalled products as though they represent actual purchase decisions and use.[14] In that sense, market share statistics might sometimes be misleading indicators of actual use. Fortunately, it appears that OEM sales are not likely to influence our results too strongly.

OEM sales, while increasingly important, are still a minority component of application markets. Office Suites are one of the more commonly included products yet the importance of OEM sales is not high. Writing in 1996, IDC analyst Mary Wardley stated:[15]

> OEM sales have suddenly grown to represent a significant percent of overall sales for office suites and thus spreadsheets ... However, OEM sales have had little to no impact on Microsoft so far, and IDC believes their impact will remain negligible throughout the forecast period.

The data on OEM sales of Office Suites in the two years for which they are available, 1996 and 1997, reveal OEM sales to have a limited impact, as illustrated in Figure 10.1. Although OEM sales are responsible for about 30 percent of unit sales in these two years, they are responsible for less than 10 percent of revenues. And for market leader Microsoft, they are responsible for only about 10 percent of sales and 7 percent of revenues.

It is worth noting, in light of the role given to Microsoft's putative attempts to control OEMs in the government's case against Microsoft, the latter's limited use of OEM sales.

Finally, statistics on market shares and prices were generated using data collected by data collection companies Dataquest and IDC. We

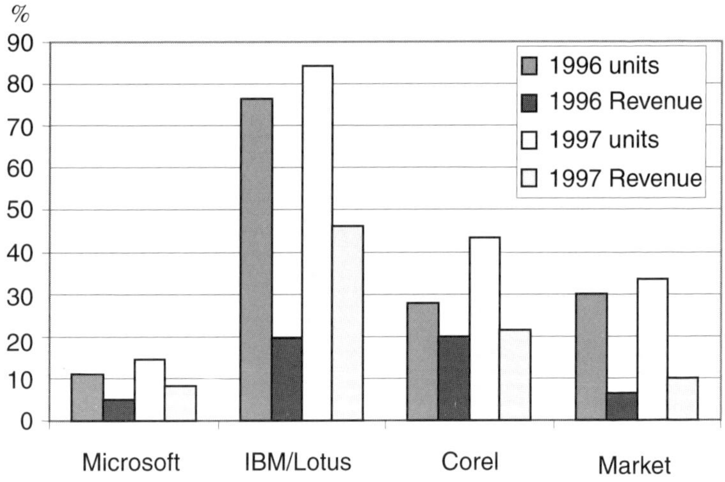

Figure 10.1 OEM sales (from the manufacturer to the retailer) as share of office suites, 1996 and 1997

concluded after a brief examination that list prices don't seem to tell us very much. For one thing, they have not varied very much. Second, it must be remembered that list prices neglect the impact of Office Suites. Third, list prices do not allow us to control for the important role of upgrades, which are less expensive than first time purchases. Also, the list prices fail to account for the units sold to OEMs, which have a far lower price. For all these reasons, we will not focus on list prices but instead on the actual transaction prices received by software producers.

Analysis of spreadsheets

Spreadsheets are one of the mainstays of computer applications. Spreadsheets allow the manipulation of numbers and formulas, and their conversion to charts. The leading spreadsheet is Excel, from Microsoft. It is one of the categories of applications where questions arise about the causes of Microsoft's success.

The evolution of the PC spreadsheet market

Credit for the invention of the spreadsheet goes to Dan Bricklin and Bob Frankston who created VisiCalc for the Apple II. VisiCalc had a list price of $250. Lotus 1–2–3 was introduced in January 1983 at a price of $495. It was immediately acknowledged to be a better product than VisiCalc. In December 1982 Gregg Williams wrote in *Byte* (p. 182) that

1–2–3 had "many more functions and commands than VisiCalc" and that 1–2–3 was "Revolutionary instead of evolutionary." *PC World* called it "state of the art."

In October 1983 *PC World* reported that 1–2–3 was outselling VisiCalc.[16] VisiCalc was removed from the market in 1985 after being purchased by Lotus. Users of VisiCalc were offered upgrades to 1–2–3.[17] In terms of market share, Lotus was to remain dominant for almost a decade.

Unfortunately we do not have detailed data on this early market. Still, from what we have pieced together, it is clear that a superior product, Lotus 1–2–3, was able to quickly wrest market share away from VisiCalc.

By 1985 most spreadsheets were meant to work with the IBM PC. Lotus 1–2–3 was the champ, with other contenders such as Computer Associates (Easy Planner, $195), Ashton-Tate (Framework, $695), Software Publishing (PFS Plan, $140), and IBM (PlannerCalc $80 and Multiplan 1.0, $250). Microsoft had Excel for the Mac (at $495) and Multiplan 2.0 ($195) for the PC.

Soon, many new spreadsheets arrived on the scene. Some were clones of 1–2–3 at lower prices (VP Planner, The Twin, and VIP Professional). Other spreadsheets, such as Javelin and SuperCalc tried to differentiate themselves by improving upon 1–2–3 in some manner, but although these alternatives received some praise, they did not receive universal acclaim and did not make much of a splash in the market.

Excel first appeared in 1985, but for the Macintosh only. Jerry Pournelle, a well-known columnist for *Byte* (and science fiction author), wrote (incorrectly but nonetheless prophetically): "Excel will make the Mac into a serious business machine."[18]

In late 1987 Microsoft ported Excel to the PC (running under an early version of Windows) and Borland introduced Quattro for DOS. Microsoft's election not to produce a DOS version of the program was something of a gamble. The success of Microsoft Windows was far from assured until version 3.0, which became available in 1990. The fact that PC users did not flock to earlier versions of Windows most likely reduced the sales of Excel since users would have had to load Windows to run the spreadsheet and then return to DOS for other applications. Also, many of the features of Excel would have worked best with a mouse, and it was rare for PCs to come with a mouse.

Thus began the market struggle between Microsoft, Borland, and Lotus. Reviews found windows-based Excel to be superior to 1–2–3, with DOS-based Quattro in second place. 1–2–3's market share was unable to stand up to the assault of superior products and Excel's market share eventually surpassed 1–2–3 and it has been firmly in first place ever since.

Spreadsheet quality

In the early and mid 1980s the closest competitor to 1–2–3 in terms of reviews appears to be SuperCalc. *PC Magazine*, in its "BEST OF 1986" review had this to say: "if market dominance were based on rational criteria, Computer Associates' SuperCalc 4 would certainly replace 1–2–3 as the leading spreadsheet program. After all, it can do anything that 1–2–3 can do and adds some notable features of its own."[19] But although various spreadsheets had attributes that were sometimes considered superior to 1–2–3's, there was no general consensus that any alternative was superior. For example, in October 1987 Michael Antonoff in *Personal Computing* stated: "SuperCalc, VP-Planner, and Twin, lack the elegance of 1–2–3 in links to applications."[20]

In late 1987 the quality of the competitors began to change. In a portentous statement, *PC Magazine*, stated: "Microsoft Corp. has just unleashed a spreadsheet that makes 1–2–3 look like a rough draft."[21] This reference was to Excel 1.0 for the PC, a port of its Macintosh Program.

According to reviewers, Lotus appeared to fall behind its competitors in terms of functionality and usability. When comparing 1–2–3 to Excel, a reviewer states "Excel offers a lot in the form of tantalizing features missing from the current version of 1–2–3."[22] Quattro was called

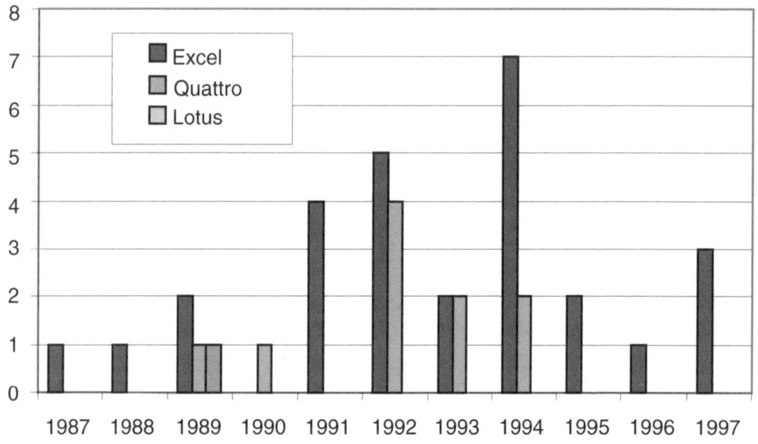

Figure 10.2 Spreadsheet wins, 1987–1997

"a powerful spreadsheet with more features than 1–2–3 Release 2.01, yet fully compatible and a better price."[23]

These were not isolated opinions. Reviewers in general had a very high opinion of Excel in the late 1980s.[24] Clearly, Excel was thought to be the best spreadsheet.

The reason for Lotus' loss of prestige is illustrated better in Figure 10.2, which represents the number of times each spreadsheet won a comparison review in a year, or was bestowed in a magazine with the claim that it was the best product. Excel clearly was the winner over the ten-year period. Between 1989 and 1994 Quattro also managed a fair share of wins, although since 1994 Excel has monopolized the victories. The remarkable feature of this chart, however, is that over the entire ten year period, Lotus 1–2–3 just barely avoids a shutout, managing but a single win out of the numerous instances where a magazine reviewer declared a winner.[25]

The message from these data is quite clear: Excel was clearly the leading spreadsheet in terms of capabilities. The main reservation about Excel was its need for powerful hardware. This last requirement was due to Excel's entirely graphical interface. As is the case with virtually all graphical software applications, Excel was slower to perform tasks than were DOS spreadsheets, even though it could show results that non-graphical (DOS) based applications could not. Once the hardware had caught up to the software (and Windows itself improved) there were no serious challengers to Excel's superiority

The role of price

This brings us to another consideration: what about price? If we are interested in explaining changes in market share we should expect both price and product quality to be important. If there are serious differences in the prices of competing products, a lower quality but lower prices product might have a larger market share than a higher quality higher priced product.

The pattern of average prices received by the manufacturer is illustrated in Figure 10.3. Borland's price discount strategy is clearly revealed. Note also that Lotus kept its prices similar to Excel's even in the face of the latter's increasing market share (as we shall see shortly) and superior reviews. Lotus only began to clearly undercut Microsoft's price in 1996, well after it had fallen below Excel in terms of market share.

But the big story is the stunning fall in prices. By 1997, the typical price (received by the vendor) for a spreadsheet had fallen to approximately $50, or a fall of over 80 percent from the typical price in 1988.

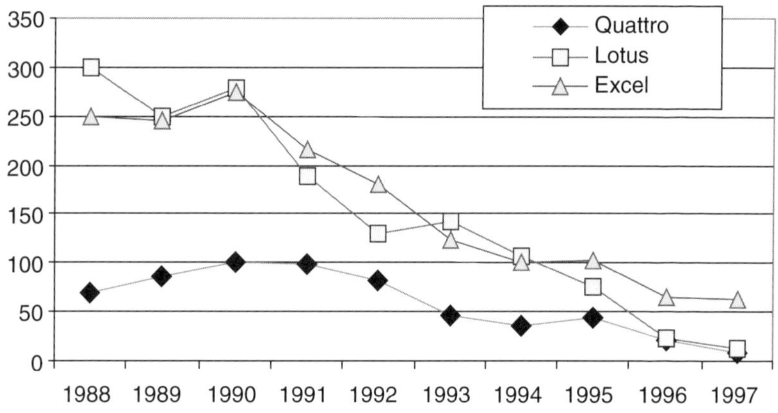

Figure 10.3 Average transaction price, spreadsheets, 1988–1997

Changes in market share: analysis

All of the above evidence indicates that if markets chose better products, Lotus should have lost market share and market dominance. After all, for a considerable period of time it was not the top ranked product. The winner should have been Excel. Is this what happened? Absolutely.

Figure 10.4 provides market share data (based on revenues) that reveals 1–2–3 losing its dominant position to Excel.

Excel had other factors increasing its likelihood of success. Not only was it the best Windows spreadsheet, but it was the first Windows spreadsheet. It was also part of the first Office Suite, and it was part of

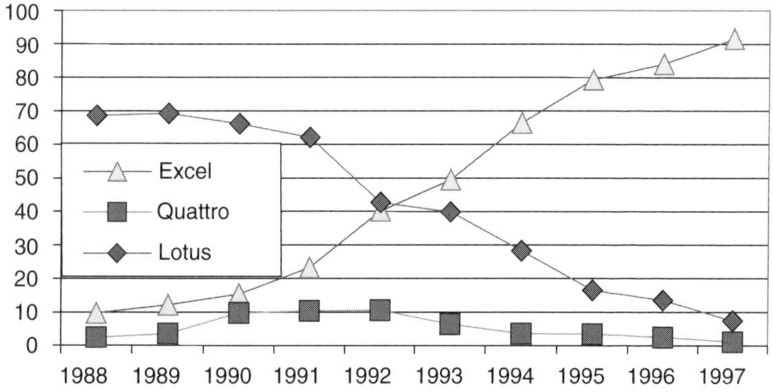

Figure 10.4 Revenue share of spreadsheets, 1988–1997

the best Office Suite. Office Suites and Windows were both strategic gambles by Microsoft that paid off handsomely.

Given the superiority of Excel, this result should be viewed as support for the view that markets choose the better products.

The market share results do not provide any empirical confirmation for the idea of markets tipping. When a product has a small market share, network effects should work to hinder increases in market share, but beyond some breakout point network effects should work in favor of market share increases. This would tend to imply some form of bend or kink, where positively sloped market share curves are flatter to the left of the breakout point, and steeper to the right. Instead what we find is a fairly steady increase in Excel's market share and a fairly steady decrease in 1–2–3's. This may mean that network effects are just not a very important factor in this market, or that their impact on market share is more complex than indicated in the concept of tipping. Either way, this does not bode well for the accuracy of the government's expert economists who discussed the concept of tipping with little or no skepticism.

There are some other issues worthy of examination. In a world of instant scalability, why did it take five years and not one, or two, for Lotus to be dethroned? We can hypothesize some answers. Users know that there is a tendency for software products to leapfrog each other in capabilities. It normally will not make sense for a consumer to switch products every time one product exceeds the capabilities of another, because of the costs of switching. Instead, it is rational for the consumer to expect that the next upgrade of a product that has fallen behind, but which has a history of technological innovation, to contain the features missing from the current version and perhaps even a few extra capabilities. Therefore, consumers will only switch when they can not wait for the missing feature to appear in the next version of their current product, or when it becomes apparent that their current vendor has fallen behind the curve and will not be able to provide a product meeting their needs in the foreseeable future. It probably took two failed generations of products for Lotus to convince the market that it was not going to catch up to Excel anytime soon. Still, Excel averaged 8 market share points a year, which by almost any other standards is quite amazing.

A second question that might arise in the mind of the reader is why Quattro never surpassed 1–2–3. It appears that we can categorize Quattro as a superior product to 1–2–3, even if it was inferior to Excel. There are two reasons, however, why Quattro might not have surpassed an inferior 1–2–3.

First, if a 1–2–3 consumer was planning to switch, it would make more sense to switch to the number 1 product than to the number 2 product. Quattro's only advantage over Excel was its lower price.[26] Instant scalability gave Microsoft the chance to meet the demand of all defecting Lotus users without incurring increases in average cost. In markets without this feature, the number 2 firm likely would pick up some of the slack due to constraints in production for the leading firm.

The second point is that between 1988 and 1995, when Quattro garnered superior reviews to Lotus the gap with Lotus did diminish. It fell from a ratio of about 7:1 in sales to a ratio of 2:1. After that, however, Quattro no longer enjoyed clear superiority over 1–2–3.

Would the Lotus hegemony over spreadsheets have ended without the advent of Windows and Office Suites? Certainly some GUI (graphic user interface) was going to replace DOS, and spreadsheets were going to have to have to be graphical in nature. Given that Lotus was unable to produce a high quality graphical spreadsheet, it would have lost the market to someone. Microsoft would have been a strong candidate to dethrone Lotus in any graphical environment because of Excel's total dominance in the Macintosh market.[27] If the market had gone to the Macintosh, where Excel was clearly the dominant product Lotus would have lost. If OS/2 had predominated, there is every reason to believe that the OS/2 version of Excel would have replaced 1–2–3. And if some third party graphical operating system had prevailed on Intel based machines, there is every reason to suspect that Microsoft would have produced a better product than Lotus because of its familiarity with graphical products.

Personal finance software

Personal finance software allows individuals to balance their checkbooks, track their investments, and plan for the future. The software has become very easy to use and very inexpensive. The major players are Quicken by Intuit, Microsoft Money, and Managing Your Money by Meca. This market is particularly interesting because it is a market in which Microsoft is a major player but not the leader in the market.

Network effects are probably smaller for these products than for many other software markets. Consumers generally are not interested in being able to switch files with other individuals.[28] With the advent of the Internet, however, the ability of software to be compatible with the offerings provided by one's banking institution has probably increased the level of network effects somewhat.

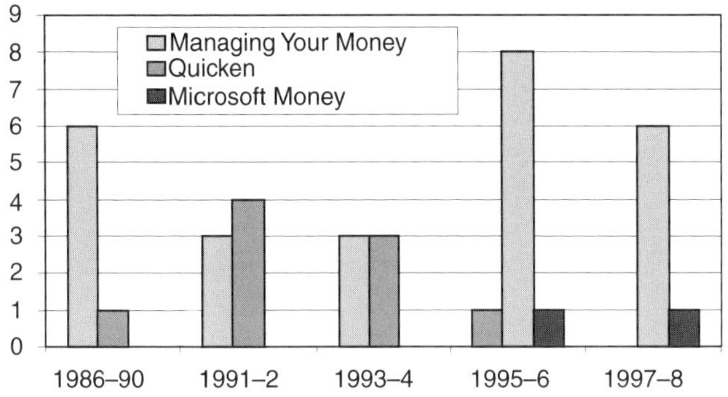

Figure 10.5 Personal finance wins, 1986–1990 to 1997–1998

Personal finance products were introduced in the early to mid 1980s. "Andrew Tobias' Managing Your Money" was the original market leader, to be replaced by Quicken.

Figure 10.5 shows the wins for the various products in the market. In the late 1980s Managing Your Money was initially considered the best and most powerful product in the category. When Quicken was introduced it received reviews that were less positive because it was not as powerful as Managing Your Money. It basically limited individuals to balancing their checkbooks and checking their budgets, but it did this quite well.[29] It also was less than one third the price of Managing Your Money.[30]

Over time Intuit improved Quicken, adding more sophisticated features, and as Figure 10.6 reveals, by the early 1990s it was considered at least the equal of Managing Your Money and by the mid 1990s Quicken was clearly considered the best product. Managing Your Money still appealed to those more interested in power, e.g. tracking sophisticated investments as opposed to just ordinary stocks and bonds. Microsoft Money, which had recently appeared, appealed to those interested in simplicity.[31]

Figure 10.6 provides information on the market shares of the three leading products. This appears to be another case of one dominant firm followed by another dominant firm, what we call serial monopoly. A market leader with 60 percent of the market is displaced within three years by another firm which then achieves a market share of greater than 60 percent. The rapidity with which Quicken overtook Managing Your Money is astonishing, although the source of the data requires some caution on our part.[32] Still, market shares changed so rapidly in

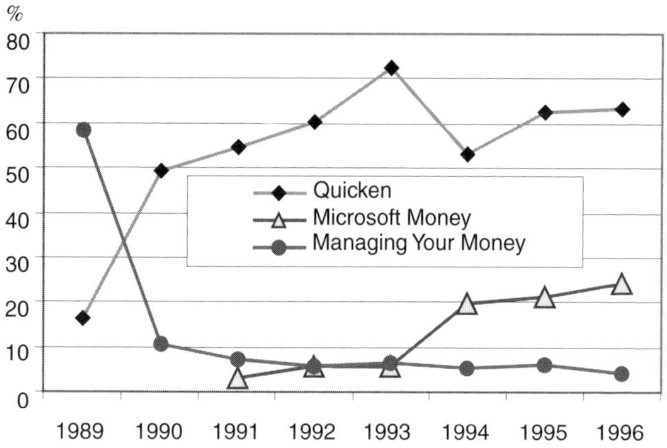

Figure 10.6 Market share of PC personal finance, 1988–1996

this market that the concepts of inertia or lock-in seem entirely out of place. Also absent is any hint of tipping in this market.

There are some differences in this market from the results found in other markets, however. It appears that Quicken became the leading product in the market when it had merely matched and before it had surpassed the quality of Managing Your Money. Figure 10.7, which represents the prices for the leading products, provides a possible explanation for Quicken's ascendancy before it surpassed the quality of Managing Your Money. The very high relative price of Managing Your Money is clearly apparent prior to 1992. Unlike many other software markets, this market caters to individuals as opposed to businesses. The retail price of Managing Your Money, being three times the price of

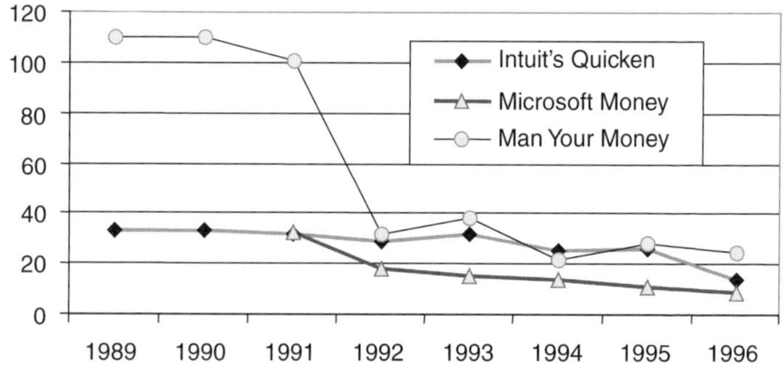

Figure 10.7 Prices of personal finance software, 1989–1996

Quicken, might well have deterred price conscious individuals from choosing it when the two products were similar in quality. This could well have led to the rapid demise of Managing Your Money.

By 1992, when Managing Your Money finally lowered its price to match the other programs in the personal finance software category, it has lost its quality advantages. Also, Managing Your Money was hurt, as were so many other products that we have examined in other markets, by its inability to provide a timely Windows version of the product; it was not until 1994 that a Windows version of Managing Your Money arrived.

We can conclude that consumers preferred Quicken's low price, simplicity, and checkbook handling to the sophisticated financial management and much higher price of Managing Your Money.

In 1991 Microsoft introduced its Money program for Windows. Unlike many of the market leaders in other applications markets, Intuit had a Windows product as early as Microsoft. In fact, its initial share of the Windows market was actually greater than its share of the DOS market. Quicken's market share in the Window's market ranged between 70–80 percent in the early 1990s, and was some ten to twenty points higher than its overall market share.

Microsoft has gained market share throughout the decade, but not from Quicken. Instead, its Windows product has replaced products in the DOS market. Microsoft's share of the Windows market has remained virtually unchanged, having actually fallen slightly since 1991. Microsoft also has had a lower price than its competitors since 1992, perhaps taking its cue from some reviewers who argued that since it was less powerful than its competitors it should have a lower price.

Quicken's retention of its market leadership is not surprising given its high quality as indicated in successful reviews. According to Microsoft's critics, however, Microsoft should have been able to leverage its ownership of the operating system to achieve a dominant position, independent of the quality of its software. The fact that Microsoft was unable to do so casts further doubt upon these claims.

Part of the reason for Quicken's success in the Windows market may have been Intuit's experience in the Macintosh market where Quicken was also the leading program, giving Intuit a clear understanding in how to write a successful GUI application.[33] This appears to be a common theme – success in the Windows market is presaged by success in the Macintosh market. Of course, it is entirely logical that it should be so.

For the purposes of our study, the important finding is that we have another case where an incumbent was quickly replaced, but only after the incumbent lost quality advantages. We also have an instance where Microsoft's ownership of the operating system has not allowed it to dislodge the dominant product, in spite of its considerably lower pricing. This reinforces our findings that achieving product quality parity or superiority is a requirement for increased market share.

Browsers

Browsers are products that allow PC owners to access the World Wide Web (WWW). The software category is relatively new since the WWW is a relatively recent phenomenon. As late as October 1994, this market was largely unformed.

Mosaic (created by the University of Illinois' National Center for Supercomputing Applications) was the first successful browser. As *PC Magazine* reported in early 1995: "NCSA's Mosaic was the first Windows-based Web browser – the killer app that started the stampede to the Web. Today, largely as a result of its stellar success, the browser field is in furious ferment, with new products released weekly and existing ones updated sometimes hourly. Browsers are even making it into operating-systems: IBM includes a browser with OS/2 Warp, Version 3, and Microsoft plans one for Windows 95."[34]

The first magazine reviews of browsers that we found were in mid 1994. Netscape, which was formed by some former programmers of Mosaic, introduced Navigator in late 1994. As far as we can tell, magazine reviews considered Navigator to be better than Mosaic from the day of its introduction. Both products were free. Internet Explorer, Microsoft's entry in this market, makes its first (beta) appearance in our magazine reviews in September 1995.

Since the browser "market" began as freeware, and largely continues as freeware, it is a somewhat unusual market in that there are no direct revenues. This is not, however, any different than the over-the-air television market, where stations do not generate any revenues from their viewers. Instead, television stations pay for their programming by selling advertising, and browser companies appear to have adopted a similar model. Revenues can come either from the sale of servers, which send out the information retrieved by browsers, or by selling advertising from the sites that browsers initially go to.[35] Although consumers can easily change the website that is the starting location for the browser, continued patronage of the original location (which is believed likely to occur) would provide considerable advertising revenues to the company that created the browser.[36]

The market for browsers is of great interest because of its role in the DOJ antitrust proceedings against Microsoft. The claims made by DOJ are that Microsoft's inclusion of its browser with the operating system has foreclosed Netscape's ability to generate market share, independent of the quality of the browsers. The government is claiming that Microsoft's bundling of the browser into Windows 98 has caused the erosion of market share that has been Netscape's recent fate.

Given our findings in other software markets that market share is strongly related to product quality, we would expect a similar relationship to hold here. In fact, since all browsers have essentially the same price (zero), there are fewer other factors at work that might disturb this relationship.[37]

In light of results from other markets, we can try to answer the following question: Has Microsoft's browser achieved a market share incommensurate with the share that might be expected given the relative quality of its browser?

Figure 10.8 indicates the wins in the browser "market" since 1995. Because this market is so new, the time span is compressed, with intervals of six months as opposed to the one or two year intervals in prior charts. Still, the trend is very clear. Netscape Navigator was clearly considered the best product until the second half of 1996, after which Internet Explorer became the superior product.[38]

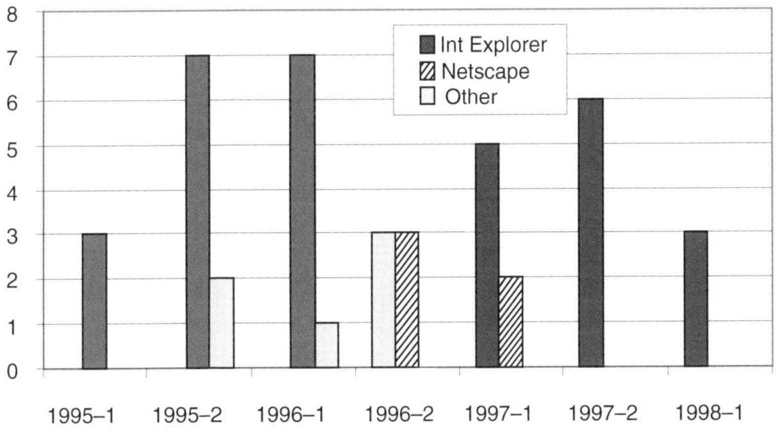

Figure 10.8 Browser wins, 1995:1–1998:1

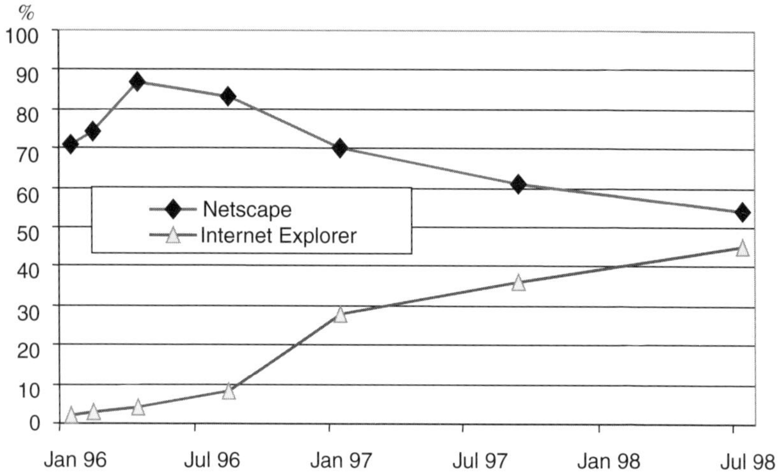

Figure 10.9 Browser shares, January 1996–July 1998

The time frame is compressed once again in Figure 10.9 which provides information on the market shares of the two products.[39] Market share here is measured differently than in other markets. Instead of measuring sales, which is the flow of new products into an already installed base, market share here reflects installed base. However, the information on use also indicates that most browsers in use are of very recent vintage, so that stock and flow magnitudes are likely to be very similar.

The actual increase in Internet Explorer's market share has been a matter of some contention. Microsoft relied on a survey that indicated a relatively small increase in Internet Explorer's market share, and the government relied on browser usage data which tend to reveal a considerably larger increase in Internet Explorer's market share.

There are serious difficulties impeding an unambiguous measurement of browser usage, including the fact that many ISPs "cache" popular web sites and that some ISPs, such as AOL put their own brand on someone else's browser.

Nevertheless, Internet Explorer has increased its market share. The Zona survey, from which Figure 10.9 is based, indicates one of the larger increases in Internet Explorer's market share.

This increase in Internet Explorer's market share has occurred concomitantly with Internet Explorer's quality improvements relative to Netscape Navigator. Internet Explorer barely grew at all, even though it was freely distributed with Windows and on the Internet, until after July 1996. This would be the same period of time where Internet Explorer achieved parity with Netscape for the first time. This is also the first time that Internet Explorer appears to have taken market share away from Netscape which had continued growing its market share even in the face of Microsoft providing a large number of free copies of Internet Explorer.

The level of superiority of Microsoft Internet Explorer after 1997, as indicated in the reviews summarized in Figure 10.9 has in our examinations of other markets always led to increased market share and even market dominance. Is there any reason to expect different results in this market?

There are several reasons that we might expect more rapid market share changes in this market than in the typical software market. First, network effects seem rather small in this market since there is little interactivity between users that might cause users to care who else uses their make of browser. Second, compatibility with prior versions seems small, since learning the idiosyncrasies of a particular browser takes far less time than learning a spreadsheet, word processor, or desktop-publishing program. Further, there is less reason to worry about incompatibility with the files created by these programs since generally the only files that remain through multiple generations of browsers are the list of "favorite" sites, and these are fairly easily translated. Finally, the price of browsers is zero, and users presumably already have access to the free downloads available on the web, since browsers are of no value without Internet access. Therefore, the concept of instant scalability, meeting shifts in market demand on a moment's notice, is even more pronounced here than in other software markets.

Thus, we should expect that market shifts would occur more rapidly in the browser market than almost any other software market that we have encountered.

There are two other markets where market shares changed by fifty or sixty percentage points within two years, one being personal finance software (the other being low-end desktop publishing). In the browser market we find a change in market share of approximately forty points within a two year interval from July 1996 to July 1998. Is the difference in browser quality such that we would expect this type of change?

We are not in a position to give a definitive answer. As noted, we should expect lower costs of switching browsers than most other software, which would enhance the speed of market share shifts. Whether the quality differential is sufficiently great to support this level of market share change we cannot know with certainty.

But given the low costs of switching browsers and the extent of the quality differentials, and given what we have learned about market share changes in software markets, Microsoft's increase in market share in the browser market seems well within reasonable levels. Our analysis indicates that the change in market share that has occurred in the browser market could have been explained entirely by quality differentials, with no appeal to the factors that the government has focused on in its case against Microsoft, i.e. ownership of the operating system or exclusionary contracts.

This is another market which doesn't seem to exhibit either inertia or tipping. Since network effects should be small in this market, it might not be a very strong test of lock-in or the tipping hypothesis, however.

Currently, Internet Explorer appears to have built up a considerable lead in market share, at least as far as usage, although some data services do not agree.[40] As long as Internet Explorer retains its advantage in quality, our analysis of other markets indicates that we can be confident that Internet Explorer will continue to take share away from Netscape – whether or not it is included in the operating system.

Microsoft, monopoly, and consumer harm

Monopolists cause harm to consumers by reducing output and raising price. Although there has been much talk about Microsoft's impact on innovation, there is no clear relationship between monopoly and innovation, nor any data to test such assertions. The question of whether Microsoft acts like a monopolist and whether it causes harm to consumers in the traditional, well-tested context should be crucial to the current DOJ case. What is the evidence?

In the sections that follow we examine the price history in various software markets. Putting several disparate pieces of this pricing puzzle together makes, we believe, a persuasive case for concluding that Microsoft has not harmed consumers.

Word processor and spreadsheet prices

Figure 10.10 reports average prices for the two largest markets, spreadsheets and word processors (in the PC, or IBM compatible, market). The most relevant feature of this chart is the very large overall fall in prices, as already noted.

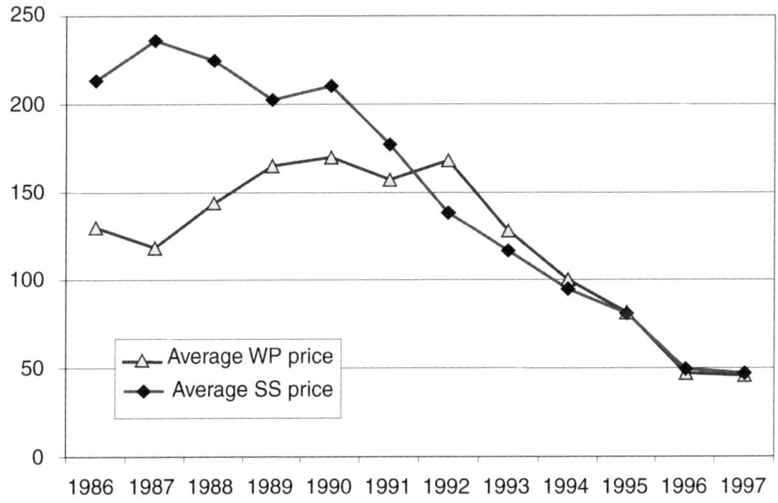

Figure 10.10 Word processor and spreadsheet prices, 1986–1997

This fall in prices is not constant throughout the period, however. From 1986 until 1992, prices were either constant or rising slightly in the word-processing market. From 1986 until 1990 prices were essentially constant in the spreadsheet market. Beginning in 1991 or 1992 prices fell in a very dramatic fashion. What is the proper interpretation of these price declines?

It will suffice for the moment to describe the early period as the Lotus era in spreadsheets and the WordPerfect era in word-processing. Although any firm, including Microsoft, could have charged whatever price it wanted when it had a small share of the market, it is likely the case that the most effective strategy was to follow the price set by the leader in the market. This conclusion is reinforced by our finding that, except in markets catering to individuals, price differentials were rather ineffective at generating additional market share.

Figure 10.10 provides information on price changes, but monopoly and competition differ in the level of prices, not in the way that they change price. However, if the market were moving from a less competitive to a more competitive market equilibrium, prices would be expected to fall during the transition. If Lotus and WordPerfect tried to use their large market shares to generate short run monopoly profits, and Microsoft didn't, we would expect prices to fall as the markets stopped taking its cues from WordPerfect and Lotus and instead started to take their cues from Microsoft. Once the new regime was in place, prices should have stabilized at their new lower level, *ceteris paribus*.

If Microsoft believed that Lotus and WordPerfect lost their dominant position because they failed to act competitively, it might have chosen a competitive price even after it achieved a dominant market shares. That appears to be what has happened since there is no evidence of prices rising even after market shares above 99 percent are achieved, as in the Macintosh spreadsheet market, and this pattern of behavior on Microsoft's part occurred in some other markets such as midrange desktop publishing which we do not cover in this paper.

By itself, this evidence might be suggestive, but would fall short of a sufficient basis on which to draw conclusions. Combined with the evidence in the next two sections, however, there is a compelling case to be told in favor of Microsoft.

Microsoft's overall impact on prices

One question that naturally arises in regard to pricing is how the markets examined in this study compare to markets overall. After all, it is possible that the pricing pattern in Figure 10.3 was reproduced in many other markets and had nothing to do with Microsoft's increased market position. We were able to perform a somewhat crude test of this claim. Dataquest provides consistent market definitions for fourteen software markets for the contiguous period 1988–1995.[41] We calculated the average price in each category for each year as if this 'average price' represented changes in prices for the underlying products.[42]

Next, we categorized markets into three main groups: one group of markets where Microsoft has a product, one group where Microsoft has no product, and a third group where the products compete with some function of Microsoft's operating system.[43] All prices are normalized to their 1988 levels to simplify comparisons.[44] The results are shown in Figure 10.11.

The results are rather striking. Although it appears that software prices in general have fallen in price over this period of time, some software prices have fallen far more than others. In particular, those categories where Microsoft participates, directly or indirectly, have had far more dramatic declines than in other markets, falling by approximately 60 percent compared to the relatively paltry 15 percent fall in prices for software in markets completely devoid of Microsoft's influence.

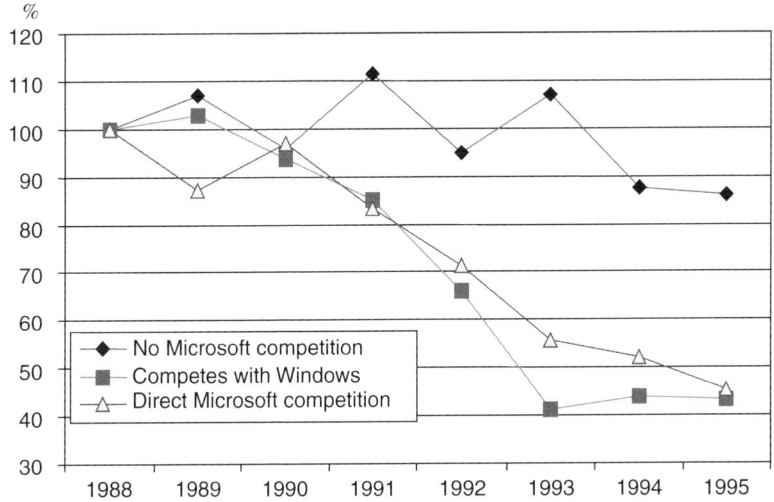

Figure 10.11 Impact of Microsoft on software, 1988–1995

PC – Macintosh price comparison

The data allow one more interesting price comparison. That is for the same product in two markets with very different market shares. We are here talking about Microsoft Word and Microsoft Excel in both the PC and the Macintosh market.

Figure 10.12 provides market shares for these two products in the PC and Macintosh markets. Examination reveals that Microsoft achieved very high market shares in the Macintosh market even while it was still struggling in the PC market. On average, Microsoft's market share was about 40 to 60 percentage points higher in the Macintosh market than in the PC market in the 1988–1990 period.[45] It wasn't until 1996 that Microsoft was able to equal in the PC market its success in the Macintosh market. These facts can be used to discredit a claim sometime heard that Microsoft only achieved success in applications because it owned the operating system, since Apple, not Microsoft, owned the Macintosh operating system and Microsoft actually competed with Apple products in these markets.

Microsoft's market share in the late 1980s in the Macintosh market is generally higher than the market shares achieved by Lotus or WordPerfect in the PC market. Microsoft's market share by the mid 1990s in the Macintosh market was considerably higher than any

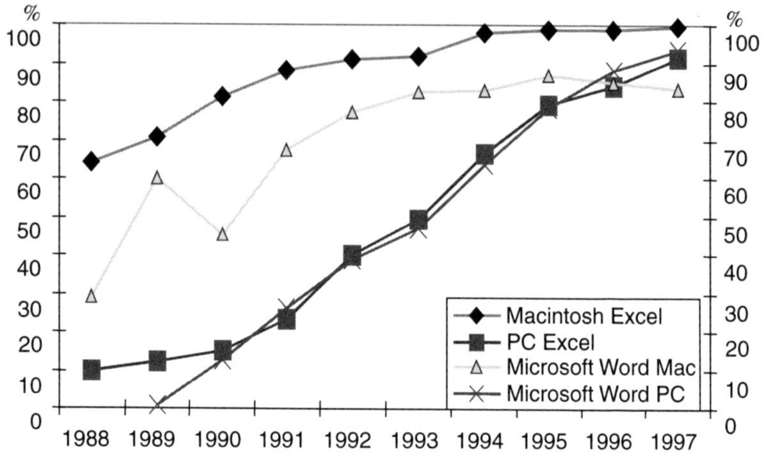

Figure 10.12 Excel and Word in Mac and PC, 1988–1997

leading firm in the DOS era. To a structuralist Microsoft would appear to enjoy a monopoly in the Macintosh market. One might expect, therefore, that its prices in the Macintosh market to be at least as great as its prices in the PC market. Additionally, since it was trying to increase its market share in the PC market in the late 1980s one might think that its prices there would be considerably lower than where it already has a "monopoly" market share.[46]

Those holding a structural view of monopoly, therefore, might expect Microsoft to charge a higher price in the Macintosh market and a lower price in the PC market.[47]

Although there is some imprecision in the data,[48] the price comparisons suggests the exact opposite of this. PC-Excel, far from being cheaper, in fact averages 13 percent higher prices than its Macintosh cousin during the period 1988–1992. PC Word's price, on average, was more than 80 percent above the price for Macintosh Word prior to 1993. After that, the prices are virtually the same. To double check this result we went to price advertisements in computer magazines from *PC Connection* and *Mac Connection*, a retailer selling to both markets, and compared prices. Excel on the PC was consistently about 33 percent higher than for the Macintosh version.[49] A similar result holds for Microsoft Word.

In other words, Microsoft was not charging high prices in the market where it clearly has a structural monopoly. If anything, the prices in the market where it was dominant were lower than in the markets where it was competing. After Microsoft had come to dominate the PC market, it might have been expected to raise prices, but it lowered them dramatically. We cannot attribute this result to some idiosyncratic difference between PC and Macintosh markets since Microsoft equalized the prices in the two markets after gaining dominance in both. What might be going on, then?

One answer, that appears consistent with all our findings, is that Microsoft worries about competitors even when it has a very large market share. Such concern about potential entrants might explain why Microsoft has not lost any markets it has gained. The decline of DOS leaders might have been partly due to an erroneous lack of such concern.

Conclusions

The concept of network effects has been a cudgel in the government's case against Microsoft. The government's use of network effects requires that certain assumptions be true if the case is to make economic sense. This paper has opened a window into the workings of software markets. To our knowledge, ours is the first systematic examination of these markets. The results have run counter to much of what passes for conventional wisdom.

The lack of evidence for market inertia and tipping should raise red flags to analysts in these markets who have treated these untested claims as established facts. The rapidity of market share changes should cause believers in market inertia to take pause. Also, the concept of tipping, which seems so reasonable in principle, seems to have no support if tipping is to mean that self-reinforcing mechanisms accelerate rates of change.

The rapid changes in market share and the close relationship between these changes and product quality that was demonstrated in this paper for three markets was repeatedly found in our more complete analysis. The large and rapid changes in market shares are counter to the claim that dominant firms become locked-in. We have seen instances of a once-dominant firm that faded into obscurity including Managing Your Money, Lotus 1–2–3 (and elsewhere, WordPerfect, PageMaker, Ventura, First Publisher and Prodigy). In some instances, the product that replaced these onetime leaders was a product from Microsoft, in other instances it was from some other company. In each instance, however, the product that replaced the incumbent was of higher quality and often cheaper.

The evidence makes clear that the most important factor for replacing an incumbent firm is to produce a better product. Other factors are undoubtedly also important, but just getting a product to the starting line of a new race was unlikely to be successful if the product was not of high quality. Sometimes price played a role, although it appeared to have a surprisingly small role (perhaps because price changes were often mimicked by other firms). Also of interest was the finding that being number two was of little value. Virtually all the shift in market share seemed to go to the number one product as measured by quality.

The other important finding is the amazing track record of Microsoft in terms of producing better products at low prices. Although it has been suggested that Microsoft did not earn its large market shares in applications, we have found the evidence to be at complete variance with this suggestion. In those instances where Microsoft moved from a low to a high market share, its products were clearly better than the market leader's. When its products were not superior, it did not make inroads against the market leader.

It has been suggested that Microsoft has used it monopoly position to refrain from lowering prices. Any claim that Microsoft harms consumers through monopolistic pricing is wholly at odds with the evidence we have uncovered. Microsoft appears to have a regime of low prices in markets it has come to dominate. Naturally, Microsoft also had to hurt its competitors by these actions.

It is true that the government has focused on the operating system and not on applications, although the states involved in the case had attempted to bring the application market into the case and seemed only to lack sufficient time to do so. Evidence on Microsoft's pricing of the operating system, although largely given behind closed doors, does not seem to be contrary to our findings in applications markets and does not seem capable of answering the basic question of monopoly power. As we have stated before, monopoly does not imply rising prices, only high prices.

We conclude that the use of network effects in antitrust cases appears to be unwarranted in the software industry. We also believe that Judge Jackson was mistaken in his findings of fact, which clearly signal that he is going to find Microsoft guilty of monopoly behavior [a prediction recently confirmed]. Since there is no evidence in any other industry indicating that network effects have the pernicious effects that have been so often attributed them, we believe that it is unwise for network effects be granted any role in antitrust whatsoever.

Notes

1. This paper is based on research conducted for our book (Liebowitz and Margolis 1999).
2. Differences in taste, however, can allow incompatible standards to coexist.
3. We have focused on a form of path dependence we call third-degree path dependence, meaning that the inability to coordinate their activity causes consumers to continue to use a product even when there would be an alternative product that would provide benefits net of switching costs.
4. See David (1985).
5. See Chapters 2 and 5 in this volume.
6. See Reback *et al.* (1995).
7. We are aware of two empirical attempts to test the strength of network effects (both using spreadsheet markets), Gandal (1994) and Brynjolfsson and Kemerer (1996). Both run hedonic regressions with putative proxies for network effects as independent variables. Gandal uses Lotus file compatibility and the ability to link to external databases to measure the strength of network effects. Brynjolfsson and Kemerer use Lotus menu structure and installed base as a measure of network effects. In general, these variables will not measure network effects. Lotus file compatibility cannot distinguish between consumers who, when upgrading, wish to remain compatible with their old files – not a network effect – from the network effect of wishing to be compatible with others. The same problem afflicts the installed base variable. These variables might have performed as hoped if the samples were limited to first time buyers, but they were not. The ability to link to external databases is a useful function, but it is not a network effect. The Lotus menu structure variable measures the importance of remaining compatible with one's old learned habits, also not a network effect.
8. One exception is the Brynjolfsson and Kemerer article cited above. Although flawed, they intended to test for this impact with their installed base variable.
9. Furbys are toys that were in short supply in the 1998 Christmas season, Cabbage Patch Dolls were in short supply during the late 1980s. The shortages in both cases caused a minor sensation.
10. "Better" here means that the costs of switching are less than the benefits, on a social scale. Obviously, any rational consumer would switch anytime his personal benefits were greater than his costs.
11. We use the term "upgrade" to imply that the product has been modified but is largely the same as before in the sense that the users do not have to learn very much new to use the product. Some market upgrades are really shifts to new products that happen to use the same name, or are owned by the same company. The text provides a few examples of upgrades that do not fit our definition, such as the introduction of WordStar 2000 as an upgrade of WordStar, and AmiPro's successor, WordPro.
12. In our 1999 book [Liebowitz and Margolis 1999] we analyze the impact of these displacements in more detail.
13. This process picks winners consistent with magazine reviewers since in every case we found, the product that produced the highest score on our constructed index also was the editor's choice.

14. Revenues and quantities are reported based on sales of software vendors (producers), and include sales to OEMs, upgrades, and retail sales. Revenues are based on the price received by the vendor, and thus represent wholesale prices.
15. P. 10, "PC Spreadsheet Market Review and Forecast," 1996–2001, IDC.
16. *PC World*, October 1983, p. 120.
17. *PC World*, December 1985, p. 221.
18. "Review of Excel Demo at Comdex, "*Byte Magazine*, September 1985, p. 347.
19. P. 115, January 13, 1987, by M. David Stone.
20. P. 101.
21. P. 33, November 10, 1987, *PC Magazine*: First Looks', by Jared Taylor.
22. Michael Antonoff, *Personal Computing*, December 1987 p. 102.
23. P. 33, Mike Falkner, *PC Magazine*, December 12, 1987, First Looks' – "Quattro: More Than 1–2–3 At Less than Half the Cost."
24. Excerpts from many reviews are provided in our book [Liebowitz and Margolis 1999].
25. We exclude the November 1993 issue of *InfoWorld* that gave Lotus the highest marks, since Excel was not included in the comparison.
26. One finding that comes from examining the fuller set of products is that prices seem to play a very limited role, particularly for products sold to businesses. This might be due to the fact that training costs swamp software costs.
27. Excel and Word had very dominant market positions in the Macintosh market long before their ascendance in the PC market.
28. There is value for some individuals in being able to share this data with their accountants. There is an accepted file format for exchanging such information, however, that most products in the category follow.
29. For example, in the September 1987 issue of *PC Magazine* on p. 482 we find the quote: "Quicken, the checkbook manager does one thing and does it well."
30. The list price for Managing Your Money in the late 1980s was $220, and for Quicken was $60. According to *Dataquest* figures, the average price received by the vendor for Quicken in 1989 was $33, and for Managing Your Money was $110 [Tables 22 and 23 in "Market Statistics 1994," *Personal Computing* software Vendor Shipment and Revenue Data, June 6, 1994].
31. For example: "But it's what Managing Your Money offers beyond basic banking that truly sets it apart from the rest ... The package provides the most comprehensive tax and financial planning and portfolio management of any product reviewed here ... This package is also the only real choice for active investors." *PC Magazine*, January 12, 1993, p. 258. Also: "If your needs are simple, you'll be especially happy with Money. Individuals who track investments or want to pay bills electronically should get one of the Quickens ... Those who want more than checkwriting – a total personal finance package – should consider Managing Your Money," *PC Magazine*, January 14, 1992
32. Because of the large price differential, market shares based on revenues may give somewhat different results than those based on units sold, making is unclear exactly when Quicken began to dominate Managing Your Money. IDC has Quicken outselling Managing Your Money 8:1 in revenues and

25:1 in unit shipments by 1991. *Dataquest* reports almost identical unit sales for the two products 1989 (a 10 percent edge to Managing Your Money, providing Managing Your Money a 3.5:1 edge in revenues. For 1990, however, *Dataquest* gives Quicken a 15:1 edge in sales and 4:1 edge in revenues in 1990. The November 1988 issue of *Money Magazine* states that Quicken "does only check-writing and budgeting, but outsells the rest." By 1990 Quicken was clearly outselling Managing Your Money in unit sales and most likely revenues.

33. Intuit had the Macintosh program with the leading market share as early as 1988, when our data on this market begin.
34. "Web Browsers: the Web untangled," *PC Magazine,* February 7, 1995
35. When a browser is first activated it goes to a preordained location (e.g. Netscape's or Microsoft's home page just as a television or radio tuner, when turned on, will be set for some frequency which may contain a station). The difference is that the browser is set to receive information from a web page that exists, whereas radio and television frequencies vary by city and thus may or may not be tuned to an actual station when first turned on.
36. According to a survey in Family *PC Magazine*: "About 38 percent set their start-up page to a site they found surfing, while 15 percent made their own start page. Most people grow so accustomed to their start-up page they never change it." The survey also examined where readers obtained their browsers, an issue of some importance given the DOJ claim that inclusion on the opening screen was crucial: "When asked where they got their browser, 42 percent said they downloaded it, 32 percent got it from their ISP, and 12 percent said it came with their computer." Browsers, October 1, 1998.
37. Netscape originally gave its Navigator browser away but later, after it achieved a dominant market share, charged a positive price. After Microsoft's Internet Explorer, which was free, began making serious inroads into Netscape's market share, Netscape again began to give its browser away.
38. A similar document was entered into the court record in the direct testimony of Microsoft witness Richard Schmalensee.
39. These data come from Zona Research who conduct periodic surveys.
40. In November 1999 information from the Web Counter, based on approximately 450 million hits a month and 475 000 web pages (many pornographic), though indicated that Internet Explorer had 76 percent of the market to Netscape's 19 percent. In March 1999, the same site reported that Internet Explorer had 68 percent of the usage market to Netscape's 31 percent. On the other hand, SuperStats, based on a smaller sample, found that Internet Explorer had 53 percent and Netscape to have 42 percent, with AOL receiving 5 percent, but it is unclear what the AOL browser is.
41. The categories are: desktop publishing, accounting, draw and paint, forms, utilities/application, communication, personal finance, presentation graphics, spreadsheets, word processors, database, project management, integrated software. We proxied for separate desktop publishing categories by putting Microsoft into midrange and everyone else into high-end.

42. Average "prices" calculated in this manner might not reflect actual prices. For example, shifts across products within a category might change the average price even if each price remained constant. we assume that such shifts are either minimal, or similar across product categories.
43. The categories where Microsoft competes are: midrange desktop publishing, personal finance, presentation graphics, spreadsheets, word processors, database, project management, and integrated software. The categories where Microsoft does not have an entrant are: accounting, draw and paint, high-end desktop publishing, and forms. The categories that compete with the operating system are utilities/application and communication.
44. Average prices are calculated as weighted averages, weighted by the revenues in each market. Unweighted average prices were also calculated and found to be almost identical.
45. This chart only examines Word for Windows, and ignores Word for DOS. The latter had a 13 percent and 16 percent market share in 1988 and 1989, respectively.
46. We have noted that low prices were not terribly effective at generating market share when the product was not the best, but they should be more effective when the product is the best.
47. E.g. the followers of Joe Bain. See Goldschmid, Mann, and Weston 1974.
48. We were forced to use *Dataquest* data for the late 1980s even though the price values are too variable to generate much confidence. That is why we looked for alternative sources.
49. In June 1990 Excel and Microsoft Word for Windows were both $329 while both products for the Macintosh were $245. In 1989 Macintosh Word and Excel were both $255 while Excel was $319. In 1988 both products were $249 in the Macintosh market, but Excel was $319 in the PC market.

References

Brynjolfsson, E. and Kemerer, C. F. 1996. "Network Externalities in Microcomputer Software: An Econometric Analysis of the Spreadsheet Market," *Management Science*, 42(12): 1627–1647.

David, P. A. 1985. "Clio and the Economics of QWERTY," *American Economic Review*, 75: 332–337.

Farrell, J. and Saloner, G. 1985. "Standardization, Compatibility, and Innovation," *Rand of Economics Journal*, 16: 70–83.

Gandal, N. 1994. "Hedonic Price Indexes for Spreadsheets and an Empirical Test for Network Externalit," *Rand Journal of Economics*, 76: 940–955.

Goldschmid, H. Mann H. and Weston J. (ed.). 1974 *Industrial Concentration: The New Learning*, Boston: Little, Brown & Co.

Katz, M. L. and Shapiro, C. 1985. "Network Externalities, Competition, and Compatibility," *American Economic Review*, 75(3): 424–440.

——— 1995. "Path Dependence, Lock-in, and History," *Journal of Law, Economics, and Organization*, 11: 205–226; reprinted as Chapter 5 in this volume.

——— 1999. *Winners, Losers, and Microsoft: Competition and Antitrust in High Technology*, Oakland, CA: The Independent Institute.

Reback, G., Creighton, S., Killam, D. and Nathanson, N. with assistance from Garth Saloner and W. Brian Arthur 1995. "Technological, Economic and Legal

Perspectives Regarding Microsoft's Business Strategy in Light of the Proposed Acquisition of Intuit, Inc.", *Upside* (February).
Roe, M. J. 1996. "Chaos and Evolution in Law and Economics," *Harvard Law Review*, 109: 641–668.
Williamson, O. E. 1993. "Contested Exchange Versus the Governance of Contractual Relations," *Journal of Economic Perspectives*, 7: 103–108.

11

The Current State of the Debate Involving the Economics of QWERTY

Peter Lewin

Introduction

Readers of this book will be aware that the economics of QWERTY is a controversial area. This chapter reports on some of details of the controversy as it has unfolded to date. In particular the nature of the incipient debate between Liebowitz and Margolis and Paul David may be of some interest.[1] This debate is complicated by the fact that neither side seems to fully realize or acknowledges the presumptions made by the other and, as a result, they often end up talking past each other. This is a motivating theme of my account. The reader should be warned, however, that this is a partisan account, in seeking to interpret the debate I have inserted my own judgments on the issues.

Somewhat paradoxically both Liebowitz and Margolis and their critics (in varying degrees) are critical of mainstream neoclassical (textbook) economics and its standards of welfare. That is to say, they are both highly critical of the kind of neoclassical economics that assumes perfect knowledge, perfect foresight, many traders, etc., the kind that derives perfect competition as a Pareto optimal efficient standard against which to judge real-world outcomes. Both focus (to a greater or lesser extent) on the importance of ignorance and uncertainty (and the importance of institutions) in rendering such a standard problematic. Where they differ decisively, however, is in the policy lessons that they take away from this.

The critics argue that the ideal of perfect competition is an ideal that, for one reason or another, the free market is incapable of attaining, and that, therefore, one should look to the government to obtain by collective action or regulation, what the market, with decentralized actors, cannot. Liebowitz and Margolis have explained clearly why the endorsement of government intervention does not follow from a valid critique of neoclassical welfare economics (and, for that matter, why a defense of neoclassical welfare economics, in itself, is insufficient to establish an argument against intervention).[2] but their insights have not always been adequately appreciated.

David's story and the lack of response

> Cicero demands of historians, first that we tell true stories. I intend fully to perform my duty on this occasion. (David 1985, 332)

With this sentence Paul David begins his story. This, as we have seen, is somewhat ironic, because, if Liebowitz and Margolis are to be believed, the account that he gives is not true. David has since objected (David 1997a, 1997b, 1999a, 1999b) that the article was not intended as an accurate historical record, but merely as an illustrative hypothetical interpretation of history, a prelude to the exhortation to economists to do more economic history. If this is the case, then the quoted sentence seems out of place.[3]

Be that as it may, from the arguments made by Liebowitz and Margolis in their 1990 article, Chapter 2 in this volume, we can conclude that some significant questions relating to the history of the evolution of the typewriter keyboard have been raised that, *at the very least*, deserve to be considered. Surprisingly, no such consideration has been forthcoming.[4] The absence of even an attempt to deal with these questions is troubling. On the matter of the history on which the economics of QWERTY is based, the case for QWERTY-nomics is under a cloud of doubt and suspicion.

It might have been expected that Paul David would have responded in one of two ways:

1. Either he could have, in all candor, conceded that Liebowitz and Margolis have a case on the historical record and that he did indeed present an incomplete picture, making the QWERTY story a poor candidate for the illustration of path dependence, lock-in and the like.
2. Or if possible, he could have jumped at the opportunity to present a more complete history while differing with the interpretation that Liebowitz and Margolis draw, providing his own, one that is more supportive of the QWERTY story as a candidate for the illustration of path dependence, lock-in and the like.

After more than ten years, he has done neither. As we shall see, he has instead attempted to avoid the issue. In the process, in some recent unpublished contributions, he has insinuated (among other things) that Liebowitz and Margolis are wrong on the facts and that he will "soon" explain (see David 1997a, 1997b, 1999a). In a direct reference to Liebowitz and Margolis he writes:

> [I will] put to one side the specific factual allegations adduced in their article ... and look instead at the logic of their analysis ... There will be time enough in the near future to put right the historical mis-allegations ... which being allowed to stand too long without the refutation it deserves, has encouraged some uncritical skeptics ... to dismiss the emblematic tale as 'the *founding myth*' of path dependence. (David 1997b, 4)

Similarly:

> there will be another, more suitable place in which to consider my detailed rejoinder to the dubious factual allegations that have circulated concerning the "true story" of QWERTY. (David 1997a, 7)

To the best of my knowledge, the response to "The Fable of the Keys" has yet to be made.[5]

On some theoretical matters

"Correct" definitions of path-dependence

While not responding on the history of the case, Paul David *has* chosen, in some of his recent, as yet unpublished, work to make an issue out of the definition of path dependence, suggesting that the technical definitions taken from the natural or statistical sciences have more validity than less technical ones and that Liebowitz and Margolis' taxonomy of path dependence is *unscientific*. I shall consider this below, but it is important to point out that David's own original definition of path dependence is not without potential problems. While logically sound it has no obvious empirical relevance, something that Liebowitz's and Margolis' taxonomy was designed to remedy.

I begin with the definition David provides in the 1985 work:

> A *path dependent* sequence of economic changes is one of which important influences upon the eventual outcome can be exerted by

> temporally remote events, including happenings dominated by chance elements rather than systematic forces.

The next sentence reads:

> Stochastic processes like that do not converge automatically to a fixed-point distribution of outcomes, and are called *non-ergodic*. (David 1985, 332, italics in original)

Note that between the first and the second sentence a number of hidden presumptions creep in. It seems to be presumed that one can meaningfully talk about real-world economic outcomes as a set of stochastic processes and that, in fact, historical processes are equilibrating processes. Otherwise what is the connection between the two sentences? A further assumption would appear to be that equilibrium in the real world is analogous to equilibrium in physical systems ("fixed-point distributions") and that such equilibrium points are relevant to an assessment of the process, whether one gets there or not.

David continues:

> In such circumstance "historical accidents" can neither be ignored, nor neatly quarantined for the purpose of economic analysis; the dynamic process itself takes on an *essentially historical* character. (David 1985, 332, italics in original)

Surely everyone would agree that *one cannot ignore history and do good economic analysis*. And it is no doubt true that neoclassical economics is hopelessly short on history. If this is all that David had wished to establish then there would be no interesting discussion. The real issue, in this particular aspect of the debate however, seems more to concern economic policy (rather than the neglect of history) and I will return to this in the next section.

Some of Paul David's recent unpublished work (1997a,b 1999a) on this subject focuses almost exclusively on Liebowitz and Margolis' theoretical contributions, or, even more narrowly, on their definitional framework. In effect he indirectly challenges Liebowitz and Margolis' suspicions of the policy relevance of path-dependence by criticizing at length their understanding of the concept. He does so brandishing the big stick of "Science."

> The time has come for me to take explicit public notice of the numerous respects in which this critical representation of the

> concept of path dependence and its significance, and even its implications in the sphere of economic policy, is *a scientifically inappropriate distortion.* (1997b, 3, italics added)
>
> I aim first to expose the many things I believe to be wrong or misleading about Professors Liebowitz and Margolis' treatment of the analytical aspects of path dependence over the course of the past seven years (1997b, 4).

He then embarks on a lengthy discussion of the definition and meaning of path dependence, which I now briefly examine. We may recall the just-quoted 1985 definition:

> A *path dependent* sequence of economic changes is one of which important influences upon the eventual outcome can be exerted by temporally remote events, including happenings dominated by chance elements rather than systematic forces. (David 1985, 332)

This is a very general common-sense definition that is clearly consistent with a variety of variations of the idea that "history matters." It is true that he goes on to attempt to make this sound more "technical" by using language borrowed from mathematical statistics, but nothing in the article appears to depend on this more "rigorous" statement.

In his more recent critique, by contrast, he makes it sound as if getting the "right" definition of path dependence and lock-in is crucial. It is not possible here to reproduce the entire argument, an attempt will be made to give the flavor.

> Path dependence, as I wish to use the term, refers to a dynamic property of allocative processes. It may be defined either with regard to the relationship between process dynamics and the outcome(s) to which it converges, or the limiting probability distribution of the stochastic process under consideration ...
>
> Path independent processes may be said to include those whose dynamics guarantee convergence to a unique, globally stable equilibrium configuration or ... those for which there exists an invariant (stationary) asymptotic probability distribution that is continuous over all the states that are compatible with the energy of the system ... Negative definition: Processes that are non-ergodic and thus unable to shake free of their history, are said to yield path dependent outcomes. (David 1997b, 5)[6]

He continues in similar vein to provide other variations. To what purpose? Two points emerge:

1. Path dependence may not imply inefficiency, and Liebowitz and Margolis are wrong to suggest that it is only if path dependence implies inefficiency that it is interesting (David 1997b, 9).

   I would merely state here that Liebowitz and Margolis do not suggest that path-dependence is interesting only if it implies inefficiency, but they do suggest that the more interesting policy implications arise when it does.
2. David seems to want to underline that, as he sees it, "path dependence is a property of *stochastic* sequential processes." He also emphasizes that it refers to "dynamic" processes.

The point here seems to be that Liebowitz and Margolis apply the idea of path-dependence incorrectly to deterministic processes (David 1997b, 7). This again would appear to be an unwarranted conclusion. In fact, I would argue that David's notion of "dynamics" in an equilibrium probabilistic situation is inappropriately "static" by comparison to Liebowitz and Margolis' implicit vision.

Other than these points, it is hard to find a relevance for David's long, argumentative discourse on correct definitions (1997a, 1999b). One need hardly add here that a particular concept which has one connotation in the natural sciences often develops important and subtly different connotations when applied to the social sciences. One need only point to concepts like "equilibrium" and "efficiency." It is hard to see how Liebowitz and Margolis' attempt to expand path-dependence in such a way as to make it more relevant to economics (by including the perceptions of economic agents in its construction) can be said to be "incorrect" or "unscientific."

Revisiting path dependence of the third degree

The reader will recall the taxonomy that Liebowitz and Margolis provide regarding the question of path-dependence. First-degree path-dependence refers to the most basic observation that "history matters" – events have enduring consequences. Second-degree path-dependence refers to the fact that some of these consequences may occasion regret. Some events, the result of ill-informed choices, may have sent the economy along a path that is, from the vantage point of present knowledge, less than optimal, so that, had we to do it over again, we might have made wiser choices.[7] Third-degree path-dependence narrows the focus still further to single out those cases of the second degree that provide an opportunity for remediation. Being on a suboptimal path, in the sense that some better world could be imagined, has no policy implications in the absence of an economical way to move toward the optimum. David has attacked this taxonomy by characterizing it as a rhetorical trick designed to empty the concept of path-dependence of any policy relevance.

Now it should be conceded that the existence of a third-degree path-dependent inefficiency is something of a paradox. Why does entrepreneurial activity not remove it? Perhaps because it does not really exist? What appears to be an inefficiency is merely an erroneous judgment made by a third party who does not understand all of the costs that would be involved in choosing an apparently superior alternative. This line of thinking appears to lead us into the Panglossian conclusion that "whatever is, is necessarily efficient," an impasse that has been noted by many theorists, for example by E. J. Mishan (1975, 699) and again by David (1997a, 1997b, 1999a) and Puffert (1999). The Panglossian impasse can be used to characterize the above type of taxonomy as a transparent attempt to foreclose any real policy discussion (as is done, for example, by David, 1997b, 13–15). I will suggest that this is an unwarranted construction, one that rests on a particular presumption of what it is necessary to do to establish a case for remedial policy intervention.[8]

The identification of robust equilibria (the result of ergodic processes) that are not sensitive to variations in the values of key variables, is fundamentally more threatening to the concept of "freedom of choice" than is the recognition that "history," including our personal choices, may make a difference. It is, however, one thing to claim to be able to understand in some way how (retrospectively) history has mattered and quite another to claim to be able to understand how it will do so in the future and to base our economic policy on this. There is, I argue, a fundamental asymmetry between understanding and prediction (much methodological discourse to the contrary notwithstanding).

Policy

What the "debate" really seems to be about is economic policy. The protagonists are on opposite sides of a fundamental policy divide and, are, in effect, talking past each other. Along these lines, I request the reader's indulgence to engage in some speculative mind-reading.

Paul David probably suspects that Liebowitz and Margolis' (and their sympathizers') work is a thinly disguised attempt to foreclose any type of antitrust policy activism and even other less-activist policies, like any form of government-sponsored activity to influence the adoption of appropriate standards. He probably suspects that they are, from the start, constitutionally predisposed against all kinds of government intervention. And he is probably largely correct.

For their part, Liebowitz and Margolis probably suspect that Paul David's work is a manifesto in support of the presumption that government *ought* to be involved in these matters and in favor of the proposition that the government can, if the circumstances are appropriate, be a force for good in the economy. They probably feel this way about most of the contributions in this area, some of which were cited above. And in this they would probably be right.

There is a difference of vision, a difference of presumptions. In this section I will illustrate how this plays out in the rhetoric of the debate. Curiously, one way to characterize my conclusion is to say that the policy recommendation that one arrives at is path-dependent. Where you end up depends crucially on where you start.

Placing the burden of proof

This can be illustrated in very familiar terms (see Table 11.1). Consider the discussion about policy relevance to be analogous (it is very closely analogous) to the conducting of an experiment with (known or unknown) probabilities. As everyone knows, the outcome of the experiment will depend crucially on which errors one seeks to avoid, that is, on which errors one considers to be Type I or Type II. To be more specific, imagine that we are "testing" for the existence or absence of an inefficiency in an established network or standard (or the adoption of a product associated with it). Then two types of experimental design

Table 11.1 Experimental design in searching for policy relevance

Experimental design	H_0 = *the null hypothesis*	H_1 = *the alternative hypothesis*
Design A	An inefficiency exists ⇒ (the status-quo is not efficient)	An inefficiency does not exist
Design B	An inefficiency does not exist ⇒ (the status quo is efficient)	An inefficiency exists

are possible depending on the choice of the null hypothesis, H_0, as illustrated in Table 11.1.

Assume that in order to establish policy relevance it is necessary to disprove the null hypothesis. The alternative designs reflect the presumptions of the experimenter. The essential difference between the two designs is *where it places the burden of proof*. Design B places it on those who lean in favor of policy interventions, while design A places it on those who presumptively oppose it. In this way Liebowitz and Margolis and David (and others who point to the theoretical "likelihood" of inefficiencies) are each trying to place the burden of proof on the other. This is why David can object to Liebowitz and Margolis' taxonomy of path dependence by suggesting that it is a rhetorical trick designed to paralyze economic policy (in reference to the Panglossian impasse discussed above) (David 1997b, 11).[9] From Liebowitz and Margolis' perspective it simply reflects where they consider the appropriate burden of proof to be placed. It is a principled position as "scientific" as any other alternative design.

It is always difficult to reject the null hypothesis (it is sometimes not possible under any practical circumstances). The experiment is designed to make it difficult. Design B is designed to minimize government intervention. Design A is designed to facilitate it. The two designs reflect differences of opinion about the likely benefits of government intervention and, thus, differences in fundamental values. In truth, of course, all empirical (historical) observation is informed by some implicit or explicit theory. The facts never "speak for themselves." One comes to every situation in life with prior presumptions. Differences in presumptions constitute the crux of the different approaches in this field. In this way *no "scientific research" is completely value free*. How is one then to choose between rival designs? Only by an appeal to common values.

In this context, Liebowitz and Margolis are, in effect, saying, "if you think you have identified a remediable inefficiency, prove it." What justification do they have for doing so? The same justification that would presume an accused person innocent unless "proven" guilty (using a stringent probability level of significance to minimize Type I errors), namely that all governmental action is essentially coercive, and if we are to err we should do so on the side of minimizing coercion. They are seeking to avoid the costs of incorrectly identifying an inefficiency, while accepting the costs of failing to identify one. Thus David is surely wrong when he attributes to them the proposition, that, absent the identification of an inefficiency, one may presume to have proven that the outcome is efficient (David 1997b, 13; see also David 1992, 137). Clearly, there is a difference between proving the existence of an inefficiency and proving its absence.

Liebowitz and Margolis are perfectly clear on this. "There is neither convincing theory or even minimal empirical support for the lock-in proposition" (1999, 15). "Although our theoretical discussion does not prove that markets must always choose the best technology, we do claim that there are good reasons to expect it to be very unusual for market participants knowingly to choose the wrong technology" (1999, 117). And so they require a heavy burden to be met. "[P]roofs of existence of inefficiency can never rely on the mechanics of production and consumption alone ... market failure ought to be a very specific and very worldly claim. Policy-makers shouldn't go about correcting markets until they have concrete proof that markets have failed" (1999, 239–240).

David places the burden in a different place. In fact he explicitly addresses this in his most recent paper on this subject (David 1999c). He does so in the context of responding to Deirdre McCloskey's persistent challenge to indicate just "how much" it mattered that QWERTY (or anything else) was an inefficient outcome. In this McCloskey was pursuing a theme she has recently developed – drawing attention to the distinction between statistical and economic significance. It is the latter that is relevant for economic history and policy, the *magnitude* of the alleged effect, the "oomph." (Presumably, the two are not unrelated, since the larger the deviation from the value implied by the null hypothesis (where the null value is zero), the more statistically significant it will be – though statistical significance is not sufficient – or even necessary – to deliver oomph.) David bristles at the challenge to demonstrate that an "economically significant" inefficiency exists. In the first instance, he points out that the very notion of "how much" implies the adoption of Pareto efficiency criteria; the QWERTY-skeptics must have some notion of "what the economy's optimum path looks like" if they are suggesting that one can measure deviations from it (David 1999c, 4). And it is this line of reasoning that allows him to suggest that the problem with his critics is that they are inappropriately wedded to static welfare economics (1999c, 5). But, secondly, "the burden of proof plainly falls on those who say that everything has turned out for the best" (1999c, 8). "Why isn't it up to the skeptics to demonstrate empirically that [departures from some theoretical optimum] only matter 'a little'? Where is it written that the burden of showing quantitative importance in this matter belongs only on the shoulders of those who keep finding grounds (in both reason and fact) for disputing the presumption of optimality or near optimality?" (1999c, 5).

This is clearly directly relevant to Liebowitz and Margolis' work, whose approach is similar to that of McCloskey. The answer to David's question is surely, as explained above, that optimality is *not* assumed (at least not by Liebowitz and Margolis). It is not addressed. What is addressed is the likelihood of government policy being able to improve matters in a world of rapid change and innovation.

In clarifying the role of the (mostly implicit) burden of proof presumptions it becomes clear that apparently value free discussions almost always harbor hidden prejudices about the desirability or otherwise of state intervention. Bringing this to light forces a discussion of the appropriate location for the burden of proof. Should those who propose state intervention shoulder the burden to show that it would, on balance, be beneficial; or should those opposing it shoulder the burden of showing that it would, on balance, be harmful? Stated in this stark manner, and remembering that all state intervention implies the abridgement of individual autonomy in some way, most economists would have to agree that the former burden is the appropriate one. Juxtaposing this with the criticisms of Liebowitz and Margolis' taxonomic and policy discussions lends the latter increased credibility.

Efficiency, policy, and knowledge

Liebowitz and Margolis and David appear to agree on what it means for a technology to be inefficient – they all agree that the criteria must involve an appeal to individual consumer valuations. For example,

> By [an inefficiency] we must mean that an alternative outcome would be preferred in some collective sense (perhaps by application of a compensation test) to the one [individuals] are now in, and that they also (collectively) be ready to incur some substantial costs to rectify the situation – assuming it was feasible to do so. (David 1997b, 13)

How then are such situations identified and corrected? David is convinced that there are historical situations in the world in which individuals were "bounded by a parochial and myopic conception of the process in which they were engaging ... [and in which they] failed entirely to foresee the complementary innovations and investments that would be influenced by their initial commitment to one rather than another course of action" (David 1997b, 15). This is clearly Liebowitz and Margolis' second-degree path-dependence, from which I said earlier no obvious policy implications emerge. What then would David propose? According to him, in a most revealing passage:

> One thing that public policy could do is to try to delay the market from committing the future inextricably, before *enough* information has been obtained about the likely technical or organizational and legal implications of an early, precedent-setting decision ... [P]reserving open options for a longer period than impatient market agents would wish is a generic wisdom that history has to offer to public policy-makers, in all its application areas where positive feedback processes [like network-effects] are likely to be preponderant over negative feedbacks. Numerous dynamic strategies can and have been suggested as ways of implementing this approach in various specific contexts where public sector action is *readily feasible*. Still more sensible and practical approaches will be found if economists *cease their exclusive obsession with traditional questions of static welfare analysis* and instead of pronouncing on the issue of where state intervention would be justified in the economy, start to ask what kind of public policy actions would be most appropriate to take at different points in the evolution of a given market process. (David 1997b, 16, italics added)

This is a remarkable passage worth analyzing in some detail. Liebowitz and Margolis emphasize the role of information (knowledge) in policy action, and establish a case sufficient to cause those who contemplate this type of policy reason for apprehension. But, in addition, I would note, that if policy-makers have knowledge of superior alternatives they surely cannot be alone in this, and if they are why not just make the knowledge public? What David seems to be suggesting here is that *policy-makers have information about what future information (or type of information) will yet be revealed, and also that they can have knowledge of when enough information has been revealed to allow competition between standards to proceed unregulated*. Somehow the policy-makers know more (about what can and will be known) than economic agents do. David may object that even if the agents had the same knowledge about future knowledge as the policy-makers do, they are not organized to, or interested in, providing a collectively rational solution. But if such a solution is "efficient," by common agreement (of what "efficient" means) it would be profitable to organize. Surely this is more than a rhetorical game. We are back to the issue of burden of proof, this time in a very literal and compelling way. One must also ask why we should be content to assume that policy-makers have the right incentives in this regard (even if by some stretch we solved the "knowledge problem")?

The "knowledge problem" is, however, the crux and it is implicit in Liebowitz and Margolis' arguments. It is ironic, therefore, to find David in this passage and in numerous other places criticizing Liebowitz and Margolis for their preoccupation with static welfare criteria. Further, he seems to be suggesting that moving beyond such a framework would support the type of policy activism he is proposing here.[10] The static welfare framework is indeed problematic and we may readily join David's call for moving the education of economists beyond it. Static welfare criteria are inapplicable to dynamic processes and, it is for this reason that, David's policy prescriptions are manifestly unworkable

Concluding remarks

Both sides of this debate proceed by waving the big stick of "Science," but in different ways. David seems to think that credibility and respectability comes from displaying an understanding of technical theoretical frameworks borrowed from the "hard" sciences. In common with much of the writers in this area, he focuses on theoretical sophistication and consistency. Liebowitz and Margolis criticize this by, correctly, pointing out that model building is not a substitute for "empirical" (historical) investigation, to find out which model, if any, is applicable. For better or worse, however, there are no investigations that could provide "knock-down" results. The way is always open for alternative counterfactual interpretations and speculations regarding future developments. The role of plausible counterfactuals is clearly relevant. Liebowitz and Margolis' work echoes (perhaps not altogether consciously) some of the important epistemologically based criticisms of standard microeconomics, and they do so in an area of applied economics that could hardly be more relevant.

Notes

1. I have made liberal use of material from Lewin (2000) In the Preface, I have acknowledged some people who helped in the preparation of this work.
2. In this they are, in many respects, close to the economists of the Austrian School. The Austrians argue not only that the perfectly competitive standard is unattainable, but that it is furthermore, "precisely irrelevant," (Boettke 1996) and the efficiency standards associated with it are mislead-

ing. Austrians are thus critical of Keynesians *and* neoclassicals for different reasons. They are critical of neoclassicals for succumbing to a naïve "positivist"-inspired "physics-envy" in their theory construction, that has led them to create an easy target for the would-be planners of our world, including the Keynesians (Machovec 1995). They are critical of the Keynesians for succumbing to the "fatal conceit" of thinking that they can achieve, through policy intervention, what the free market cannot, and, in the process, threatening the very valuable achievements of the *real-world* market process. In policy matters, Austrians do not see themselves as utopians, they see themselves as realists. On the other hand, they see both Keynesians and neoclassicals as utopians – albeit of different stripes. The protagonists in the debate discussed in the text unconsciously mirror the same two sides of this policy divide. Both are critical of neoclassical economics, one in muted and somewhat superficial terms, the other more fundamentally. And yet they are clearly opposed to each other.

3. In support of this reading we may note the following

   > Standing alone, my story will be simply illustrative and does not establish how much of the world works this way. That is an open empirical issue and I would be presumptuous to claim to have settled it, or to instruct you in what to do about it. Let us just hope the tale proves mildly diverting for those waiting to be told if and why the study of economic history is a necessity in the making of economists. (David 1985, 332)

   But David then proceeds to a series of quite provocative unsupported assertions that have, indeed, formed the basis of presumptuous historical judgments and related policy prescriptions, some offered by David himself (of which more below). Also, as we shall note, apart from the incongruence of this reading with the first sentence quoted above, David's failure to concede Liebowitz and Margolis' case, or even to respond on the issue of the veracity of the story he tells, leaves the distinct impression that he is more wedded to his particular interpretation than the above paragraph would suggest.
4. A notable recent exception is the online discussion on the EH.NET and also Puffert (1999).
5. In his most recent contribution (1999b, 7) David seems to have deflected the issue entirely. He writes: "As this was not a direction in which I felt it would be particularly useful to encourage others to invest their time, it seemed best to decline invitations to become engaged in debates with the die-hard skeptics whose attacks on path dependence were formulated as disputations of the historical evidence regarding the story of QWERTY."
6. Similarly for lock-in, "lock-in ... is simply a vivid way to describe the entry of a system into a trapping region ... When a dynamical (sic) economic system enters such a region, it cannot escape except through the intervention of some external force or shock ... [and] may thus become locked-in to attractors that are optimal, or just as good as any others [or not]" (David 1997b, 11).
7. David opines: "notice that while incomplete information may be critical in blocking spontaneous escapes from dominated coordinated equilibria [read outcomes] it is not a necessary condition for decentralized market processes to select such states." One wonders then what is? What other explanation is

there for why voluntary economic agents would choose inferior situations other than ignorance (of the advantages or of the coordination costs)?

8. This is relevant to the typewriter case discussed earlier. Paul David clearly implies that QWERTY is a case of third-degree path-dependence. Deirdre McCloskey has commented: "I am astonished that Paul [David] does not reply to the empirical, historical question: if QWERTY ... is such a costly constraint on typing industries, why have none of them, not a single typing division of any company, large or small, capable of internalizing the allegedly important externality in retraining its typists as you could retrain someone to play a clarinet who knew the saxophone, ever changed?" (McCloskey 1999).
9. For example he refers to, "quite transparent resorts to the stratagem favored by Humpty-Dumpty, 'It's not what the words mean, but who shall be master!'" (David 1997b, 11) and to "Strategic redefinitions, playing with words ... a form of rhetoric that is essentially obscurantist ... the purely semantic trick ... the taxonomic gambit ... deployment of taxonomic non-sequiturs ... rhetorical games ..." (1997b, 13), which leaves one wondering whether all this name-calling is itself some sort of "rhetorical game."
10. At first I wondered how such a *non sequitur* could ever arise, but then I read David (1999b) and realized that it was associated with the dialogue with McCloskey as explained above. Another remarkable thing about this passage is that he seems to be asserting that we ought to forget about discussing the justification for policy action in principle and simply talk about what *kinds* of policy action would be most appropriate.

References

Boettke, P. J. 1996. "What is Wrong With Neoclassical Economics (and What is Still Wrong With Austrian Economics)?," in Foldvary, F. E., *Beyond Neoclassical Economics*, Aldershot: Edward Elgar.

David, P. A. 1985. "Clio and the Economics of QWERTY," *American Economic Review*, 75: 332–337.

——— 1986. "Understanding the Economics of QWERTY: The Necessity of History," in Parker W. N. (ed.), *Economic History and the Modern Economist*, New York: Basil Blackwell.

——— 1997a. "Path Dependence and the Quest for Historical Economics: One More Chorus of the Ballad of QWERTY," University of Oxford, *Discussion Papers in Economic and Social History* (November 20) *<http://www.nuff.ox.ac.uk/economics/history/paper20/david3.pdf>*.

——— 1997b. "Path Dependence, Its Critics, and the Quest for 'Historical Economics': Keynote Address to the European Association for Evolutionary Political Economy" Athens Meetings (November 7–9).

——— 1999a. ``'Myth'-Informing The Public About Public Goods and QWERTY," *<http://www.eh.net/ehnet/Archives/eh.res/apr-1999/0006.html>*.

——— 1999b. "At last, a Remedy for Chronic QWERTY-skepticism!," prepared for presentation at the European Summer School in Industrial Dynamics (ESSID), held at l'Institute d'Etudes Scientifique de Cargèse (Corsica), (September 5–12, 1999) *<http://www.eh.net/Publications/remedy.shtml>*.

Lewin, P. 2000. "The Market Process and the Economics of QWERTY: Two Views," *Review of Austrian Economics*, forthcoming.

Liebowitz, S. J. and Margolis, S. E. 1994. "Network Externality: An Uncommon Tragedy," *Journal of Economic Perspectives*, 8: 133–150; reprinted as Chapter 3 in this volume.

——— 1995a. "Are Network Externalities a New Source of Market Failure?," *Research in Law and Economics*, 17: 1–22; reprinted as Chapter 4 in this volume.

——— 1995b. "Path Dependence, Lock-in, and History," *Journal of Law, Economics and Organization*, 11: 205–226; reprinted as Chapter 5 in this volume.

——— 1996. "Should Technology Choice be a Concern of Antitrust Policy?," *Harvard Journal of Law and Technology*, 9: 283–318; reprinted as Chapter 6 in this volume.

——— 1998a. "Path Dependence," entry in *The New Palgrave Dictionary of Economics and Law*, ed. P. Newman, London: Macmillan, 17–23; reprinted as Chapter 7 in this volume.

——— 1998b. "Network Externalities (Effects)," entry in *The New Palgrave Dictionary of Economics and Law*, ed. P. Newman (London: Macmillan), 671–675; reprinted as Chapter 8 in this volume.

——— 1998c. "Dismal Science Fictions: Network Effects, Microsoft, and Antitrust Speculation," Washington, DC, *Cato Institute, Policy Analysis* 324; reprinted as Chapter 9 in this volume.

Machovec, F. M. 1995. *Perfect Competition and the Transformation of Economics*, London and New York: Routledge.

McCloskey, D. N. 1999 *<http://www.eh.net/ehnet/Archives/eh.res/apr-1999/0005.html>*.

Mishan, E. J. 1975. "The Folklore of the Market," *Journal of Economic Issues*, 9: 690–720.

Puffert, D. J. 1999. "Path Dependence in Economic History" *<www.vwl.uni-muenchen.de/ls_komlos/pathe.pdf>*.

Author Index

Subject Index